Which Path to Heaven?
A Satirical Look at Political and Religious Bigotry

Reginald Scot

As told to Ken Boutwell

Which Path to Heaven? A Satirical Look at Political and Religious Bigotry
ISBN: Softcover 978-1-949888-05-8
Copyright © 2017 by Ken Boutwell

All rights reserved. No part of this book may be reproduced or transmitted in any form or by any means, electronic or mechanical, including photocopying, recording, or by any information storage and retrieval system, without permission in writing from the publisher.

To order additional copies of this book, contact:

Parson's Porch Books
1-423-475-7308
www.parsonsporch.com

Parson's Porch Books is an imprint of **Parson's Porch & Book Publishers** in Cleveland, Tennessee, which has double focus. We focus on the needs of creative writers who need a professional publisher to get their work to market, **&** we also focus on the needs of others by sharing our profits with those who struggle in poverty to meet their basic needs of food, clothing, shelter and safety.

Which Path to Heaven?

Dedication

The author and his scribe dedicate this book to all who have been and are the victims of religious bigotry.

Contents

Dedication v
About the Author viii
About the Scribe ix
Author's Appreciation x
Scribe's Appreciation xi
Preface xiii
Friend's Email 1
Slight Turn of Events 4
Visitation 17
The Funeral Service 39
Graveside Service 51
A Journey Back to Niceville 63
Sunday — Time for Church 89
A Visit with Martha 129
A Visit to Washington, DC 147
Final Judgment 164
Author's Confession 194
Final Judgment 195
Track Number Per Minute 213
Quick Visit with Martha 220
Trip after Judgment 224
Selected Reviews 225
Scribe's Experience 228
As You Will, My Son 229

About the Author

Reginald (Reggie) Scot, who now resides with God in heaven, was a successful English land owner who served as a member of parliament in the 1500's. He is most remembered today as the author of *The Discoverie of Witchcraft*, published in 1584. In it, he courageously argued that the belief in witchcraft was based on untrue and irrational superstitions promoted by the church as well as the communities, at large. His writing was attacked by leading clergy and philosophers of his day. King James VI (remembered for the King James version of the bible) called Scot's work "damnable".

Although Reggie has now been a resident of heaven for over 400 years, in July 2015, he felt that he had been called to again confront the evils of man's religious bigotry. Instead of a direct assault on bigotry as in his first book, however, he decided, this time, to fulfill his calling through the unique approach of acquainting people with the events, issues and memories they are likely to face immediately after their death. To do this, he chose to discretely monitor and document the experiences of a strong and committed Christian during the first few days after his death as he searched for the path to heaven. After reviewing God's list of scheduled deaths, Reggie chose John Willis who was slated to die on July 2, 2015. John was a highly successful accountant and respected citizen in Columbia, South Carolina who was also a strong and compassionate Southern Baptist Christian totally committed to obeying all of God's biblical laws.

About the Scribe

Although, as a resident of heaven, Reggie would have full access to John Willis' thoughts and activities after his death, Reggie had no ability whatsoever to write the book. He needed an earthly scribe. After an extensive search, he chose Ken Boutwell, an unknown and not very talented writer in Tallahassee, Florida. Ken did, however, have the advantages of being about the same age as John, having grown up in the South and having been a member of a Southern

Baptist church all his adult life. Hence, it would be easy for Ken to see things through John's eyes.

Through ways that Ken still does not understand, Reggie contacted him about 2 AM one morning to inform him that he had been selected to serve as the scribe to write this book. When Ken objected, Reggie carefully explained that he would tell him exactly what to write. All Ken had to do was type. When Ken objected the second, third and fourth times, Reggie used the age-old technique of blackmail, threatening to tell Ken's fellow church members that he was a left-wing liberal if he did not fully cooperate. That did it. Ken knew that he could never hold his head up again if his fellow Southern Baptist church members thought that he was a liberal, especially a left-wing liberal. He went to his computer and waited for Reggie's words.

Author's Appreciation

The author expresses his deepest appreciation to his earthly scribe, Ken Boutwell, for diligently following the directions given to him in the actual writing of the book, even when the directions conflicted with Ken's own beliefs. Reggie also thanks John Willis for dying early in the book and for letting him discretely monitor John's thoughts and activities immediately after his death. A big thanks goes to Pastor Alex Flake for remaining true to his beliefs throughout the book without which the book would have little meaning. Appreciation is also extended to the Association of Sin Search Saints for opening not only its association records, but also the records of its members for the author's review. And the book could have never been written without the help of Sally and Aaron Barfield, Martha Grissett, Pat and Buddy Parker, and Cecil and Judy Willis (John Willis' parents) in sharing their lives with the reader. And, of course, a huge thanks goes to Danny, the hero who chose to respond to hatred with love, something that is very rare in today's world.

Scribe's Appreciation

Ken thanks the author, Reggie Scot, for giving him the opportunity to do the actual writing of the author's messages which changed Ken's life forever—hopefully for the better. Ken also wants to express his appreciation to his wife, Jean, his brother, Wayne, his daughter, Julie, and his grandsons, Casey and Michael, his brother in law and sister in law, Bill and Nancy Youngblood and his friends Clint Gill, Patricia and Buddy Barker, George Borders, Hazel Rosser, Jon Mark McKinley, Ed Carter, Linda Culbreth, Ned Couey and Fred Seamon all of whom were frank and open in their critiques of early drafts. The support and encouragement from Ken's daughter, Jennifer, and son Jeff, which came at critical points when Ken and Reggie were in the middle of their many disagreements, are greatly appreciated. A special thanks goes to daughter Julie, friend Chis Koumas and Kevin Anderson and Associates for their critical edits. At times, Ken found himself caught between Reggie's writing directions and the critiques from his family, friends and editors but, hopefully, in the end everything came together to help you, the reader, find your way to heaven where we can all spend our eternity in peace, love and fellowship.

Preface

"Silence in the face of evil is itself evil: God will not hold us guiltless. Not to speak is to speak. Not to act is to act."

Dietrich Bonhoeffer

How long will good people remain silent in the face of the religious bigotry that has captured our Christian faith in America? How long will we sit silently by while religious bigotry overshadows love, tolerance and grace?

How long before we finally stand up and say, "Enough is enough. This is not who we are?"

Reginald Scot, the author, boldly answers this question for himself in this book. He will no longer be silent and hopes that the book's stories will encourage you to join him and others in speaking out against religious bigotry and all its sanctimonious forms of evil.

A day does not go by that white political and religious leaders, somewhere, do not play to their support bases by demeaning others. They denounce court orders that grant equality and call on school boards and local, state and national governments to force their religious agendas, including funding their schools, on the rest of the nation, all under the umbrella of "religious freedom". Within their own churches, women are relegated to subservient roles, the LGBT community demonized, sexual assaults of women excused, other faiths damned, and demeaning jokes about blacks and other minorities laughed at.

Outside the church walls, transgender people are being murdered at the highest rate ever, white extremist march through the streets with their guns shouting, "Jews will not replace us", and synagogues, mosques and Black churches are vandalized, bombed and burned. While all of this is happening, local and national religious leaders grant their support by remaining deafeningly silent for fear of losing members and their money. In those rare cases where a national church leader dares to speak out, his or her job is quickly threatened when pastors of large churches threaten to cut off their financial support.

Meanwhile, national church denominations expel churches accepting LGBT members as well as those with women pastors, local churches expel LGBT members and split from denominations who ordain LGBT ministers. Local pastors preach intolerant religious and political sermons to expand their church memberships and budgets. Extremist pastors call for the death of LGBT individuals. A pastor publicly burns a copy of the Quran. Priests sexually abuse little children and their superiors cover up the abuse. Christians pack the airways with emails, tweets, texts and Facebook postings that ridicule other races, immigrants, LGBTs, women and the liberals who support them. Politically, Christians boastfully support men who sexually assault women and ridicule the women who report the assaults. Church members even give a standing ovation to an alleged assaulter of teen age girls. And the list goes on and on.

No wonder the image of religious people as caring, loving and tolerant people has given way to the image of the angry, intolerant religious bully. Within this hostile environment, too many of us have yielded to the bullies by remaining silent because of concerns that we, ourselves, will become the victims of the bullying or will lose friends or cause church and/or family splits or even, in some cases, lose our jobs if we are on a church staff. Others of us just do not want to "rock the boat" or think that our voices do not count. Our silence, however, sends a strong message to the world that we are a part of and fully support the week after week intolerance and bigotry. By not speaking, we are speaking a lot louder than we think.

And while we remain silent, more and more thoughtful people are simply rejecting Christianity in all its forms. And who can blame them?

Religious bigotry, of course, has existed as long as recorded history and caused millions of deaths through religious wars. It has even caused religious people to burn people with different beliefs at the stake and murder their own children for dating a person of a different faith. Many Southern white churches in the United States, from the 1950s through the 1970s, bullied African Americans eager

Which Path to Heaven?

to throw off the sinful bonds of segregation and the whites who supported them. In so doing, they created an environment where extremists felt free to beat and even murder innocent victims. Today, both in the United States and around the world, homosexuals are the new targeted group, as evidenced by the hate speeches and sermons delivered in churches and at political and religious rallies. Churches welcoming gay members remain rare, again, because of the fear of losing members and their dollars.

After watching the desecration of his Christian faith for several decades, Reginald Scot felt that he could no longer silently bask in the comforts of heaven while so many of his earthly fellowmen suffered at the hands of religious people---just as they did back during his time on earth in the 1500s when the churches were falsely accusing people of being witches and then showing God's love by murdering them. He had to speak out again through this satirical novel about a strong Christian's search for the path to heaven immediately after his death. As the novel unfolds, it vividly shows the meanness, the silliness, the ugliness, the cruelty and the hypocrisy of religious bigotry and the challenges facing those who oppose such bigotry. A surprise chapter shows how God would look if he shared the intolerant beliefs of many Christians today and reveals God's plan to return America to its white Christian roots.

Reggie realizes, however, that his voice alone will do little to win the battle. It will take the voices of thousands, probably millions. Accordingly, he humbly asks (really, begs) that you join him and others who are beginning to speak out in favor of treating all people with respect, dignity, love and equality. While this book concentrates primarily on Christianity, it applies equally to all faiths where hatred and religious bigotry now rule supreme. Those of us who care can no longer roll over and play dead while our individual faiths are distorted and destroyed by religious bigotry.

The time has come for us to speak out. Every single one of our voices count, including yours and mine. You do not have to be as forceful as Reggie is in this book. But, if you can without losing your job, please find a way to speak out. You can talk quietly with your friends. You can organize informal small groups of like-minded people to discuss how to respond to bigotry. You can talk to small groups in your church, synagogue or mosque. You can write your own book. You can distribute copies of this and other similar books. You can discuss this book in your book club or small group or your bible study group. You can write letters to your local newspaper. You can write guest editorials. You can speak out in response to hate emails, texts, tweets and Facebook postings. You can talk to your pastor and let him or her know that they are not alone. If you are a pastor, you can talk to other pastors, you can talk to your lay leaders, you can participate in public community dialogues with other faith leaders, you can write and sign joint letters with other pastors to denominational leaders and you can preach a series of sermons on "Is this really who we are"? All of us can pray for opportunities to speak out and respond quickly when those opportunities arise. But whatever you do, please do not remain silent because, as Bonhoeffer says, "Not to speak is to speak" and, in this case, our silence shouts to the high heavens.

Chapter 1

Friend's Email

*"O wad some Pow'r the giftie gie us
To see oursels as ithers see us!"*

Robert Burns

It was late, and John was turning his computer off for the evening when he noticed an email from his friend, Chris, pop up.

After serving two assignments in Afghanistan, Chris now works as a highly sought-after contract undercover agent for the CIA, DEA and FBI. He is a delightful person but, probably because of his career, is skeptical of and analyzes everything, including his religious beliefs. Chris seldom attends a church service and, just today at lunch, John had shared with him the peace and love that can come from accepting Christ as one's personal savior.

"Then why don't Christians show that love and peace in what they say and do instead of being such holier than thou bigots?" Chris had replied. John countered, "It may seem like bigotry to you, but we do it because we want you and everybody else to know the love of God and to be able to spend all eternity with Him. Don't you want to go to heaven when you die?"

Chris suddenly looked at his watch, jumped up and said, "Rats, gotta go. I am late for my appointment" and then, in half jest, added as he grabbed his rain coat and headed towards the door "Not sure that I want to spend eternity with a bunch of bigots. That might be worse than hell."

When John got back to his office he followed up with an email to Chris telling him how much he had enjoyed their lunch, ending with "I would love to continue our discussions."

Chris had now responded, and John was anxious to see what he had to say.

Reginald Scot

John,

Thanks for your email and for lunch today. I would also like to continue our discussions. I must go out of town tomorrow morning on an emergency assignment but should return by late Sunday evening. Mondays are the days that I do volunteer work down at the Veterans home. So how about lunch next Tuesday? Call me tomorrow morning.

As you can tell from our conversations, earlier today, however, I have a really hard time coming to terms with all the religious bigotry. I have an even harder time believing that God condones such bigotry in His name. I went to your church last Sunday and it was more of the same. You will see my letter to the editor in Sunday's paper.

It's always more of the same. A few years ago, I met a family and became very good friends with them. The wife was Jewish and the husband—ole South Carolina Baptist and he was very active with the church. She converted to Baptist and raised their two children as Baptists. One day I found her crying. I asked, "Why are you crying?" She said the Pastor of her church pulled her aside and flatly told her that her parents were going to hell because they were Jewish and there was no way she would be joined with them in heaven after their deaths. She was horrified. The Pastor told her the only way her parents would go to heaven was if they renounced their Jewish faith and became Christians. The husband, after hearing this, sided with the Pastor and added more pressure on her to, in turn, put more pressure on her parents. Of course, her parents were not going to convert.

Well, as you know, I have my own personal issues with organized religion and seeing her so upset and now almost estranged from her parents, I really wanted to meet this pastor. So, I called and made an appointment with him telling him I was troubled and needed faith. I didn't say off the bat what was troubling me. So, I went to the meeting trying to keep my temper in-check to see where he was really coming from. He flat out tells me that anyone who is not a Christian is going to hell. Plain and simple. So, I gave him a scenario. "Hey, I was in Afghan and my best friend was killed when he saw that I was about to step on a land mine and shoved me to the side. He tripped and fell on the mine and it exploded. I am alive today only because my friend gave his life for me. He was Muslim. Soooo, what? He's in hell?"

Yep.

Well, how about all those babies and innocent children who were killed as collateral damage who didn't have a chance to even know who Jesus was. Are they in hell?

Yep.

An image of these innocent young children screaming in pain as they burned in the pits of hell with no hope of ever escaping was thrust like a piercing arrow into my mind's eye. I couldn't believe this guy actually believed God would do that to these little children. So, just to make sure I understood him, I gave him another similar question: "What about all of the Native Americans who died before the European Christians came over and told them about Jesus. Are they all burning in hell today?

Yep.

Well now I started to feel my head spin around and wanted to throw up. So, I laid one more on him.

I said, "a guy just rapes and kills my wife and I catch this guy in the street and beat the hell out of him. An ambulance shows up and this guy is muttering to the paramedics that he wants a minister before he dies. This minister shows up and asks him if he accepts Christ and the bad guy says "yes.". "So, did this guy really go to heaven?" and the minister answers "yes." So, I say, "my wife was just raped and killed, and she was Jewish. Where did she go." And the minister says, "she would go to hell." So, I shot the Minister.

Chris

Chris always did like to sneak in a "shock you" in his conversations to emphasize his point. Of course, he would not shoot the pastor. But, one thing was clear as a bell, he must have had a bad experience somewhere back in his earlier church life that turned him so bitter against organized religion. Winning him to Christ was going to be a real challenge. As John turned his computer screen off and headed to bed, he felt deep down, however, that that was exactly what God was calling him to do. Tomorrow, he would call Chris and confirm their lunch next Tuesday.

Chapter 2

Slight Turn of Events

"If you live each day as it was your last, someday you'll most certainly be right"

Steve Jobs

John got a good night's sleep. Sometimes, however, the best laid plans of mice and men go awry. Instead of waking up ready to call Chris, John woke up dead.

At first, he did not realize that he was dead. He thought that he was in the midst of one of his many dreams as he floated around the ceiling looking down at his body lying there, motionless, in the bed. He tried pinching himself but found that he had nothing to pinch. He tried calling JoAnn, but no sound came out. Instead, everything was just nice, peaceful and quiet as he floated around the room near the ceiling—a strange, but very pleasant and delightful feeling—a feeling that he had never experienced before.

Then the question hit him. *Am I dead? Could death come this easily?* No suffering, no months-long battle for life, no relentless pain. He had always thought death would be that way—hard and miserable—but if this was death, it wasn't hard and miserable. It was wonderful. He had simply gone to sleep and when he woke up, he was floating around the ceiling looking down at his body. He loved the feeling and was hesitant to run any further "dream" tests but wanted confirmation. So, he tried moving from the ceiling back down to the bed and into his body. To his delight, nothing happened. His body remained lifeless and he remained floating near the ceiling. He really was dead…and he loved it. He had feared death all his life, but this was nothing like he had feared. Instead it was nice and peaceful. *I could get used to this*, he quickly concluded.

Given this slight turn of events, he forgot all about calling Chris as his thoughts turned to his family—his wife, their two sons and their wives, his grandchildren. His sons and their families had come for the weekend and they had plans that morning, the lake and a cookout.

Even as he thought about them, however, he was not overcome with grief. Instead, he felt an overwhelming emotion of pure relief, free of all worries. He felt that he had been given a new life and the future awaited him. Not just a vague future, but a joyful—blissful, unfettered, God-giving future—awaited him for all eternity because he was a strong bible believing Christian.

Then he saw JoAnn walk into the room. She had gotten up about an hour earlier and gone down to the kitchen to prepare breakfast for everyone. She had slipped out of bed without noticing that he was no longer inside his body. As she walked back into the room, she reached down to pick up a Barbie doll in a crisp blue sailor dress that Sophia had left there the night before. "John, time to get up. Everyone'll be ready for breakfast in a few minutes," she said, her face turned toward his dead body, which was only partly covered by the sheets. John watched as she headed out the door smiling at the doll. Then she turned and called again a little louder, "John! Get up!" *How could she not know I'm dead?* John wondered. Did his soul slip away that quietly? Was death so much like sleep? Was his lack of presence in his body all that unnoticeable?

He saw JoAnn re-enter the room, walk over to the bed, and shake his body to wake him. He noted the horror on her face as his body gave no response. She ran from the room shouting to their sons, "Billy! Bo! Come here! Something's wrong! Dad won't wake up!"

Both boys came running and began shaking his body shouting, "Dad! Dad! Wake up! Wake up!"

John felt a sudden deep sadness. He had not said goodbye. He had not told them how much he loved them.

He continued to watch as Bo called 911, the ambulance arrived, and the EMT medics tried to revive him before finally telling JoAnn and the family that he was dead. They cried and held each other before the hearse came and hauled his old body away.

To his surprise, John was glad to see it go. After all, he was finished with it. It was not in good shape. He had developed a big "pot belly" or as his father used to say, "he had a furniture problem: his chest had fallen into his drawers". His bad knee was always acting up, and he had to go to the bathroom every hour, it seemed. He suffered from heartburn constantly, and sometimes he got an intense tightness in his chest, with pain shooting down his arm. He had wondered if he should have the tightness in his chest checked but had told himself it was just indigestion.

John had never been dead before and did not know exactly what to expect. But he was surprised that he was still in his house and able to see his family, hear them talk, watch them mourn. He was everything he had been before, except now he was in a spirit form.

In the back of his mind, he had always thought that when death came, he would die one moment and be in heaven the very next. That was what he had heard the preachers say at many funerals. They would say, "Betty is in a far better place, now in the presence of God." And he remembered that Jesus said to one of the men on the cross next to Him, "Truly I tell you, today you will be with me in paradise." So, that must mean that the man went to heaven immediately after his death.

So why am I still here? He had already been dead a couple of hours and should be in heaven---not still in the same bed room where he had died. Was there something that he needed to do? He now wished that he had studied his Bible a lot more about what one should do immediately after death to get to heaven. He remembered lots of things that the Bible said that he needed to do before he died to get to heaven, but nothing about what he was supposed to do after dying. In fact, he wondered why preachers did not talk a lot more about this. They needed to lay out the exact process for getting to heaven immediately after death, not leave it for each person to figure out on his own.

Should I go somewhere, or will God send someone to get me? What if I miss my ride and have to spend all eternity hanging around here? That would not be funny. Then he thought, s*tupid me, floating around here in my bedroom. They* *can't get a chariot in here. They are probably waiting for me right outside in the driveway.*

Without even thinking about whether he could move, he zoomed through the walls, right through his closed front door, and out onto his porch, just like a radio wave. But there was no chariot and no angel. No one was waiting for him. Not in his driveway, not on the street, not anywhere. He looked up and down the streets and they were completely deserted. There were not even any spiritual signs with an arrow pointing which way to heaven. Then he thought, *maybe they are waiting out back!* He zoomed back through the walls to his backyard. But it was the same: no one waiting. No signs. No nothing.

Now panicking, he thought, *I really am crazy. I should have thought of this before. Heaven is up in the sky. Not down here on earth. I need to be looking on top of the house, not on the sides. That is where they are coming for me.* With full anticipation, he zoomed through the walls, through the ceiling, through the roof and onto the rooftop. He could now see for blocks and there was .... nothing. Nothing at all. Then he thought, *The clouds. That's where the angels will be coming from.* He searched every cloud, all the big ones, all the little ones, and all the openings in between, looking for a chariot breaking through and headed his way or the appearance of an angel or a sign of some type. But nothing appeared. Absolutely nothing.

Then a terrible thought hit him. There is one other place. A place down below. *What if, instead of an angel, the devil is coming to get me?* He would be coming up from hell, so he might be waiting under the house. John was confident that he was headed for heaven, but there was that nagging possibility. One can never be a hundred percent sure. There was that one time when the clerk gave him an extra ten dollars in change and even though he knew he should tell her, he didn't. Maybe, just in case, he should check under the house, but do it in an inconspicuous way so that if the devil were down there waiting for him, the man with horns wouldn't see him.

John went to the back corner of his family room that was just above the part of the house farthest from the crawl space opening. If the devil were waiting for him down there, it would be difficult for him to see John's spirit in that back corner. Slowly and cautiously, and with some fear, he slid through the floor into the darkest corner under the house. From there he could see the light coming from the opening at the other end and everything in between. His spiritual eyes searched every nook and cranny. To his relief, there was no devil--nothing unusual. Then, just in case, knowing that it was a silly idea but doing it anyway, he searched for openings to a tunnel that might lead to hell down below. Again, to his relief, he found none. Everything was just like it had always been.

Relieved that the devil had not come for him, John eased back through the floor into the house. This all seemed so crazy but being dead was totally new to him and he simply did not know what to expect. He was having to learn as he went along, and, at this moment, he was totally lost with nothing to do except......except wait.

Hearing his family talking in the kitchen, he moved to where they were. JoAnn was muttering through her tears, "I tried and tried to get him to see his doctor, but no, he would not go. Now look. He's gone and left me here all alone."

Momentarily forgetting his own anxieties, John turned his attention to JoAnn. He wished he could reach out and put his arms around her and tell her how much he loved her, but it dawned on him that he no longer had any arms, or a voice, or even a mouth. Now, he could do nothing but watch as she wept.

They moved into the family room, and John moved with them, glancing out the window just in case his ride to heaven had arrived. It had not, so he took a position in the upper corner of the room just a few inches from the ceiling. He looked down on the coffee table and saw a stack of *Snow Rabbit* children's books. He smiled at the thought of how much the grandkids loved for him to read those books to them. Those had been some great times. In the books, only the children could see the magical Snow Rabbit. So, after reading one of the books, the kids claimed they had just seen the Snow Rabbit right behind him. He turned and claimed he also saw the rabbit, but they shouted, "No! Only kids." Those were wonderful times and he planned to carry those and lots of other similar happy memories with him to heaven.

John glanced outside once more but saw no chariots or angels or anything unusual. Not having found the devil, he had regained his confidence that heaven was his destination, but he was growing a little concerned about when. Surely, he would be there before his funeral, and Pastor Flake would be able to truthfully say, "Today, John's in a far better place, in the presence of God." In the meantime, he would just have to wait.

His death had occurred early Thursday morning while he was sleeping. The medics pronounced him dead at about 8:30 a.m., and his body was transferred to the funeral home before noon. For the rest of Thursday and all-day Friday, John hovered near the ceiling in his home, changing rooms every now and then to be with different family members. He especially enjoyed Friday when lots of friends dropped by to bring food and tell his family how sorry they were about his death. Except, every time the doorbell rang, he would rush to the door just to make sure that it was not Jesus or an angel coming for him. It never was.

He and JoAnn had built strong friendships since they had moved to Columbia in 1969, right after they were married. He enjoyed listening to the nice things his friends said about him. He even laughed, as much as a sentient radio wave can laugh, when Joe, his fishing buddy, recounted the time that the two of them knocked a hole in their boat while trying to maneuver through one of the tributaries of Lake Murray. They had to spend the entire night trying to walk out. Fortunately, JoAnn had gotten worried and called the park ranger, who found them wandering around in the woods at 3 a.m. Joe told how the mosquitoes came in droves, big as helicopters and thirsty as desert dogs. Mosquitoes—that was one thing that he would never have to worry about again .... unless mosquitoes also go to heaven.

John was pleased when Sally, their maid for almost forty years, came by with a beautiful strawberry cake. *The kids will love that*, he thought. He had always liked Sally. In some ways, she was like family, and he was glad that she had come by to comfort JoAnn and the boys. Immediately upon entering the room, Sally started crying and hugging JoAnn. "I'm so sorry," she said. "I don't know what we'll do without John."

JoAnn responded by wrapping her arms around Sally and resting her head on her shoulder. The two remained in a loving embrace, both crying. "Sally, thanks so much for being here," JoAnn said through her tears. "It means the world to me."

Sally responded with characteristic kindness. "I asked the Smiths if I could come help you today," she explained gently. "You do what you need to do, and I will take care of things here." She then walked to the kitchen, put on an apron, and started rinsing the dishes and loading the dishwasher. John knew that Sally and her husband, Aaron, were struggling financially, and that every dollar counted. Taking a day off was a major sacrifice. Yet here she was, bringing a beautiful cake and showing her love by offering to spend her day helping his family.

After Sally moved to the kitchen, Pastor Flake arrived. John was grateful to see that his pastor was one of the first ones to get there. Friday was Pastor Flake's day to prepare his sermon, but when he heard the news about John he dropped everything and came immediately. As he walked into the room and saw JoAnn and the family, Pastor Flake began to cry and was briefly unable to talk. He hugged JoAnn and wept. John noticed that JoAnn seemed a little cold to the pastor. Instead of returning his embrace, she just stood there frozen, glancing at the others in the room. John was moved by his pastor's affection for him, however. He was a good man. John would miss him when he got to heaven.

"How can I help?" Pastor Flake asked. His voice sounded sincere.

"I'm not sure, JoAnn answered. "This has all happened so . . . so suddenly."

"What about the funeral plans? Can I help with anything there?"

"We have an appointment this afternoon at Sunset Funeral. I know John would want you to be a part of the service."

"Of course," Pastor Flake answered. "I'd be happy to. Have you written the obituary yet?"

"Not yet."

"Well, why don't we go to the dining room table and do that right now?" Pastor Flake suggested.

JoAnn and the boys gathered with Pastor Flake around the table, and they began to talk, with the pastor taking notes. After only a few minutes, Pastor Flake stood and said, "Okay, why don't I take this back to my office and type it up? I will get it back to you in an hour or so."

John's attention had been temporarily diverted watching the grandchildren chase each other around the house and was surprised that the conversation about his obituary was over before he had a chance to hear any of it. He wanted to say—in fact he did say, but no one heard him— "Hey, wait, it takes more than a few minutes to write down my life!" But Pastor Flake was leaving with his notes, and there was nothing John could do to stop him.

John grew disturbed at the self-satisfied smile that Pastor Flake had on his face as he departed, a significant enough smile to make John worry about what his obituary might say. Was Pastor Flake going to play a joke on him in the obituary? *This is not the time to be funny*, he thought. Because this was all so new to him, he worried that he might need a good obituary to help him get into heaven.

For the rest of the day, John floated around his home, periodically glancing out the window for his never-arriving escort to heaven. Otherwise, he spent his time looking at pictures, knick-knacks, mementos, and other reminders of his life. Wonderful memories came flooding back, but so did some not-so-good memories. It was a mixed bag. But, overall, John loved his life and felt that it was good enough to get him into heaven in very short order. His funeral was scheduled for Saturday morning, and he was sure that he would be in heaven by then.

Friday night passed slowly—John wandered around his house, watching over his family. He spent a lot of time hovering over JoAnn. His thoughts wandered back to their first date and how he had fallen in love with her before they even got to the movie theater. He didn't remember the name of the movie, just how beautiful she was and how he kept glancing over just to see her face, particularly her shining eyes. When she turned and smiled at him on the way to the theater, his legs turned to putty and he almost stumbled.

Now, he looked down as she slept and wanted to hold her one more time, tell her how much he loved her, and apologize for any pain he had caused her over the years. He remembered again with a start that he no longer had arms or a voice. He wished that he had told her a thousand more times that he loved her and was so thankful that she had been his wife for those fleeting forty-six years, in spite of the major crisis that almost tore their marriage apart a few years ago.

Since he seemed not to need sleep anymore, he decided to visit his sons' rooms, first Bo and then Billy's. He settled into his ceiling corner in Bo's room and looked down to see Bo and his wife, Jenny, sleeping peacefully.

He remembered the moment that he first saw Bo as a baby. He was the most handsome baby ever born, of course, and John could not take his eyes off him. The first time he held him was just like being in heaven, or at least it seemed that way at the time. His mind raced through years of "Bo" memories. Bo's first smile. His first steps. The first time he rode a bike down the street, shouting, "Look at me, Daddy! I'm going minety niles a myer!"

There were lots of little league baseball games and camping trips, including the one where Bo slipped off a log and fell into a mountain stream with a current that seemed to rush by at a hundred miles per hour. Fortunately, the rapid waters pushed him almost immediately onto another log that had fallen across the stream, and they were

Which Path to Heaven?

able to pull him to safety. Just thinking about that event scared John all over again.

Now John's thoughts shifted to how happy he and JoAnn had been when Bo and Jenny had their first date for their high school prom. John and JoAnn were friends with Jenny's parents and adored Jenny. She was everything they wanted for their son: kind, enthusiastic, smart, admired both by her peers and adults, and a natural leader respected by others. They were thrilled to watch their romance bloom.

As he watched them sleeping so peacefully, his mind raced through the years. He remembered Jenny giving birth, first to Bobby and then to Sophia. What a blessing those two grandchildren had been in their lives.

Then John's mind moved to their second son, Billy, and he shifted to his room. John was amazed at how quickly, as a spirit, he could transfer from one place to another. Immediately upon thinking that he wanted to be in Billy's room he was there. No time delay. Just the thought and he was there—right through the wall.

He looked down at Beth sound asleep on Billy's outstretched arm. This would make a perfect picture he thought. John remembered thinking when Bo was born that one could not love a second child nearly as much as the first. But he had been wrong. Billy triggered the same outpouring of love as Bo had when John first saw him. He could not stop holding Billy—even when both JoAnn and the hospital nurse told him that Billy was hungry and needed to nurse. Had Billy not started to scream loud enough to disturb the whole hospital, he might still be holding him today.

As John thought about his family, he rejoiced that over the years he had often expressed to JoAnn how truly blessed the two of them were with a wonderful, healthy, and happy family. In his mind, he credited those blessings to the high moral life that he and JoAnn had lived. They had graduated from college, worked hard, and been rewarded with successful careers. They had never asked for or received a government handout. Neither of them gambled or had ever had an alcohol or drug problem. They, of course, had never been divorced or had an abortion. On the gay issue, there had been the one big crisis that almost tore their marriage apart, but John remained truly pleased that he had had the faith and courage to handle it exactly as God wanted. He had been tested and remained strong and obedient to God's word. He knew that God would be proud of him when he reviewed his record—which he hoped would be soon.

John's thoughts then moved on to the couple's obedience to God in other areas. They had both, especially JoAnn, who loved to help others, been active in their community. Both had taught Sunday school as members of Christ Episcopal Church and more recently at Zealot Baptist Church. In fact, they were part of the co-founding group who led the split from Christ Episcopal to found Zealot Baptist when the national Episcopal Church endorsed the ordination of gay ministers. He and JoAnn had dipped into their savings to give more than $300,000 to help build the new church building, which became a beautiful tribute to God. Their names were inscribed on a plaque listing major donors in the sanctuary entrance. John once took a picture of the plaque, joking that he was going to take the picture with him when he died to show God his and JoAnn's dedication and commitment.

At Christ Episcopal, he had swallowed hard but accepted the Episcopal endorsement of the ordination of women pastors. He never thought, however, that he would see the day that the church would endorse the ordination of gay pastors. It was an uncompromising moral issue for him, and he would never put his grandchildren in a situation where they might be tempted into the gay lifestyle. That would be like throwing them to the wolves. He simply loved them too much. The more he thought about his adherence to the highest of biblical moral standards, the prouder he became and the more he was sure that he would soon be in heaven, basking in all its glory.

But why was he not there already? What was the holdup? Was there something else he needed to do? Maybe he needed to find that picture of the plaque—but suddenly realized that finding it would do him no good. It finally hit him. After death, all one has is one's spirit and one's lifetime record—no material things whatsoever. He had absolutely nothing except the person he had been.

Daylight came on Saturday morning and John was still floating around like an invisible cloud. There had been no word whatsoever from God about when he would be transported to heaven. Meanwhile, his family prepared to go to the funeral home. They had scheduled the visitation at 10 a.m. followed by the funeral service at 11 a.m. and then the burial at noon. This was to be followed by a luncheon for those who wanted to visit with the family. John had always thought that the visitation would be the night before, but his brothers and their families were coming from Cincinnati and could not get there before 10 a.m. JoAnn wanted to wait for them.

John had never been really close to his two older brothers, Clint and Jeremy, who had thoroughly embarrassed the family when they participated in the Selma Civil Rights March back in 1965. Their father had disowned them for years after that and had reconciled with them only a couple of years before his death.

Since his father's death, John and JoAnn had visited his brothers only a handful of times. Those occasions had been tense to say the least. They lived far away, and John had never quite forgiven them for the embarrassment that they had caused their parents. And there was that telephone call from his brothers a few years ago when John faced the biggest crises of his life and his brothers, instead of showing sympathy, had admonished him. It was really none of their business, he told them. Now, however, it felt good that they were driving all that distance to be at his funeral. Given he was not yet in heaven and did not need to take any chances, John wished the thought had not hit him, but it did. *Maybe his brothers just wanted to make sure that he was dead.*

Putting that thought aside, John realized that unless something happened soon, Pastor Flake would be lying when he said at the burial, "We can all rejoice because John is in heaven with God looking down on us at this very moment, hoping we're not mourning, but rather celebrating his life." *Maybe he won't say that today.*

Maybe he will just say, "John is looking down on us today and wanting us to not grieve, but to celebrate his life." That would be true because he planned to be hovering inside the burial tent just under the top unless he got moved to heaven in the next hour or so. He just hoped that Pastor Flake did not say, "Today we're lowering John's body into the ground where he will rest until Jesus comes again to receive him unto Himself." That was his worst fear. He liked the idea of looking down from heaven a lot better than spending maybe a few hundred years just lying there in one place waiting for Jesus. What if God decided to wait ten thousand years before sending Christ back to earth? That's a very long time to just be lying there in the cold, dark ground.

Chapter 3

Visitation

"I could not escape a feeling that this was my own funeral, and you do not cry in that case."

--- John Knowles

His family left at about 9:30 a.m. to go to the visitation. John waited a little longer, still hoping that some angels or maybe a chariot would arrive to escort him to heaven. *What if they didn't get the message that I died?* He briefly wondered. That would explain everything. One thing was certain; he had never planned to attend his own funeral.

As he anxiously waited, he looked around the room again at all the food their friends had brought and felt good that so many had come by. He noticed that the cake that Sally had brought was almost gone. He had watched with some amusement earlier as the grandkids kept easing into the dining room to sneak slices of the cake. Sally definitely made a great strawberry cake, which made him wonder if they had strawberry cakes in heaven.

As he looked at the remaining few crumbs of the cake, he thought of Sally again. It did not seem like it, but she really had been with them for almost forty years, coming one day each week to do laundry and clean their house. He and JoAnn had always paid her well, starting out at $2.00 per hour in 1974 and, most recently, paying $15 per hour for the four hours she worked every Wednesday. Sally wore a constant smile and was a terrific cleaner. She worked hard from the time she arrived until she left. But neither Sally nor her husband Aaron were good with money, maybe because both had grown up in poverty and simply never learned to manage money.

Their parents had been sharecroppers, and both families had worked in the same cotton fields. Neither family had enough money to send their children to college and, as teenagers, Sally and Aaron were often kept out of school to help plant or harvest crops. So, it was doubtful if either could have succeeded in college even if their families had had enough money. Sally and Aaron got married after high school and got a sharecroppers' deal with a big cotton and corn plantation.

John knew about the sharecropping rules back in those days, and they were often not good for the sharecropper, but they were the best jobs that many poor white and black folks could get, especially poor blacks like Sally and Aaron. The plantation provided the farmland and equipment for crops, free housing, and loans during the year for living expenses. The sharecropper and his family provided all the labor to plant, cultivate, and harvest the crop, and when the harvest was sold, the plantation owner split the profits with the family, usually fifty-fifty. The sharecropper's share of the money was seldom large enough to fully pay off debts to the owner. Hence, few sharecroppers ever accumulated any savings, much less enough money to buy their own land or to send their children to college, thereby perpetuating the system from generation to generation.

Sally and Aaron stayed on the plantation for almost seven years and then had to move in 1974 when the owner died, and his heirs decided to set the entire farm out in pine trees. They had no savings, but Sally did have a sister who lived in Columbia. So, they moved in with her sister and Sally started looking for house-cleaning jobs.

Sally had first come to work for John and JoAnn soon after Bo was born, and she had remained with them ever since. Aaron was a hard worker and got a job as an auto mechanic at a local auto repair shop. When he started in 1974, he was making $3.00 per hour, but over the years his salary had increased, so that he was now making $14.00 an hour. Sally and Aaron had scrimped, saved, worked extra jobs, and borrowed enough to send both of their children to college. It had been a struggle, but they were determined to see their children graduate from college.

They had also bought a Rob Coles home that was their pride and joy. They had been delighted when the Rob Coles agent offered to loan them the money to purchase one of their prefab homes. They knew that Rob Coles preyed on low-income people, particularly low-income black people who could not get bank loans, and that the 14 percent annual interest rate was more than double the rate charged by banks. Yet, this was their only hope to ever own a home. Besides, the Rob Coles agent had convinced them that they could easily make the payments based on their current incomes.

After moving into their new home, however, they found that the mortgage payments were about $300 more per month than the agent had promised. When they complained, the company showed them the contract that they had signed and said that they could either make the payment or move out, losing their $10,000 down payment—which had been their entire savings. After that, Sally and Aaron never quite had enough to pay all their bills, especially when unforeseen emergencies happened. That put them in the position of frequently needing to borrow money to pay for utilities, get their heater fixed, or make a mortgage payment.

Sally often called John, with tears in her voice, to ask for an advance on her pay. John always agreed, but over the years, her advances had gotten two and three months into the future and Sally was too embarrassed to ask for another loan. So, Aaron had gone to a payday loan store and borrowed $200 to get their utilities turned back on. He signed all the papers but did not understand that he was agreeing to a 285 percent interest rate plus large penalties if he was even a day late on a payment. Within just four months, the $200 payday loan had increased to over $700, despite the $150 that he had repaid, and the company had garnisheed Aaron's salary at the auto repair shop. By the time the loan was paid off, it had cost Aaron and Sally over $900.

Sally had talked to John about the loan payments and John had taken the papers that Aaron had signed to an attorney friend, who said that there was nothing that could be done. All the penalties and high interest rates were perfectly legal under current federal and state laws.

Sally no longer smiled when she came to do housework. In fact, most days you could tell that she had been crying. Then it happened: Aaron was diagnosed with cancer. They had no health insurance. Aaron could no longer work, although he tried for almost six months. They first tried to live off Sally's maid service income, but she could earn only about $500 per week at best, sometimes less, and their monthly mortgage payment was $1050. In the meantime, medical bills piled up. They had to frequently change doctors when the doctor who Aaron was seeing would inform them that he could not see him again unless they paid their bill. In the meantime, collection agencies sent demanding letters and made threatening telephone calls trying to collect the $55,000 that they had been charged for his surgery and the four days that he had been in the hospital.

Their utilities had been shut off, and they found themselves living on handouts from friends, churches, and government programs when they could qualify. John thought that he might be able to help them get a new bank mortgage at the 4.9 percent rate most other home owners were paying at the time, but he could not get the Rob Coles office to even call him back to learn what the loan balance was. Instead, Rob Coles moved quickly to repossess the home and had them evicted. They moved back in with Sally's sister until their oldest son graduated from college a year later, got a job and started sending them enough money to rent a small apartment. Aaron, fortunately, recovered from his cancer and, although still weak, had returned to work. But Sally and Aaron were now in their late sixties and had no hope of ever retiring. It had been a long time since John had seen Sally smile.

John had no idea why all these memories about Sally and Aaron came to him out of the blue, except that it seemed so unfair that he and JoAnn had been in a school in Niceville, South Carolina, at the same time as Sally and Aaron, only John and JoAnn were in the new all-white school that had received a AAA award from the state for the quality of its academic programs. Sally and Aaron were in the all black school that used to be the old, run down white school. While all four had started out in the same town at the same time, one couple had a wonderful, successful life, while the other was never without stress and worry.

John, now that he was only moments from his final judgment, wished that he had shown more compassion for Sally and Aaron and maybe even helped them a little with their financial problems,

Which Path to Heaven?

instead of criticizing them in his thoughts as poor money managers and labeling them as "welfare queens." Perhaps such a mindset had taken roots in his early years at Rock Bottom Baptist church back in his hometown, but John had always felt that people who were on government welfare programs were worthless, living off those who were willing to work and pay taxes. He often expressed such feelings aloud and told jokes about welfare queens in his Sunday school lessons. On one Sunday, he remembered that when he made fun about Sally and Aaron being welfare queens, everyone in the class laughed—except for Martha.

He did not know Martha very well, although she had been in the class for a couple of years. She was a very quiet person who kept to herself. He did not know her nationality. She had slightly dark skin and facial features as if she might be from Egypt or Morocco or some other North African country. She had no accent, however, so she must have been born in this country. But it bothered him at the time that rather than laughing, she just looked at him with sadness. *What was she saying with that look?* he wondered at the time, but he had promptly forgotten about it until now.

An even more disturbing thought hit him. *Is Sally and Aaron's tragic life playing any role in my still being here rather than in heaven?* Then he recalled again the $300,000 that he and JoAnn had given to build the new Zealot Baptist Church. That money helped build a beautiful church home for God's people and his plaque on the wall would last forever. That was a lot more important than giving money to people who would quickly spend it. No one would ever even know that he gave it. So, he quickly dismissed the question and remembered that he needed to go to his own visitation down at the funeral home.

Even though he no longer had his body, this spirit thing did have some good advantages—transportation, for one. He simply thought to himself, *I want to be at the funeral home in the visitation room,* and *swoosh,* he was there, hovering comfortably just below the ceiling.

He noticed his body in the casket before anything else. He looked really good in his black suit and all that makeup, if he may say so. It was a little late now, but he should have been wearing makeup for years.

Glancing around, John noticed the handsome wreath on the casket. It featured his favorite yellow roses. But beyond that, there was only one other wreath next to the casket. *Why haven't they brought the rest of the flowers in?* He wondered. He had always imagined that he would have a truckload of flowers at his funeral. He would be able to measure his success in life by the number of floral wreaths at his funeral.

Now he was here and there were only two wreaths. Not the sendoff he had expected. He wondered, momentarily, if God was also going to measure his success in life by the number of floral wreaths. Then he heard a comment that floored him—well, to the extent that a hovering spirit can be floored. One of the funeral home staff said, "This is the first time I've ever heard of a family asking that donations be sent to a political organization in lieu of flowers."

The other staff member replied, "What is the Columbia Women's Conservative Club, anyhow?"

What was JoAnn thinking? Sending his flowers to a political club! She was not even a member! No one in his family was a member! Then it hit him like a ton of South Carolina bricks! Pastor Flake's wife, Lucretia, was the incoming president of the club and Pastor Flake had, just last week, asked for a donation because Lucretia had to raise $30,000 while she was president.

Pastor Flake had said, "John, the devil and his liberal minions have taken our country away from us and from God. We've got to take it back or your grandchildren will have no country. Christians have to stand together, and each of us has to do our small part."

John listened with respect as he always did when the pastor spoke to him one-on-one. This time, however, he sensed the pastor's political talk laced with added urgency.

"Lucretia has a great program lined up for the women's club next year," he explained. "She's already seeking a commitment from

Alabama Chief Justice Roy Moore who, you remember, stood up for God like no man has ever done before in displaying the Ten Commandments on public property. Justice Moore is a true man of God, John, who will not yield to the devils stealing our country. Just yesterday, Justice Moore defied Obama and his minions on the Supreme Court by telling Alabama court clerks that they don't have to issue marriage licenses to gays—at least for now."

John nodded knowingly as if he were well aware of this, although he wasn't.

"And that's not all, Lucretia is also working on getting Franklin Graham to speak to the club. What a coup that will be! Franklin is to the gay movement what George Wallace and Lester Maddox were to the civil rights movement—true men of God who will speak out against the liberals who have kidnapped our country. John, we need your financial help in taking our country back."

John, remembered responding, "Let me talk to JoAnn. We'll help, of course, just terrible these things. The gall of these left-wing liberals!" He thought that they would probably donate a couple hundred dollars. After all, that would be a cheap price to get the country back from wherever the liberals were hiding it.

Unfortunately, he had died before he could get back with Pastor Flake, and now he had no money—another limitation of death that he had never thought about before. It all made sense now. Pastor Flake had talked his family into donating his flower money to the Columbia Women's Conservatives Club, probably telling them that that was what he would want. That explained the wry smile on Pastor Flake's face when he had left yesterday. It was not a joke that he was planning. It was out and out theft.

Pastor Flake has stolen my flowers. That may very well be why I am not yet in heaven. If I don't get into heaven, it will be his fault, John concluded in no uncertain terms.

Although he always quietly consented and nodded seriously every time Pastor Flake gave one of his political sermons, a part of John suspected that all this talk about "taking our country back" was really just a crock of slop. *No one has stolen the country, but Pastor Flake has stolen my flowers,* John concluded now in a fit of spiritual rage. *A funeral without flowers is no funeral, at all.* Again, death has its limits. There was nothing he could do, now, except look at his two floral wreaths, the one on the casket and the one standing next to it.

John knew that the wreath on the casket was from JoAnn and his sons, but who sent the other one? Probably someone who had not read the obituary. So, he drifted down closer to look at the card. All it said was, "I still love you and am praying for you," with no name. John instantly knew who the wreath was from, but he was not about to admit it. That chapter of his life was over, gone, and forgotten. He had been tested and did not yield.

After a few minutes, he looked around the room and saw that it was filling up fast with extended family members, friends, co-workers, and church friends. Maybe he could convince God to count the number of people rather than the number of wreaths. People are a lot more important than flowers, except he distinctly remembered Jesus talking about the lilies of the field, and there were absolutely no lilies in this room. Pastor Flake had probably stolen those, too.

There was nothing he could do, so he turned his attention to looking for his family. There near the casket, he watched as JoAnn, Bo and Jenny, and Billy and Beth formed a receiving line. The grandchildren chased each other around the room as if they were at a birthday party. At least there was no danger of them knocking over a floral wreath.

In spite of the absence of flowers, if John had had a chest it would have burst, he was so proud of his family. JoAnn looked absolutely beautiful. He had kidded her over the years that he wanted her to wear that beautiful purple dress with her pink scarf to his funeral. "None of that black stuff," he had told her. She abided by his wishes, donning the purple dress and pink scarf. His sons were exceedingly handsome, their wives beautiful. They looked every bit the successful professionals they had become.

John had only one concern. His sons had become somewhat liberal, religiously and politically, especially on the gay issue. However, those political differences had not boiled over into any major disputes similar to the differences that he had had with his brothers. He felt that he could now go to heaven with his earthly job completely fulfilled—well, mostly fulfilled. That is, if someone or something would come along to show him the way.

The flower thief was the first in the receiving line and the first to speak to JoAnn, who stood by the casket. Pastor Flake turned to the casket, laid his hand on John's handsome body, and said a short prayer. John was not quite sure what the prayer was, but it sounded like, "Lord, please accept this poor sinner with all of his warts and blemishes into thy kingdom."

Poor sinner! Warts and blemishes? What is he talking about? If anyone has warts and blemishes, it's the flower thief.

Pastor Flake's prayer definitely delivered a blow to John's cause and made him think about the pastor's full name, which was Alexander Reel Flake. Reel had been Pastor Flake's mother's maiden name. Cheated of flowers and now cursed with warts and blemishes, John decided to shorten the pastor's name to A. Reel Flake. But then remembered that after death, he might be in a place where he could no longer ask for and receive forgiveness, so he dropped the "Reel" and just called him A. Flake.

Pastor Flake was now talking to JoAnn and saying what a great man John was and that he did not know what the church was going to do without him. John thought, *if something doesn't happen soon, looks like I'll be right there, warts, blemishes, and all.*

Pastor Flake had exerted a major influence on John's life. While John had always viewed homosexuality as a sin, he had never realized what a dangerous sin it truly was until the national Episcopal Church authorized the ordination of gay pastors, and until he heard Pastor Flake preach about it one Sunday morning about five years ago.

Pastor Flake, in the middle of his sermon, brandished his fist in the air, and then slammed it on the wooden pulpit with a force that John thought would crack it. "Make no mistake! God's word is clear and beyond doubt," he shouted, his face ruddy and engorged. "Homosexual sex, whether by those married or not, is an abomination and a sin against God and his people and will destroy our nation. Those are not my words. Those are the words of the God we serve."

John had been startled by both the message and the force and anger with which it was delivered. *Strange*, he thought. While he had always been strongly opposed to homosexuality, he had never viewed it as a danger to our nation. But the words that followed in the sermon really caught John's attention.

With even more determination, Pastor Flake warned his audience, "And those who do not take a stand against such lifestyles are equally guilty because those who remain silent in the face of evil are just as guilty as those who commit the sin." He paused for several seconds, looked around the sanctuary with a look of great concern, and delivered the final blow: "As for me and my house, we will serve the Lord, our God." He paused again, lowered his voice to a whisper and asked, "What will you and *your* house do?"

The congregation was stone silent almost as if everyone had stopped breathing while they weighed this critical question from God's servant.

Pleased with the reaction, Pastor Flake then compelled his congregants to respond to his question with a commitment to each other and to God: "If you choose to stand with God against gay lifestyles and gay priests, I invite you to join me down front at God's altar. If you choose to stay with the Devil, then you may stay in your seat or leave. For, as God says, no man can serve two masters. Either he will hate one and love the other, or he will hold to the one and despise the other."

John thought that he knew his Bible pretty well and had always thought that parable was about money. Perhaps he had read it all wrong and it was, indeed, about homosexuality.

Anyway, he looked around the sanctuary as congregants rose and moved toward the altar. As a Sunday school teacher, he had to lead by example, so he too rose and stepped out into the aisle, waiting for JoAnn to join him. She remained seated with a look of deep concern on her face, almost like she knew something he didn't. John motioned to her, but she still did not stand. He reached and softly grabbed her arm and gave a gentle pull. To his relief, she began to stand. He pulled some more, and she walked toward him with tears welling up in her eyes and beginning to slide down her cheeks.

Together, they slowly made their way down to the front with about a hundred other people. Without saying a word, JoAnn looked at him with tears still running down her face, as if this walk would change their lives forever. As they turned around to face the congregation, John saw Martha walking out the back door.

Back at the visitation, Pastor Flake finished talking with JoAnn, gave her a tight hug, and then quickly shook hands with Bo, Jenny, Billy, and Beth, not exchanging a single word with any of them. He then moved through the room, laughing and slapping people on the back, until he came to Don Gravendale, where he settled in for a longer conversation. John shifted a little closer, but the noise of the crowd made it difficult for him to hear. In spite of the noise, however, it was pretty clear that they were talking about the recent Supreme Court ruling in favor of same-sex marriage and about the sermon that Pastor Flake planned to deliver at tomorrow morning's church service.

John heard Pastor Flake claim in a defiant voice, "Christians are being persecuted because they dare speak out against this grievous sin. Our own government is turning on us, my friend, and we must take a stand here and now. We must take our country back from the devil and his liberal minions, starting this Sunday!"

Don responded, "I think that we need to get some state legislators to introduce a protection-of-pastors bill so that pastors are not arrested by our government for refusing to participate in this gross sin. I know a legislator named Alton Beany from down in Red Hills. Good Christian man, he will be glad to do it because I know too much about his extracurricular activities! Want me to call him?"

John could not tell for sure, but it sounded as if Pastor Flake laughed and said, "Yes. Sounds like our kind of a man."

Don had inherited millions of dollars from his parents and used the money to build a large real estate fortune. He had thought that life could not get any better when it got worse—in fact, a lot worse—when his son came home from college and told his parents that he had something that he wanted to talk to them about.

"I'm gay," their son announced to them, "and I have a friend that I want you to meet."

Don simply could not accept this. He immediately sought counseling from Pastor Flake. After counseling, Don accused the gay community in Columbia of recruiting his son into their wicked ways and vowed to destroy them. At Pastor Flake's suggestion, Don begged his son to get counseling, and when he refused, Don reacted in a fit of anger and ordered him out of his house. He told him to not come back until he had changed his ways and repented for his sins.

Two days later, Don's son committed suicide. Don pledged, from that day forward, to do whatever he could to totally destroy gays and their abilities to recruit young lives into their sinful ways. He said, "If I can prevent just one parent from having to endure this kind of tragedy, I'll consider myself a success."

A few weeks after the burial of his son, Don approached Pastor Flake about leading all the Christ Episcopal members who disagreed with ordaining gay ministers out of the church to form a new Southern Baptist church, Zealot Baptist. He was adamant about both the name of the church and that it be associated with the

Southern Baptists because, as he said, "They have a full history of fighting against the devil's intrusion in our lives."

"In fact," he said, "their very formation was based on fighting the devil's attempt to take away the rights of innocent slave owners, and many of their churches fought long and hard to prevent women from voting in the 1920s. In the fifties and sixties, many of their churches fought every step of the way when the left-wing liberals tried to force racial integration on this nation."

Don went on to emphasize that the Southern Baptists were not shy about pointing out the Biblical passages that supported racial segregation, adding that to this day, almost all their churches are lilywhite. And they're steadfast, even today, in keeping women, who the Bible says must always be subordinate to men, out of ordained deacon and ministerial positions."

But most importantly to Don, of course, Southern Baptists had recently taken a strong stand against the ordination of gay ministers, lumping such actions into the same category as the sinful practice of ordaining women. He was confident that it would be a cold day in hell before the Southern Baptists would ordain either gay or women ministers, and hell will be completely frozen over if they ever sanctioned gay marriages.

"Pastor Flake," he exclaimed confidently. "They're our kind of people!"

Don was just as adamant about the name Zealot Baptist because he said that the congregants would be zealots in enforcing God's laws. No one else liked the name at first, but when Don offered to donate the first two million dollars to help build the new Zealot Baptist Church, everyone started to like it a lot more.

Over the next few weeks, Don and Pastor Flake received pledges for more than $10 million to build the new church, including John and JoAnn's $300,000. Almost 600 people agreed to leave Christ's Episcopal Church and other local churches to form the new church. They were off and running.

Turning his focus back to the visitation, John noticed the arrival of his old business partner, Clyde Jenson. At about the same time, John and Clyde had started to work for one of Columbia's small but highly respected accounting firms, Smith & Crowdy. Although they had other clients, Smith & Crowdy primarily served real estate developers. That proved to be a great market, and the firm prospered.

After about ten years, the founders decided to retire. They sold the business to John and Clyde. The firm continued to grow, and they added offices in Greenville and Spartanburg. Currently, they employed about 135 full-time accountants. The firm was highly profitable, and John and Clyde had been doing well financially.

The two had a fabulous working relationship even though they were miles apart when it came to political views and religious beliefs. Clyde was a Democrat and John a Republican, but they never discussed politics except to periodically kid each other. For example, just last week Clyde asked John if he had heard about the Republican lifeguard who refused to throw a life jacket to a drowning man because the man would just become dependent on it. John responded by asking Clyde if he knew the difference between a Republican and a Democrat. After hesitant shake of the head from Clyde, John said, "Both are generous, but the Democrat is generous with his money and yours." They laughed at each other's jokes as they always did.

Beyond their business relationship, both were Christians, but Clyde was much more interested in missions and helping others, while John was more focused on preventing sin, especially the last several years.

Clyde walked over to the casket and placed his hand on John's lifeless hands. "John, I don't know how we'll carry on without you," he said quietly. "It won't be the same. So long, friend." His old friend then wept uncontrollably. JoAnn walked over, put her arms around Clyde, and the two of them just stood there, crying and hugging each other. Finally, JoAnn loosened her arms and said, "Clyde, he loved you like a brother." Composing himself, Clyde moved on to greet Bo, Jenny,

Billy, and Beth, hugging each one, continuing to weep and unable to get a word out. Yet, unlike what he had witnessed with Pastor Flake, John could tell that there was a special bond between his sons and Clyde—a bond of love and mutual respect.

As Clyde finished tearfully hugging the family, John noticed his friend Chris standing in front of his casket. He must have come back early from his out of town trip. As Chris looked down at John's body, every muscle in his face was distorted as he tried to maintain his reputation as a tough, take-no-prisoners private investigator. But he couldn't, and the tears came flooding out. In the midst of his tears, he muttered more to himself than to anyone else, "John, thank you for being my friend. I wish that all Christians showed your same love and concern. Say a special prayer to God for me and ask Him why he tolerates so much bigotry in His name. I will keep our luncheon appointment at the restaurant next Tuesday in your honor."

Still trying to hold back his tears, Chris noticed Pastor Flake and Don Gravendale standing a little to his left. With a devious grin on his tear stained face that said, "I know that I shouldn't do this", Chris pulled out his minuscule detective recorder and eased over to quietly stand behind the two men so that he could record their conversation. Once a detective, always a detective. For their own sake, John hoped that Don and Pastor Flake had taken a break from condemning gays and lesbians, but there was little chance of that. Don, with a face that had turned as red as a sliced beet, released his bitterness, as he often did to whomever would listen: "Alex, they killed my son. Every last one of them will roast in hell." Chris grimaced and turned as if to confront them, but, instead, wisely turned and walked away. As he did, he whispered into his recorder, "No, Don, you and your pious church friends killed your son. I pity all of you on your judgement day."

As Chris left the room, John glanced toward the door and saw Martha, someone he had not seen since that day four years ago when she walked out the back door at Christ Episcopal. What was she doing here? Did she come to give him one last chance to re-examine his life?

If she had, it was too late. His book had been closed. He was on his way to heaven, now having convinced himself that his trip to heaven would start as soon as they lowered his now-useless body into the ground. His earthly responsibilities would then be complete, and he would be on his way.

It had to be heaven, he reasoned again, *because if one is going to hell that's immediate. The devil does not mess around. He wants you burning as soon as possible. On the other hand, God is more interested in helping people make a smooth transition, giving them time to see their friends one last time.*

That was it. He had figured it out.

Martha walked over to the casket and stood by it with that same sad expression on her face she had shown in Sunday school. John would have given anything to know what she was thinking. After standing by his casket and staring at his body for a long time, she leaned over, whispered something, and then softly kissed his cheek.

John was touched but wondered why she was so sad about his death. They had never been very close, but she seemed to genuinely care for him. He wondered even more about what she had whispered to him.

Martha remained by his casket for a while longer, and then started sobbing, dropping to her knees, shaking all over. After a few moments, JoAnn stepped over and helped Martha stand, hugging her tightly. Gaining control of her emotions, Martha finally turned to face JoAnn and gave her the most caring hug John had ever seen. She then did the same to Bo, Jenny, Billy, and Beth before slowly walking out of the room as her gushing tears returned.

John could not figure it out. It was as if Martha had come to deliver one last important message. He wished that he had been close enough to hear what she had whispered. Maybe it was the message that she had wanted to deliver to him back when she was in his Christ Episcopal Sunday school class. What was it? Maybe she knew something about why he was not already in heaven. He went into a deep reverie, pondering, something he had seldom done in life.

But John's pondering was quickly interrupted when his brothers, Clint and Jeremy, walked into the room with their wives. John was struck by how much older they looked since he had last seen them. Then he remembered it had been about seven years, and they were both now in their seventies. Somehow, at this moment, the anger toward them that he and his father had nurtured seemed silly. The whole idea that it would destroy the nation to give blacks the same freedom and civil rights as everyone else enjoyed, as George Wallace, Lester Maddox, and his father so strongly argued, seemed utterly stupid now.

Actually, their father had not disowned them after their participation in the Selma march. Instead, the final straw came when Clint brought a black friend home with him from college.

Welcoming a black person into his home to spend the night would wreck his father's image in the community. How could he face his white friends—especially Rob Coles, his banker and builder friend—if he let a black person sleep in his house, eat at his table, and use his bathroom? Rob Coles would find out and tell everyone in Niceville, and he could never hold his head up again.

After a long, heated argument, Clint and his friend left, with Clint pledging to never come back and their father shouting, "That's just fine with me!" John remembered that moment as if had occurred just seconds before. With mixed emotions, John had watched Clint and his friend leave. He cared for his brother, but Clint knew how strongly their dad felt about segregation. He should have never put him in that situation. The next day, their dad went out and bought the largest Confederate flag he could find and raised it over his used car dealership in downtown Niceville.

Years later, John learned that Rob Coles served as the Niceville KKK Grand Dragon, and that their dad held an ongoing line of credit with Rob Coles' bank that he used to buy vehicles for the used truck and car lot. The line of credit was critical to the survival of their father's business.

Yes, this was the same Rob Coles who owned the company that twenty-five years later sold Sally and Aaron their home with a 14 percent mortgage, the same company that would not return John's calls when he tried to help Sally and Aaron after Aaron's cancer diagnosis, and the same company that evicted them a few months later—only now the company was owned and operated by Rob's son, Rob, Jr.

Jeremy was not there the night that their father had kicked Clint and his friend out, but a few weeks later, he had his own run-in with their father. Jeremy had caught a ride with some friends to Washington, DC to participate in the Martin Luther King march on the nation's capital. Rob Coles saw Jeremy's picture in the paper as a part of the crowd and notified their father. Three weeks after Clint and his friend were asked to leave, Jeremy and their father had their own confrontation ending with Jeremy's promise that he would never come back.

Yet, here they were, exhausted after driving from Cincinnati to be at John's funeral. Perhaps because of their shared feud with their dad, the brothers had remained very close their whole life. Both had successful careers as attorneys in Cincinnati, and now retired, they owned second homes near each other in Florida.

John immediately regretted not having spent more time with them. His brothers had reached out to him on several occasions, but John hoarded the rancor about how embarrassed he had been as a teenager over his "nigger loving" older brothers. He had watched as his dad struggled to hold his head up in the community as word spread about Jeremy's and Clint's participation in civil rights marches. He could not forget their dad's devastation when Rob Coles canceled the line of credit for his car lot, telling him that a man who cannot control his sons is no man at all, an embarrassment to his white race and to God Almighty. And that was not the worst. Because of Rob Coles' connections, no other bank in Niceville or the surrounding towns would extend their dad a line of credit. Soon thereafter, their father closed his used truck and car lot and went to work as a salesman for a used car dealer in neighboring Cold Rock.

Rob Coles refused to let the issue drop. He peppered Cold Rock with leaflets containing a picture of their father with the caption, "Father of Nigger Lovers." One night around 2 a.m., a gun was fired outside their home. The next morning, they found a sign taped to their front door: "Home of Nigger Lovers." They never called the police, and it never happened again, but they lived in fear for years. Their father struggled until his retirement to earn enough money to support his family and in his final years, stripped of his dignity, had to depend on John for financial help.

During those years of his father's harassment, John was fortunate to keep his high school grades high enough to earn a full scholarship to Furman University. He had to work to cover other expenses, but he was able to graduate on time and pay for his dates with JoAnn, who was also attending the college. They got married the day after graduation in 1969. His father forbade Clint and Jeremy from attending the wedding.

Turning his thoughts back to his visitation, John shifted closer to his brothers and watched as they both stood at his casket with tears flowing softly. Clint spoke first. "John," he whispered. "Things should have been different. I hardly knew you."

Then, Jeremy spoke, also softly, directly to John's body as if it could hear him, "Why did we let our differences keep us apart so long?"

Both brothers fell apart and their wives had to steady them. For the first time, John began to understand the impact of injustice on people's lives. Cruel injustice hurts not only those who are beaten down by it, but those who try to fight it—and sometimes those, like their father, who are caught in its crossfire.

When people choose to make outcasts of others, whether because of race, gender, class, educational level, religion, politics, wealth or even place of birth, families can be divided forever, friendships destroyed, livelihoods stolen, and self-dignity lost.

John wondered, *Why did I have to die to see this? Why could I have not seen this when I was alive and could have done something about it?*

John's brothers and their wives went through the family receiving line embracing each family member and expressing how sorry they were about John's death. Their sorrow seemed as earnest as any expression of sorrow John had ever seen. They then moved toward the sanctuary for the funeral.

As they were leaving the room, Sally and Aaron entered. John looked, specifically, to see if Sally smiled as people greeted her. She did not. The couple walked quickly to the casket and, arms around each other, just stood there, not saying anything. What were they thinking? Were they contrasting their lives to his and JoAnn's?

He felt horrible again that Sally and Aaron had lived such a life of stress and worry, never having enough money to feel secure, while he and JoAnn had not only been free of financial worries, but also enjoyed all the extras that money could buy.

As John watched Sally and Aaron move on through the receiving line, he realized the enormity of this inequality and wondered why God allowed such a system to exist. If God could create the earth and all that it is in it in seven days, why could He have not also used His power to create a social and economic system where all people could live happy, healthy and successful lives? He certainly should not have left that task to mankind.

Sally and Aaron finished greeting his family, including the three rowdy grandchildren, and then quickly left the room, as if they felt uneasy being there. John did not fully understand what mandated such a hurried exit but was very glad that they had come because he realized now that they had been an important part of his life.

As Sally and Aaron left the room through the side door, the deacons from Zealot Baptist entered the front door. John wondered why they came as a group, all ten of them. Then he saw that they had been assigned his pallbearers. He had never thought about who his pallbearers would be; he guessed that the Zealot Baptist deacons would be as good as any. He picked out a couple of them as leaders in the Columbia community.

Henry had served as a city commissioner and, along with Jerry, who had served as president of the Chamber of Commerce, had been fighting hard over the past few weeks to prevent the legislature from removing the Confederate flag from the state capital. They claimed that their campaign had nothing to do with race, but John knew differently. Their frequent racist jokes at deacons' meetings showed their true colors.

Just last week, immediately after the opening prayer at the deacons' meeting, Jerry had said, "Hey, before we get started, I have a good one. Why is there cotton in pill bottles? To remind black people that they were cotton pickers before they were drug dealers." Everybody in the room laughed. Now that he was only moments away from his heaven entrance exam, John no longer found the joke funny.

He might have been more pleased with his deacon pallbearers had he not been doing all his thinking and reminiscing for the past few hours. These were his co-deacons, but their more-moral-than-you stance now bothered him. A week ago, he had been one of them. Now, they disturbed him for reasons he could not quite put into words. Perhaps the feeling sprang from his concern about why he was not already in heaven.

He was no longer in control of the situation, though—another death limitation—so he decided that there were enough dedicated Christians in his pallbearer group that his body would not get contaminated on the way to its grave. Just in case God's procedure was that his spirit would be reunited with his body during the burial process and he had to stay in the ground until Jesus came again, he didn't want a contaminated body. He suddenly wished again that he had studied his Bible more to know better what happens to people's souls when they die. He desperately hoped that staying in the ground for ages with a contaminated body was not the way to heaven.

John watched as friend after friend, members of Zealot Baptist Church, old friends from Christ Episcopal Church, and members of the Smith & Crowdy accounting firm filed past his casket, looked at his handsome body, and moved through the family receiving line, each person expressing condolences.

He had often wondered if anyone would come to his funeral, He even joked a few times about hiring mourners and paying more the louder they cried. Yes, he certainly had nothing to worry about today, except whether he was ever going to make it to heaven. Everyone gradually moved into the other room. It was now time for his funeral service.

He couldn't let go of his anger at Pastor Flake for stealing his flowers and for his earlier comment about "warts and blemishes," and now wished that JoAnn had gotten somebody else to speak at his service. *Pastor A. Reel Flake has a few warts of his own,* he thought. But alas, John realized that he was not in control of that either.

Before he left the room, he looked for one more person who he thought might show up, but did not see the person, so he willed himself to the funeral parlor.

Chapter 4

The Funeral Service

If you want something good said about you at your funeral, you may want to do something good while you are alive.

K. Boutwell

The shock of the day came when the door opened and Rev. Love, who had been the pastor of Christ Episcopal Church before Pastor Flake, led his casket and his family into the room. *What's this all about? Where's Pastor Flake?* Then he saw him sitting in a pew near the back with a scowl on his face. Apparently, JoAnn and his sons had asked Rev. Love to conduct the funeral. He knew that their relationship with Pastor Flake had been strained for quite some time now.

There was no love lost between Rev. Love and Pastor Flake even though Pastor Flake had come to Christ Episcopal as the senior pastor when Rev. Love retired. Rev. Love and his wife, Ann, had always been compassionate, caring people. Rev. Love often quoted Mathew 25 in which Jesus explained that God divides people into two groups: the sheep who help people in need and the goats who refuse to do so. Jesus, Rev. Love always explained slowly so that his congregation would not miss the point, assured all that the sheep would be given everlasting life and the goats sent to eternal punishment.

For a fleeting moment, John panicked that he, himself, might be more of a goat than a sheep. He remembered how he and JoAnn were so active in helping those in need when they were members of Christ Episcopal, but struggled to remember the last time he had helped the least of these in the last few years since they had been at Zealot Baptist. He finally remembered that it was when he gave a dollar to a homeless man who approached him as he and JoAnn were coming out of the downtown Governor's Dining Club a few weeks ago.

Since he had helped found Zealot Baptist, his emphasis had been on fighting the sin that was destroying the nation. He wondered, now that he was perhaps only moments away from being judged, whether he would be given credit for all the help that he and JoAnn had given to others while they were at Christ Episcopal. Then he wondered whether he had made a mistake by changing his emphasis to fighting sin to save the nation.

Just in time, it dawned on him that there are two paths to heaven. God and Pastor Flake had called on him to travel the second path. Pastor Flake was a master at the second path, a pro at leading people down that path. There were no sheep or goats on Pastor Flake's path to heaven, just saints and sinners, and it was easy to distinguish between the two.

The saints hated sin and the sinners loved sin, and the beauty of this path was that the saints decided what was sin and who the sinners were. All one had to do to get to heaven, according to Pastor Flake, was to believe that the Bible was God's holy word and to obey every law in the Bible.

It occurred to John that he did not know all the laws in the Bible, but Pastor Flake did, and he had said that the most important laws were those prohibiting other religions, divorce, abortion, and homosexuality.

He was not sure how Pastor Flake chose these four out of the hundreds, more likely thousands, of laws mentioned in the Bible, but he did know the time and place when Pastor Flake learned that, sometimes, it is best to play like some of the laws were no longer in effect.

It had happened at a Wednesday night business meeting at Christ Episcopal about eight months after Pastor Flake had become the church's new senior pastor. At the meeting, Lucretia, Pastor Flake's wife, suggested that the third-grade Sunday school class was getting too large and needed to be split into two smaller classes. Someone asked how large the class was, and Lucretia rose to respond when Pastor Flake said, "Lu, honey, you need to let the men do the talking because the Bible says in 1 Corinthians 14:34 that women should be silent during church meetings. They're not to take part in the discussion for they are subordinate to men."

The meeting grew quiet as a church mouse, except for a couple of young boys who started giggling.

Lucretia turned and glared at Pastor Flake with a look that could have set a swamp on fire. The best John could remember, the glare lasted over an hour---or at least seemed that way before she said with a voice that left no doubt about how she felt, "Alex, honey, you know where you can stick that verse!"—with a long, heavy emphasis on the word "stick". She then very slowly gathered her belongings, gave a dry smile to those around her and marched out of the church.

Things were a little awkward for a moment until someone moved that the meeting adjourn. The third-grade class remained the same size until Pastor Flake led the breakaway a year later.

After that meeting, Pastor Flake never again mentioned the law in 1 Corinthians. Instead, he started preaching about a few other sins and laws, such as Muslims, divorce, abortion, and homosexuality. John had guessed that God and Lucretia told him which ones to pick. Anyway, it sure made things a lot easier to have only a few major laws to worry about. Since John could not immediately remember many cases in the last few years where he had helped the least of these, he was relieved to remember Pastor Flake's alternative route to heaven.

The alternative sin-hating, law abiding route was definitely easier than doing unto the least of these. To hate, all you had to do was just sit around and spew out words of hate at the devil, liberals, immigrants, Muslims and gay people every now and then, and John was proud to say that he had become very good at that in the past few years. He grew especially proud as he remembered the hundreds of anti-gay and anti-liberal emails that he had received and forwarded. His mind immediately went to one that he had sent to his friends just this past week. It was a good one because it killed two birds with one stone by hitting both gays and liberals in the same short email. The email read:

I love it when a plan comes together, don't you?

>   *A. Back off and let those men who want to marry men, marry men.*
>   *B. Allow those women who want to marry women, marry women.*
>   *C. Allow all women who want abortions to get abortions*
>   *D. And, voila! In three generations, there will be no more liberals."*

As he fondly remembered all his anti-gay and anti-liberal emails, he thought, *God has to be so proud of me*! He paused for a moment. *Unless I'm supposed to go after some of these sins more than the others.* Pastor Flake seemed to be a little soft on divorce and remarriage, even though Jesus had clearly said in Mathew 19:9, "Anyone who divorces his wife, except for fornication, and marries another commits adultery." In Leviticus 20:10, God clearly mandates that the punishment for adultery is death.

Apparently, Pastor Flake got a modern-day exemption from God on that one because Deacon Fred Wilkens had been divorced three times. John guessed that Pastor Flake got the exemption based on Fred's $150,000 donation to the Zealot Baptist building fund. Then a funny question came to John. Would Pastor Flake marry a gay couple for $150,000 since the Bible calls for the same death punishment for homosexuality as for adultery? Continuing to chuckle at his question, he thought *If he will sell out for one, he ought to be willing to sell out for the other.* The first gay couple, however, might have to offer him $200,000 because he would have to change some of the words in his standard wedding message. After the changes had been made, however, the price should drop back to $150,000.

After another laugh, John got more serious and wondered what had happened to the third way to get to heaven, which he had learned at the Rock Bottom Baptist Church when he was growing up in Niceville. It was really a lot easier than either of the other two. According to John 3:16, one is required only to believe: "For God so loved the world that He gave his only begotten son that whosoever believes in him shall not perish but have everlasting life."

The beauty of this road to heaven is that one does not have to do anything else. John knew a lot of Christians on this road. They sometimes came to church on Sundays, but then spent the rest of the week doing whatever they wanted. That just did not seem right.

In fact, people could wait until the last day of their lives to believe and still get to heaven—unless, of course, like John, they died in their sleep just before believing. In that case, they might be in deep trouble.

Although John was a strong believer, there was one part of "just believing in Christ" that really bothered him. He never discussed it with anyone because he was afraid that they would accuse him of questioning the Bible and that wouldn't do for a Sunday school teacher.

But he had always wondered if people who believed that Jesus was the son of God, just as stated in John 3:16, but who tortured and murdered people, would still go to heaven. People like the Christians who tortured and executed the innocent men and women accused of witchcraft: did they go to heaven when they died because they believed with all their heart that Jesus was the Son of God?

As Rev. Love walked to the lectern and started to speak, John was reminded that his funeral service was about to begin. He turned his attention back to Rev. Love.

"Family and friends, we're gathered here today to celebrate the life of John Willis. John was born on March 6, 1947, in Niceville, South Carolina, and died on July 2, 2015. His parents were Cecil Willis and Judy Simmons Willis. " Rev. Love paused for a moment to clear his throat and then continued, "John graduated from Niceville High School in 1965 and from the Furman University in 1969. He married his high school sweetheart, JoAnn Wilson, to whom he had been married almost 47 years at his passing. John is survived by JoAnn, his son, Bo and his wife Jenny; son, Billy and his wife Beth, three grandchildren, Bobby, Sophia and Jim and ah…..." as he started to mention another name or say something else, but, after glancing down at JoAnn, apparently changed his mind. Instead, he said, "Today, I want to talk about the John Willis that I knew."

John immediately recognized the past tense of the word and wondered why Rev. Love said "knew" rather than "know." Was he going to talk about the big event? Since Pastor Flake had been his counselor, he would not bring it up, but Rev. Love might. Had John a heart, it would have been racing.

Rev. Love proceeded, "The John Willis that I knew would want me to read the following scripture from the King James Version. Mathew 25: 31-46: 'When the son of Man shall come in his glory, and all the holy angels with him, then shall he sit upon the throne of his glory; and before him shall be gathered all nations; and he shall separate them one from another, as a shepherd divideth his sheep from the goats; And he shall set the sheep on his right hand, but the goats on the left. Then shall the King say unto them on his right hand, come, ye blessed of my Father, inherit the kingdom prepared for you from the foundation of the world; For I was hungered, and ye gave me meat; I was thirsty and ye gave me drink; I was a stranger and ye took me in; Naked and ye clothed me; I was sick and ye visited me; I was in prison and ye came unto me. Then shall the righteous answer him, saying, Lord when saw we thee hungered, and fed thee? Or thirsty and gave thee drink? When saw we thee a stranger and took thee in or naked, and clothed thee? Or when saw we thee sick or in prison and came unto thee? And the King shall answer and say unto them, verily I say unto you, inasmuch as ye have done it unto one of the least of these my brethren, ye have done it unto me.'"

John, unaware that a spirit could actually get sick, suddenly felt very sick. He used to quote this scripture in his Sunday school lessons at Christ Episcopal Church frequently. But he could not remember quoting it a single time since the split. He did, however, give that dollar to the homeless guy a few weeks ago. John now thought that maybe he should have given him a hundred dollars, maybe a thousand.

Rev. Love paused, knowingly for a second, and looked around the chapel as if he were searching for someone or something. Did John imagine it, or had the Reverend just cast a quick glance at his spot near the ceiling? Rev. Love then continued with his reading, "'Then he shall say unto them on the left hand, depart from me, ye cursed, into everlasting fire, prepared for the devil and his angels; for I was hungry, and ye gave me no meat; I was thirsty, and ye gave me no drink; for I was a stranger, and ye took me not in; naked and ye clothed me not; sick and, in prison and ye visited me not. Then shall they also answer him, saying Lord, when saw we thee hungered or thirsty, or a stranger, or naked, or sick, or in prison, and did not minister unto thee? Then shall he answer them, saying, verily, I say unto you, inasmuch as ye did it not to one of the least of these, ye did it not to me. And these shall go away into everlasting punishment; but the righteous into eternal life.'"

Feeling even sicker, John now felt that he should have given that homeless man $10,000, maybe even a hundred thousand. Eternity in hell is a long time. But he did give that $300,000 to help build that beautiful Zealot Baptist church building. So that should count for something, except he could not remember a single passage in the Bible where God said that building a beautiful building would get a person into heaven.

Completing the reading of God's word, Rev. Love paused again and said, "Pray with me please: Our Lord and Savior, we come today asking that you receive John Willis, our valued friend, family member, and brother, into your kingdom. We know that when that happens, heaven will be a different place. We acknowledge that we hurt because John is no longer with us and ask that you help our hurt. John spent a long time with us and made this a better place for many of us and, for that, we're thankful. Amen."

John immediately analyzed the prayer. Boy, that was a short prayer, but to the point, asking God to let me into heaven, which means that he must have an inkling that I'm not there yet. *Did he really notice my presence up here when he glanced up?*

But someone like Rev. Love asking God to let me in has got to help my cause. But why did he say that "Heaven will be a different place" when I get there? Why did he not say that it would be a "better" place? That would have been a much better recommendation! And why did he say that I made this a better place for "many" of us instead of "all" of us? That's not going to help!

Rev. Love continued. "John and JoAnn were members of Christ Episcopal for my entire twenty years as its pastor," he explained. "I know that the story of the sheep and goats is a strange scripture for celebrating the life of one who has gone to be with our Lord, but Mathew 25 was a passage that John and I often discussed and one that I know he would want you to consider today as you evaluate your own life's work."

John now wished that Rev. Love had chosen another biblical passage. Given John's record over the past several years, this one was not a good sendoff passage for him. There was no reason to bring this passage to God's attention just moments before his final judgment.

"John was particularly interested in the sheep and the goats, and the fact that goats were sent to eternal damnation while the sheep received eternal life," Rev. Love continued. "A big question for John, and I believe a big question for all of us, is 'What makes a person a goat?' Obviously, we all want to be sheep—or, at least, we ought to want to be sheep. But in our world of governmental programs for the least of these for which all of us are forced to pay taxes, the water sometimes gets murky. John often asked, 'If we're being forced by our government to pay taxes to feed the hungry and clothe the naked, is that sufficient to make us sheep? Or do we need to do more?' This was a huge dilemma for John, who, as all of you know was politically opposed to governmental welfare programs because he thought that they stifled initiative and created dependency. But he worried that opposing those programs made him a goat, and we often discussed the fact that Christ allowed no alibis. One either helped those in need or one didn't. This was a dilemma that John is now carrying to his grave, but not a dilemma for JoAnn at all. JoAnn has, ever since I've known her, been a sheep who gives of her time and money to help those in need."

JoAnn lowered her head, a gesture that John thought expressed more her concern for his eternal soul than any sign of humility at Rev. Love's commendations of her good deeds.

"With their concern about helping those in need when they were at Christ Episcopal, John and JoAnn were leaders in establishing the church's first clothes closet way back in 1989. They helped establish Christ Episcopal's prison ministry, and they were active participants until they left the church. They volunteered at the Columbia homeless shelter for at least eight years, if my memory is correct.

Truly, during their time at Christ Episcopal, they were sheep in the truest sense of the word."

Again, John's eyes would have filled with tears as visions of his and JoAnn's service at Christ Episcopal came back to him. What had happened to him these past few years? He knew, of course that it was the breakaway and the big event that followed soon thereafter that started him on the new path. He glanced back at Pastor Flake and noticed that he had developed an intense scowl as the eulogy went on.

"But the John Willis I knew was not just a good Christian at church, he was a strong leader in our community," Rev. Love continued. "He served on the Columbia United Way board for several years and was the citywide campaign chair in 1997 when United Way raised the most funds in its history, a level that has not been reached again in the following eighteen years. He was a Rotarian, serving twice as president of the downtown club. Along with his business partner Clyde, he founded the South Columbia Teen Club to combat the influence of gangs. That club alone has provided college scholarships for more than ninety kids over the past fifteen years. Truly, Columbia will miss John Willis."

John was immensely proud that Rev. Love had mentioned his contributions to his community. Those were activities that he had really enjoyed, and Rev. Love's proud listing definitely ought to help him get into heaven.

But Rev. Love was not finished and moved on to another topic. "Many of you who know John also know, however, that over the past several years he and I have had our differences.," he said. "We both, jokingly, claimed that we were political moderates. He called me a 'liberal moderate' and I called him a 'conservative moderate.' But these two moderate positions put us at odds during elections, and we often had, you might say, interesting discussions. As far as I can remember, I never won one of these discussions, but neither did John." After smiling, he paused, then reflected, "We differed on another subject as well, and that subject caused us so much stress and tribulation that we agreed to simply not discuss the topic. That subject was the treatment of homosexuality by Christians."

John was startled. *What is he doing? This is not the type of stuff he needs to be saying at my funeral. He needs to keep talking about what a great Christian I was, how I loved and respected everyone, how much I will be missed, and how I will soon be in heaven with God looking down on everyone. Not all this stuff about gays. I know what he is doing: He's just trying to get the last word in. Well, he's not! If he wants an argument right here in front of everyone, then he is going to get one.*

Then it hit John, he could not speak so that anyone could hear him—these death limitations were getting to him. He glanced back again at Pastor Flake who had now folded his arms tightly in front of him and his scowl had turned into a mask worthy of a Halloween parade float.

"I've always felt that being gay is not a choice," Rev. Love continued. "It's a gift from God, made a sin only in the minds of those who have chosen to believe as they do. By the grace of God, one is born gay. But being anti-gay is a choice. Hence, the sin is not in being gay but in being anti-gay. I read recently of a pastor down in Georgia who disowned his own son because he was gay. I cannot imagine such ignorant cruelty. If I had a gay son or daughter, I would love him or her to the end of the Earth and thank God for bringing him or her into my life."

Pastor Flake now looked as if he were trying his darndest to lay an egg! For a moment, John became concerned, because of the very large veins pulsating near the Pastor's temples, that he was going to have a stroke and would be joining him as a spirit any minute now on the ceiling. He definitely did not want that to happen. He had enough to worry about getting himself into heaven without having to also worry about getting Pastor Flake in.

But Rev. Love kept on. "John, on the other hand, believed strongly that being gay was a choice and that making that choice was a sin of the highest order. He often quoted biblical passages to support his position."

John agreed that he had, indeed, quoted those biblical laws, but they did not seem nearly as important now that he was on his way to his final judgment as they had back then.

Rev. Love continued, "This past week when the Supreme Court approved gay marriage as the law of the land, John and I almost severed our friendship because he felt that the courts had overruled God, and I thought that they had made a major move to prevent religious tyranny in our nation. Now I'm sad to say that John and I will not be able to finish this argument until we're both in heaven, and I'm sure that God will have put the issue to bed by then."

John hoped that that was the end of that discussion and that Rev. Love would get back to talking about all the good things that John had done for others--good things that needed to be brought to God's attention at his final judgment.

And Rev. Love did just that by turning his attention to JoAnn and the family. "JoAnn, Bo, Billy, family, as you go from this service today, I encourage you to remember the good that was in John and the good that he did. This community will miss him, and I know that you will miss him."

After a long pause, Rev. Love concluded with, "Let us pray."

"Our God and our Father, we pray that you will forgive John of those sins that he did not know he was committing and accept his soul into heaven this day. Amen."

What was that all about? John thought. *You cannot sin unless you know you are sinning, and I know that I've not sinned. Just ask Pastor Flake. Well, maybe not him, because he just stole my flowers! Not Fred Wilkens, the deacon who is on his third divorce, after being caught having affairs by his first two wives. Ask the national saints. Yeah, them. Wait, wait, maybe not them, either. Everything they see is sin! Look, God's just gonna have to trust me on this one.*

As John pondered how he was going to convince God that he did not have any unknown sins, the pallbearers carried his casket to the cemetery just outside the funeral parlor where his grave had already been dug.

John's family and the crowd followed, and he wondered what Rev. Love could possibly say at the graveside service that he had not already said. John certainly didn't want any more attention given to sins that he might have committed without knowing they were sins. He had never thought about such sins before and did not want to start at this late date.

Chapter 5

Graveside Service

"Religion is great at instilling the fear of hell, but awful at giving a taste of heaven."

Mokokoma Mokhonoana

John's casket was a little heavy for the pallbearers and some of the funeral home staff had to help, but they succeeded in placing it on the rack above the grave. John took a position inside near the top of the burial tent and waited for Rev. Love to say a few words before the final prayer. He hoped that the service would be short; he didn't want to take a chance on anything else being said that would make it more difficult for him to get into heaven. And he absolutely did not want Rev. Love to say, "We now bury John's body where he will stay until Jesus comes again to call him unto Himself." The thought made him shudder.

John's family, including his brothers and their wives, now sat in the chairs under the tent with JoAnn and his sons and their wives sitting in the chairs nearest the casket. A few of the guests stood under the shade of the tent, but most were forced to stand outside in the boiling sun. South Carolina's famous black gnats were busy with their games of flying into peoples' eyes, up their noses, and into their ears. The sun bore down, the temperature soared near ninety-eight degrees, and the air was still as a frightened mouse, which brought even more gnats. In other words, it was hot as, well, hot as blue blazes, because it might be a bad omen to mention that other word at this junction. Sweat poured down the faces of the guests, and the women frantically batted the gnats with their cardboard funeral home fans, not understanding that the gnats were experts at that cat-and-mouse game. John concluded that any fool should recognize that the service needed to be short and sweet. Besides, he needed to get the service over so that he could be on his way to heaven. Yet Rev. Love remained standing outside the tent in the back, making no effort, whatsoever, to give John his final farewell. "Why doesn't he come on up and get the service started?" John wondered.

Then, an *Oh, no!* involuntarily escaped from John's spiritual lips. Pastor Flake was making his way toward the casket with a microphone in his hand. Apparently in deference to John, JoAnn and the boys had asked Pastor Flake to perform the burial service, probably thinking that it would be a short one.

This is not good, John thought. *Pastor Flake is going to lay that dinosaur egg he has been hatching in his gut, and it's going to splatter everywhere.* If he could have done so, John would have grabbed the microphone, thrown it into the grave and, when Pastor Flake crawled in to retrieve it, lowered the casket on top of him. He knew that Pastor Flake was not going to let Rev. Love get away with what he had said back in the parlor. *There is going to be a knockdown drag-out here and I'm going to be caught in the crossfire. My chances of getting into heaven are gone! I might as well get my fire extinguisher and head down below."* Then he remembered that he had no ability to even hold a fire extinguisher. *This death thing is just not working out,* he thought. *No wonder hell is so hot; you can't bring a fire extinguisher with you!*

Pastor Flake began to speak.

"Family and friends," he said, "when I thought about what I should say to you as we lower John into the ground to await the return of Christ, I remembered John's total commitment to saving our nation from Hollywood, the liberals, and the Supreme Court justices who have all committed themselves to the devil to destroy our country."

He did it! He did it! John was beside himself. *Pastor A. Reel Flake said that I'm going into the ground until Christ comes again. How will I ever get to heaven buried six feet under? This guy stole my flowers and is now trying to bury me for no telling how many years. If he says one more thing that hurts my chances of getting into heaven, I'm going to have to take him out!*

Then John realized that he had no ability whatsoever to take Pastor Flake out.

Pastor Flake continued, "So I decided to let John use my voice to give us his final warning of what the devil is doing to our children, our children's children, and all our children from here on. Before I do that, however, I'm going to ask Deacon Fred to open the casket so that we can see John as he speaks through me."

While Fred moved to the casket and opened it after searching for the lever which he couldn't find because there wasn't one, John noticed the large stack of speaking notes in the Pastor's hands. *This is terrible,* he thought. *This is not going to be a short service. We will be lucky to get away by dark.*

Pastor Flake looked out at his audience with grave concern, as if he were about to announce the end of the world. In a very serious and religious voice, he began, "As he goes down into the ground to await Christ's return, John wants us to know that those of us who remain here have a responsibility to save our nation from the devil's grip."

Then, raising his voice a notch or two, he declared, "John wants me to tell you that this past week, five minion lawyers—yes, just five lawyers, who have given their souls to the devil himself—overruled our Lord and Savior's laws. How can we look this nation's Founding Fathers in the eyes and admit that we let this Christian nation that they so carefully designed come under the control of the devil? We need to be ashamed of ourselves!"

John glanced back at Rev. Love and noticed that he had lowered his head, shaking it slightly as if embarrassed by John's words, as if these words were, indeed, being uttered by John himself, who was helpless to stop it.

Pastor Flake continued. "As he goes to his grave, John challenges us to never surrender," he proclaimed. "We must take a stand and never yield. Those five Supreme Court lawyers who betrayed our Lord by ruling that our states and counties must issue marriage licenses to same-gender couples think that they have overruled God's laws, but God always wins. His laws will be true until the end of time and not one lawyer or millions of lawyers can overturn them. God's law in Leviticus 18:22 unequivocally states, and I quote verbatim, 'Homosexuality is absolutely forbidden, for it's an enormous sin.' Even a fool lawyer ought to be able to understand that. But that's not all. In Leviticus 20:13, the God we serve states again his absolute law and I quote, 'The penalty for homosexual acts is death to both parties.' How many times and in how many ways does God have to tell this nation his unequivocal law on homosexuals? These are the words of God. No man may overturn them, especially not five lawyers sitting in Washington, DC."

John glanced back at Rev Love. His demeanor had changed from one of embarrassed resignation to rage. Rev. Love leaned over to Chris, who was standing nearby, and said loud enough for those close by to hear, "This guy is a fool!"

Chris responded, "I agree" and, then, patting the concealed weapon in his suit jacket, laughingly, asked "Want me to help him get to heaven early?" To which Rev. Love responded "Tempting, but we don't want to make heaven hell for everybody else."

Pastor Flake, happy that he had a captured audience, continued unflustered and determined. "You may say that the polls show that the majority of the young people in our country support gay marriages, and those polls may be right. But why do our young people have this opinion? I'll tell you why. Hollywood and the liberal media have pulled one of the greatest coups of all times by convincing this nation's young people that God's laws are no longer relevant.

"Look at John in that casket. He wants me to tell you that God's laws are never irrelevant. He knows and wants you to know that there will be a day of reckoning—a day when God will bring this nation to its knees for violating His laws. Just as God had a whale swallow Jonah to get him to go tell the people of Nineveh to repent of their sins, God is now having this grave swallow John so that he can tell us to repent of our homosexual sins."

Listening intently, although somewhat wary of what Pastor Flake may say or do next, John suddenly understood why God had taken his life this week. God had to take his life, so Pastor Flake could use him and his grave to warn God's people about the sin of homosexuality. Just like Christ, John had been called to make the ultimate sacrifice, only this time it was to save the nation from homosexuals. His worries were over. His ultimate sacrifice should definitely get him into heaven, regardless of what Rev. Love thought.

But Pastor Flake was just getting started. "Not only does John want us to repent and stand strong against Hollywood, the liberal media, and all the other forces that the devil has commandeered to his service, he wants us to mount a counterattack. Yes, with God's help, we will, John. We will not let you down! We will not! Christians all over this great nation will rise to defeat the devil and his minions. Already, Franklin Graham, who understands the horror that homosexual marriages will inflict on our children, is set to lead a national revival in every state capital. In his Facebook announcement, Franklin tells us: 'America is in trouble. At 62 years of age, I've lived long enough to learn that neither the Democrats nor the Republicans can turn this country around; no political party or politician is the answer. The only hope for this country is Almighty God and His Son, Jesus Christ. Next year I'm planning to travel to all fifty states to conduct prayer rallies—we're calling this the Decision America Tour. I want to challenge Christians to boldly live out their faith and to pray for our nation and its leaders.'"

As Pastor Flake expounded on Graham's upcoming national tour, John glanced down at JoAnn and could tell from the tightness in her face that she had had about all of Pastor Flake she could take. John was now worried that she might get up, walk out, and pop Pastor Flake one as she passed. In fact, he was sure that JoAnn had been watching Rev. Love and they had been non-verbally planning just such an action.

Pastor Flake, of course, noticed nothing and went on, "Franklin Graham understands that homosexuals will recruit our children to their sinful lifestyle and, in doing so, violate God's laws. His website warns us with these words: 'We are to speak the truth of God's Word to a society that's racing toward moral decline at warp speed.' So, John, from his grave and through my voice, asks you now to join us in praying for Graham's Decision America Tour and to give generously to help those who are fighting the evil forced on us by those five devil-lawyers in Washington. Before we go on, however, John wants Lucretia to say a few words."

What? John thought. *What I want is for Lucretia to shut up and go home.* But his death limitations, he had come to accept, were very serious limitations when it came to speaking up for himself.

Lucretia smiled as she walked to the front. Pastor Flake handed her the microphone. She smiled again and began, "Before John passed, Alex talked to him about supporting the Columbia Women's Conservative Club in our efforts to take our country back. John had enthusiastically committed to helping. So, I know that as he looks down on us from heaven right now, he wants me to ask you to join him in participating in our current fundraising campaign. In honor of John's commitment, JoAnn and the family enthusiastically asked that you send money to our club in lieu of flowers. This is what John wanted."

No! That is not what I wanted. I wanted flowers! John tried to shout but couldn't. All he could do was remain in his not-so-comfortable hovering position near the top of the tent, mad as a setting hen.

Lucretia continued, "As John, through Alex, has so beautifully told you today, our nation is under attack from the left, which has taken our country from us and hidden it beneath their sinful ways. Well, the Columbia Women's Conservative Club will not let our nation remain buried in sin, and we will not pay a ransom to the left-wing devils to get it back. Instead, we will fight with every last ounce in our Christian bodies until we, too, lie in our graves beside John. And even then, we will keep on fighting, like John today. Yes, John continues to fight as he lies there in his casket. Look at him! See the determination and commitment on his face! He pleads with you to join him in fighting against this terrible tragedy forced on our nation."

John looked at the face on his old body and saw no pleading whatsoever, except maybe a pleading look for her to shut up.

Lucretia glanced at her audience and must have liked what she saw, although John could not imagine why. So, she went on, "Before he died, we explained our battle plan to John and he loved it. In fact, he helped develop it. That plan includes inviting Roy Moore, the chief justice from Alabama, to speak on how we can defy the sinful court rulings forced on our nation. We also hope to get Franklin Graham to give our club a special visit when he is in Columbia on his Decision Tour. As John has already told you, Franklin is a man of God who clearly sees the moral decline in our nation and is committed to organizing an army of Christians to fight back. If John could rise up out of that casket, he would be the first to volunteer as a captain in Graham's army."

Turning toward the casket and looking directly at John's body, Lucretia said, "Since you cannot rise up, John, we're pinning your captain's bars on you today as you lie here in your place of honor." She walked over to the casket and, with radiant pride, pinned the bars on the collars of John's black suit.

Taking a few steps back, Lucretia exclaimed, "As a captain in God's army, John is in heaven right now, talking to God on our behalf."

No, I'm not. I'm right here! Never had John wanted arms to wave so badly.

Lucretia plodded right along. "He wants each of you to join him and also be captains. And you can do just that by contributing at the captain's level to our campaign. That level is only a thousand dollars. If you cannot do that, you can contribute at the lieutenant level, five hundred, or the sergeant level, two hundred and fifty. We have set up a table where you can make your donations and receive a certificate showing your rank in God's army as you leave today."

Captain's bars? Captain's bars! They took far more than a thousand dollars from me. They took my flowers. She ought to be making me a five-star general! John wanted to shout.

Lucretia was on a roll. "Finally, John wants all of you to join the Women's Conservative Club next Wednesday at noon on the fourth floor of the capitol to pray for our state and our nation to return to God. John will not be there because he will still be in heaven speaking directly with God and asking for His blessing on our club and for His guidance as we fight in His army. Thank you. And God bless America, and God bless the great state of South Carolina. And thank you, John, for your message today!"

John was at a total loss. Was all this good for his chances of getting into heaven or had he just been doomed to hell? In the last few minutes, Pastor Flake had buried him at the bottom of his grave waiting for Christ's return to Earth, and Lucretia had lifted him to heaven where he chatted with God. Did they know something that he didn't? All John knew was that he was still here, and he had either just become a charter member of Columbia's hatemongers club or played a major role in organizing God's army of Christians to take back the nation. One way, he would soon be shoveling coal in hell. The other, he would soon be riding in the lead chariot with Pastor Flake in God's victory parade, with the deacons from Zealot Baptist proudly carrying the rescued nation on their backs.

While John considered his own fate, he looked around at the guests, who were still frantically swatting gnats while being burned like roasting hotdogs by the scorching sun. They were not happy, but too courteous to leave, that is, except for Chris and Rev. Love, who were on their way to the parking lot.

He thought that Pastor Flake, who was standing in the shade of the tent, would be wise enough to see what was happening and close the service, but that was only wishful thinking.

For some reason, Lucretia then handed the microphone to Deacons Henry and Jerry. Henry began, "It would not be appropriate for us to send John off without recognizing his contributions over the last almost seventy years to maintaining our South Carolina way of life. So, Jerry and I have a surprise! We want to drape his casket with this confederate flag and say to John, 'The left-wing liberals have tried to destroy our South Carolina history and way of life, but you have stood firm. John, we want you to know that, in your absence, we will continue to carry the torch, and with that torch, our beloved confederate flag.'" Henry and Jerry then had a little ceremony to unfold and drape the flag over the closed part of the casket. Upon completion, the rest of the pallbearers clapped loudly.

As the deacons finished, John glanced at his brothers and did not like what he saw. Jeremy had his hand on Clint's leg and was whispering, "Just let it ride, Clint. Let it ride. We'll be out of here in a few minutes." He heard Clint respond in a much louder whisper, "We better be or I'm gonna stuff that flag down his stupid throat."

John was now getting worried. *Any minute, now, this burial is going to come unglued and I'm going to be caught in the middle.*

If Pastor Flake heard the whispers, however, he chose to ignore them because he took the microphone and said with a very satisfied smile, "Thank you, Lucretia, and thank you, Deacons Henry and Jerry. You can look at John's face in the casket and tell that he is proud to be a captain in God's army and to have his casket wrapped in the confederate flag."

John looked again at his old body and saw no change, except that now it was covered with gnats and the makeup was beginning to melt and run down the sides of his face.

Then Pastor Flake spoke in a very adamant and determined voice, "John, we want you to know that we at Zealot Baptist are right beside you. We'll also stand up to the devil's tyrants. We'll never ever, even under the threat of arrest by our morally corrupt government, marry a same-gender couple in God's house. Nor will we ever let a married gay couple become members of our church. But, John, just as you and JoAnn often challenged us, we'll always show the love of God to gays. We want all of Columbia, indeed, all the nation, to know that Zealot Baptist is a church of love. We love single gays and lesbians who stay in their closets, welcome them into our worship services, and will do everything that we can to save their souls from eternal damnation."

John looked at JoAnn's watch. Pastor Flake, with Lucretia's and the deacons' interludes, had now been speaking for forty-five minutes, and it looked like he was just getting warmed up. The temperature had to be over a hundred now and those who could not find shade under the tent were in the final stages of cooking to a crisp. Most had given up on fighting the gnats and glanced around at each other with pleading looks that said, "Will this guy ever stop?" Then, from the back of the sun scorched crowd, a red-faced, sweat-soaked elderly man, who had already taken his suit coat off and was using it to keep the sun from blistering his bald head, called out in a muffled tone that was still loud enough for all to hear, "Hey, Preacher, it's hot as hell out here in the sun." To which an elderly lady shouted through the funeral home fan she was using to shield her face, "Amen, brother, hot as hell! And these gnats are eating us alive."

Totally missing the message but seizing the moment, Pastor Flake exclaimed in a commanding voice, "And that is exactly where these left-wing gay lovers are going when they die!"

John looked immediately at JoAnn and knew that she was going to explode.

But Pastor Flake saw nothing and returned to a calmer, more loving and religious voice as he looked directly at Bo and Billy, saying, "Because of your mom and dad's admonition that, as God's people, we must love all people, including our gay brothers and sisters, I am proud to announce today that next week, Zealot Baptist church will start a new conversion counseling program for our gay brothers and sisters to help them understand and repent of their sin."

Then, turning towards the casket, Pastor Flake addressed John directly with a huge grin: "John, before you enter the ground to await Christ's return, I'm even prouder to announce that this unique program will be named, 'The John and JoAnn Willis Gay Rescue Program.'"

It was at that point that all hell broke loose. JoAnn jumped up. "You yellow-bellied, arrogant bastard!" she shouted. "You will not use my name or John's name to inflict harm on any of God's children! You want a Biblical quote, well, I'll give you a Biblical quote: Deuteronomy 23:2: 'A bastard shall not enter into the congregation of the Lord; even to his tenth generation shall he not enter into the congregation of the Lord.' You and your snooty wife have prostituted John's burial today to promote your hate, and you did it in God's name. I knew we should never have asked you to do this service. I stayed quiet over the past five years while you killed our marriage and destroyed our family with your stupid hate. You're the one who sins, not our gay sons and daughters and friends. It's you and all of your hatemongering friends who are going to hell, not them!"

John panicked. *What is JoAnn doing? I will never get into heaven now.*

But that was just the beginning. Bo jumped up, grabbed the microphone from Pastor Flake, and beat him over the head with it. Deacon Fred tried to intervene, but Billy cold-cocked him. People dashed off in all directions, knocking the tent poles down and collapsing the tent, trapping nine people who frantically struggled to crawl out.

John's spirit got thrust into the open casket, which was quickly knocked closed by a falling tent pole, trapping him inside with his body. If that were not bad enough, the jolt caused the casket to start its descent into the grave. John, temporarily forgetting that he was a spirit, went into a death panic, thinking that he was on his way to the bottom where he would have to stay until Christ returned.

Fortunately, John, remembering that he was a spirit, was able to pass right through the top of the casket and rise into the air. It was at that point that he realized that death certainly had some major advantages along with its limitations. Quickly looking around, he could not miss noting that a down-home South Carolina brawl had broken out and was now in full swing. The Zealot Baptist deacons were squared off against the Smith & Crowdy staff. His business partner, Clyde, had one of the Zealot Baptist deacons in a headlock. Deacon Fred was still out cold from his encounter with Billy. Martha held a handful of hair that she had just removed from Lucretia's head. Despite their ages, his brothers had Deacons Henry and Jerry down on the ground and were wrapping the Confederate flag around their heads. He heard Clint say to Deacon Henry, "I didn't get beaten half to death in Selma to have you drape a Confederate flag over my brother's casket." In the meantime, Rev. Love and Chris were taking advantage of the mayhem to let the air out of Pastor Flake's car tires.

The funeral staff had locked themselves inside the building and called the police.

John's first thought was, *Well, I guess JoAnn will not be going back to Zealot Baptist.* That was followed by a horrible thought: *My chances of getting into heaven have just been shot. God will definitely not let anyone in whose wife has just called God's messenger, Pastor Flake, a yellow-bellied bastard.* How was he going to explain the ruckus that just happened? Then, he got it! He would blame the devil! But which side was the devil?

As sometimes happen, a photographer from the *The State* newspaper was driving by and saw the commotion. He got some great photos, which went viral within an hour with the caption, "A typical South Carolina funeral." The best picture of all was the one with the microphone stuffed in Pastor Flake's mouth with the caption, "Pastor eats his words." Voted second best was the picture of Deacon Henry eating the Confederate flag. The police arrived and loaded three paddy wagons full. The photographer followed the paddy wagons to the jail and got some more great pictures of the deacons getting their mug shots taken.

The reception luncheon was canceled for obvious reasons and, as the last paddy wagon left, John found himself all alone in the cemetery.

With nothing else to do, John decided to watch his grave as the workers filled it with dirt. Given what almost happened, he was glad to be able to watch looking down on it rather than looking up from the bottom. He was really glad when it was completely filled, and he was still above it. Now, if he only knew when his ride to heaven would show up.

Chapter 6

A Journey Back to Niceville

"History will have to record that the greatest tragedy of this period of social transition was not the strident clamor of the bad people, but the appalling silence of the good people."

Martin Luther King

The day had been draining on John's family, and when they got home from the police station, it was late. They decided to eat a quick bite, and all go to bed. Fortunately, they had not been charged with any crime as a result of the melee at the cemetery, so they could take that off their worry list. Pastor Flake and the deacons could not say the same. After they accused the police chief of being part of the left-wing liberal plot to take over the country and deliver it to the devil, things kind of went downhill. When the family left to come home, Pastor Flake and the deacons had completed their mug shots and were posting bond.

John was still down at the cemetery waiting for a message from God. He had been sure that as soon as his funeral and burial were finished, someone from heaven, maybe Jesus himself, would come for him. But so far that had not happened.

It made sense that cemeteries would be pick up points for new spirits whose bodies had just been buried. With over 6000 people dying per hour, it would be a lot more efficient to pick up spirits at the cemetery rather than making 6000 individual house calls per hour. So, after his grave was filled, John roamed the entire cemetery searching for a chariot stop or at least some signs pointing towards heaven. But, again, found nothing. Not even a guardian angel watching over him. Everybody was dead and he was all alone--without any idea of what to do or where to go.

He was afraid to leave, however, because the cemetery seemed like the most likely place for his ride to heaven to appear. He just needed to wait in his Sunset Funeral Home "waiting room" next door to the cemetery until his ride arrived.

Unfortunately, his waiting room had no magazines or even a television. So, he settled in and began his wait for his name to be called with nothing to do except think and worry.

Perhaps this is what I'm supposed to be doing: just thinking and assessing my life so that I will be ready to answer questions when I'm interviewed for my final entry into heaven.

With that thought, he decided to review his life, starting with his childhood years in Niceville, to see if there were any messages or information that he might need in his final interview--anything he might need to explain.

John remembered that his father had been a very strict but loving man, and a devout Christian. From John's first memory, his father had owned the Dixie Truck and Car Lot down on Plantation Road. Almost every business in Niceville used the word "Dixie" in its name. There was the Dixie Café, the Dixie Feed and Seed, Dixie Groceries, Dixie 5 and 10, the Dixie Dry Cleaners, and even the Dixie Methodist Church.

John's dad, or Mr. Willis as most people called him, was at the lot six days a week, but he took Sunday off to go with his family to the downtown Rock Bottom Baptist Church. The name "Rock Bottom" was chosen by the church's founding fathers to note that their faith in Christ gave each member a strong, rock-bottom foundation for their life.

Sunday was the Lord's Day, his father always said, and they needed to keep it holy. Sunday afternoons were always for rest. His father taught the adult men's Sunday school class, and Saturday nights were set aside to prepare his Sunday school lesson. No one messed with him while he was preparing. Onetime John and his brother Jeremy got into a fight on the porch just outside of the dining room where their father always worked. That was a major mistake. The lesson that Sunday must have been about the wrath of God, because that is what they got in response. Their father had each of them go cut a switch off a tree and bring it inside. In previous wrath-of-God situations, their father had them swap switches when they returned, so, thinking ahead, John had cut the largest one he could find, while Jeremy cut a much smaller one. To this very day, John still thought that Jeremy had advance information, because, this time, their father used the one each brought to "tan his hide." John still remembered being confused at the time. Next time, should he cut a large or small switch? However, after a few of these hide tannings, their father never had any more Saturday night interruptions.

As John now thought of that little episode, he felt sure there could be no big message here, except maybe never to generate the wrath of God in people who use switches.

John remembered his mother as a sweet, generous person who mostly managed the house and vegetable garden while their father worked down at the truck and car lot. Dad usually stayed at the lot during lunch because that was when a lot of buyers came by. But he always came home right at seven each night, expecting his supper to be on the table waiting for him. It always was.

Their mother also taught Sunday school, but hers was the fourth-grade class. John and his two brothers went to the same K-12 school. It was the only school in Niceville, except for the black school out on the edge of town. John's oldest brother Clint was a straight-A student. His second-oldest brother, Jeremy, was an okay student but a star football player. John surprised everyone by being both a straight-A student and a star athlete, excelling in both baseball and football.

During the summer when he and his brothers were young, all three boys helped their father down at the used car lot by doing odd jobs. Joe Jackson, a black man who worked for their father doing jobs like cleaning the cars and the grounds, often brought his two sons, Ben and Hank, with him during the summer to help out. The five boys often played together. In fact, Clint and Jeremy became really good friends with Ben and Hank. In fact, best friends ever. At their ages, the fact that he and his brothers were white, and Ben and Hank were black never entered their minds.

All five boys were having a fantastic time that summer. Joe had set up a contest in which the boys would each wash a vehicle without Joe watching. When all were finished, Joe tried to guess which boy washed which car or truck. When not washing cars or doing other chores, all five boys played war games, with the trucks and cars serving as boulders to shield each boy from an enemy's attack.

It was always Clint and Ben against the other three. It had been their best summer ever.

It was, that is, until Claude Stoner came down to the Dixie lot to talk to their dad about buying some more log trucks. Claude was in his early fifties and had inherited the largest logging company in Niceville. He bought almost all his trucks from their dad, and he was his biggest customer. A big man, Claude chewed tobacco, always wore his cowboy boots and hat, and had a big belt buckle with a picture of the Confederate flag on it. Claude and Rob Coles, the banker, shared a close friendship, and they often had coffee at the Dixie Café next door, telling one "nigger joke" after another.

On this particular day, Claude was checking out some log trucks with their dad when Ben and Clint came running by to escape their enemies. Joe had temporarily joined the other team, but then faked that he had been shot.

With a fury that the boys had never seen before, Claude, out of the cold blue, shouted to their dad, "What the hell are you doing letting your boys play with these niggers?" Pointing toward Joe, he shouted even louder and with more anger, "If you want my business, you'll fire this nigger who thinks that he can play with white boys. I'll be back when this nigger's gone." Claude then turned, stalked to his truck, got in, slammed the door closed, raced the motor a couple of times, and peeled off, slinging gravel all over the nearby cars and trucks to let everyone know that he meant what he had just said.

Even now as he shifted around his Sunset Funeral Home waiting room, John remembered the look of horror, hurt, and fear on both their father's and Joe's faces. The war game had stopped. No one said anything until Joe finally said, "Mr. Willis, I need to go. I'll find another job………. somewhere." For the first time in their lives, the boys saw their dad cry as he and Joe hugged each other, each knowing that he had no choice.

Totally humiliated in front of Ben and Hank, Joe and his two sons got into his car and slowly drove off. There were no goodbye waves or see-you-laters. John never forgot watching Clint cry his heart out, knowing that he might never see his friend again.

John still could not get the horror of that summer day out of his mind—even as he now floated around the waiting room patiently biding his time before his escort to heaven arrived.

While he wondered if a message was buried somewhere in the memory of that day, he remembered the news that flew through Niceville the following day as told by some of Joe's neighbors.

That night, five hooded KKK members, reeking of South Carolina moonshine, came screeching up to Joe's house after dark in two pickup trucks. The trucks had Confederate flags flying from rigged up flag poles in back and poster paper signs taped on the truck doors proclaiming in large handwritten letters, "KKK—PROUD ENFORCERS OF GOD'S LAWS." The lights of one truck shined directly on the front door of Joe's house and the other lights on a nearby oak tree. The hooded servants of God piled out with burning torches in their hands and rushed in masse onto the porch of Joe's house and gave him the choice of coming out or having his home burned to the ground. Fearing for the lives of his family, Joe came out and was immediately grabbed, stripped of his shirt, and tied to an oak tree that was close enough to the house that his wife and sons could see what happens when a nigger gets "uppity" and plays with white boys. Four of the hooded brothers gathered around Joe to watch the fun, while the largest man, a barrel-chested, red haired guy known in the KKK circles as the "Whupper," waved his whip and backed up a few paces to deliver the lesson. Before doing so, however, he snarled in his slow southern, moonshine slur, "Don't know why y'all niggers ne'er learn. Y'all can't play with white foks. Y'got that nigger? We's gonna let you off easy dis time. Yu're only gonna get five lashes tonight—one fer each boy. Next time, it'll be two lashes fer each. Di'ye hear that, nigger?"

With the force of the wrath of God, the first lash made a big slash down Joe's back and blood immediately dripped down on to his pants. However, either because of the moonshine or the stupidity of the Whuper, the next lash completely missed Joe and caught one of the nearby hooded brothers around his neck, drawing blood that quickly made a bright red spot on the bottom of his white hood. The KKK brother, apparently, did not like the lash and turned and shouted, "You stoopid idiot, I'm gonna wrap that whup around yo fat, dirty neck!" He lunged at his hooded brother, who had turned, dropped his whip, and started running the other way like a spotted ape. Before the wounded saint could reach his attacker, however, he tripped over a tree root, fell, and hit his head on the bumper of the truck, knocking himself completely out of this world. His nearby brother rushed to pick him up but tripped over the same root and hit his head first on the truck door and then on the running board, also knocking himself into nether land. The hit ripped the paper "KKK—PROUD ENFORCERS OF GOD'S LAWS" sign into shreds, revealing a painted sign on the truck door: "Stoner's Logging Company."

Forgetting about Joe, the hooded enforcers of God's laws loaded their two unconscious brothers into the back of one of the trucks. One of the three remaining conscious brothers got into the back of the truck with his two laid-out buddies just in case they came to and wanted to know where they were. The other two drove the trucks.

Almost as quickly as they had appeared, the hooded protectors of Niceville's way of life gunned their truck motors and sped away with their unconscious brothers in the back of their truck and their Confederate flags flying high.

Well, they almost sped away. As the truck with the unconscious KKK members in the back was turning the corner out of Joe's yard, its high-flying confederate flagpole hit a low hanging tree limb, causing the pole to slam the only conscious saint in the back of the truck upside of the head, knocking him out of the truck and onto the hard ground, head first. Now there were three hooded brothers in nether land. The two drivers stopped, stacked their third buddy on top of the other two like pine logs and drove away more slowly this time with only one Confederate flag flying high.

As soon as the white hoods were out of sight, Ben and Hank ran to the tree and untied their father, their mother wiping the blood off his back. She wanted Joe to call the police, but he refused. Then she begged him to go to the hospital emergency room and he also refused, although he wanted to go just to hear the wounded hooded servants of God explaining to the hospital staff what had happened to them. But Joe knew all too well what had happened to other blacks when they had gone to the police or the hospital after a KKK visit.

Now remembering the KKK story more than fifty years later, John wondered what message he was supposed to extract from it. He decided that it was that if most KKK members' brains were put in a matchbox, they would rattle like BBs in a box car. After a spirit chortle, he knew this might not be the message that he was looking for.

Turning back to those days in Niceville, John remembered that Clint was the most hurt by the news of Joe's whipping and kept asking their dad if Joe's sons had been hurt. Dad kept saying that he didn't know. Clint then wanted to go see Ben, but their dad refused and never answered Clint's repeated question, "But why, Dad?"

John did remember his mom and dad talking about what to do, eventually agreeing that his dad should discreetly send Joe a check for six months' pay but should not risk delivering it himself.

A few weeks later, Joe moved his family without leaving any trace as to where they were going.

That experience was John's first real encounter with what it meant to be black in Niceville back in those days. It also made clear to him how cruel adults could be for no apparent reason. John then asked himself if he had ever been that cruel to anyone and concluded that he had not. He could remember a few occasions, especially one, when he had taken a strong stand against both sin and sinner. That was different. So, that could not be why his trip to heaven was being delayed. There had to be another reason and he needed to find it before his judgment interview.

John's thoughts wandered back to what had happened right after Joe left his job at the lot. He remembered his father talking to his mother about who would replace Joe. He certainly did not want to ever go through that experience again. He finally decided that he would hire a woman with no children and sent the word out into the black community. Blacks were cheaper to hire. After several interviews, their dad hired Charlene Grissett, a thirty-something single black woman who had been taking care of her mother. Her mother had recently died, and Charlene needed work.

Dad tried her on washing the cars and trucks and cleaning the lot and even though she was a woman, she was even better than Joe. Charlene had the added advantage of being almost white. In fact, she was half white. So, hopefully, there would be no more problems from Claude Stoner. Their dad told their mother that he had never heard of the KKK hurting a woman.

Charlene worked out well, and Claude came in and bought three more trucks as if nothing had ever happened.

John quickly assessed his entire memory of those two days involving Joe and his family. He decided that the message was that one must work within the social rules of the society in which you live to avoid trouble. That may sound like a solid message, but somehow John did not feel that it would help him very much in his final interview, especially if those rules hurt other people.

While he waited, his thoughts moved on to other memories of his youth. During the next few years after Joe left, the Civil Rights movement was picking up steam in other parts of the South. However, Niceville had no marches and the Confederate flags flew proudly, along with the American flags, both at City Hall and at the county court house as well as at many businesses. Local blacks remained quiet and obeyed all the segregation rules placed on them.

Looking back on those days, John wondered how black parents were able to teach their children all the written and unwritten rules of segregation. It was critical that they did so because one little slip, even on their children's part, could cause a black person to be humiliated, or lose a job, or even receive a late-night visit from the Niceville KKK. They had to remember that they could only drink from public "Colored" water fountains and use "Colored" public bathrooms—if there were any at all labeled "Colored," which often they weren't. They had to remember that they could not go into any white restaurants or white hotels. They could not enter white churches or white theaters. The bus station had two waiting rooms--one for whites and one for blacks--and blacks dare not enter the white room. In fact, blacks were never allowed to use the same waiting rooms as whites anywhere. And, of course, blacks had to always sit at the back of the bus. Traveling out of town in the South was always a problem for blacks because many towns had no black restaurants, no black restrooms, and no black hotels. A few white restaurants, but only a few, had a dining room out back with a "Colored" sign on the door where blacks could get a meal, but they were not advertised and hard to find.

The only blacks allowed in white homes were maids, but they could not eat at the same table as the white family. Black men could never smile at or even look a white woman in the eyes. Blacks had to live in black neighborhoods and attend black schools. No sports team from a black school could play a sports team from a white school. And, of course, no white school sports team could ever have a black player and vice versa. Blacks were to treat all whites with respect and dignity, always saying, "Yes, sir," and "No, sir," or "Yes, ma'am," and "No, ma'am."

The same was not true for whites. Whites could, and did, ridicule, humiliate and offend blacks anytime they wanted. Although no decent person would use it today, the word "nigger" was commonly used in white conversations in Niceville. John distinctly remembered a speech by Darrel Evans, a local politician, at the county courthouse.

Everyone stood on the courthouse lawn as Evans shouted his speech from the porch. White people were the first group standing nearest the speaker, and black people, knowing their place, stood in the back. Evans started out talking about what a great place Niceville was to live and raise a family, and then went on to talk about all that he would do to make Niceville an even better place to live.

Pointing to the Confederate flag flying behind him, he launched into how that flag symbolized Niceville's way of life. No one would ever bring that flag down as long as he was in office. "We're a peaceful community," he said. "We will always be a peaceful community as long as I'm in office. There will never be a freedom march in Niceville because we all know our place. Our whites have their communities and our niggers have theirs where we can socialize, each with our own, as God intended."

"But," he said, "I want the world to know, and for our local niggers to know, that you will not mess with Niceville as long as I'm in office. You mess with Niceville and I will personally go to Atlanta and buy a train load of Governor Maddox's ax handles. And in Niceville, we know how to use ax handles!"

Obviously, Evans did not have to worry about losing the votes of black people because very few could afford the required poll tax or meet the other stringent voter requirements imposed by the ruling whites. He did, however, need to show that he was more committed to maintaining Niceville's segregated way of life than his opponents. He had to "out-nigger" his opponents, he often joked with his white buddies.

Appealing to the racial bigotry of his white voters, Evans shouted, "I've nothing against niggers." Lifting his head to see over the whites gathered close by and directly address the blacks in the back, he said, "In fact, I love all ya'll. I love you so much I want to send every one of you back to Africa." The blacks knew from experience that at such a point, for their own safety, they should leave. In the meantime, many of the whites shouted and clapped, just as enthusiastically as the members at Zealot Baptist clapped when Pastor Flake delivered one of his anti-gay sermons.

John remembered, as clearly as if he were still standing in that crowd right now, the hurt on the faces of some of the blacks, especially those black parents with their children with them, as they eased away. Evans, however, was not the only white racist speaking out against integration in those days. National leaders such as George Wallace, Lester Maddox, Ross Barnett, Orval Faubus, and Bob Jones up at Bob Jones University created a favorable environment for people like Evans with their segregationist speeches. John could not remember the exact words of these national leaders, but he did remember their tones of defiance and hatred towards blacks as well as white left-wing liberals who were forcing racial integration on innocent whites.

John wondered how Evans and the national segregationist leaders could get away with such hate speech and then realized that they were speaking to white audiences who loved their messages. After a little more pondering, John decided that a speech reflects the audience to which one is speaking. If you're speaking to racial bigots, you need to speak bigotry. He started to extend this analogy to modern day television networks but stopped himself because he didn't know which networks God watched.

Speaking of bigots, John wondered if Darrel Evans and the national segregationist leaders ever got into heaven. *Surely, they're all dead by now,* he thought. *So, where are they today?* He wondered again why he was recalling those events in such detail just now. Was there a message in here somewhere for him? Something that he needed to know for his final interview?

Clearly, the whole Southern culture was organized against blacks in those days. Whites held all the power positions and blacks held none. Whites held all elected governmental positions, all law enforcement positions, and all the professional jobs that earned higher salaries. They strongly enforced keeping blacks in their subservient roles— no wonder Joe didn't want his wife to call the police. The police were part of the system that enforced the current culture and would do nothing to ensure that Joe received protection. In fact, they would most likely feel that he deserved what he got because he had violated the unwritten rule that blacks and whites don't socialize in any manner.

For the first time ever, it was totally clear to John that the whole legal, cultural, and economic system back then was intentionally organized by the whites against the blacks. And that there was very little, in fact nothing, that a black person could do to avoid becoming a victim of that system. He could now see the sins perpetrated on blacks by whites who had both designed and enforced the system, but few white people saw them as sins back then—just the way things were-----and needed to be kept.

And blacks were not the only ones affected. The system would turn on a white just as quickly as it did on blacks if a white threatened the system. John remembered a specific event that happened to his brother Jeremy.

Jeremy was a junior in high school and had dated a lovely girl named Sandy who had just recently moved to Niceville with her family. Sandy's father was Jimmy McCormick, a Church of God minister from upstate Illinois, who had moved to Niceville to start a new church.

Where Rev. McCormick came from, blacks and whites often worshiped together, so he followed the same practice in his initial house church. In addition to worshiping together, they were also working together to build a small, cinderblock church building. Given that they were in Niceville, South Carolina, they only had twelve members, seven black and five white. Everyone else in the community understood the risk far too well to take a chance on attending an integrated church.

One Saturday afternoon, Jeremy stopped by the Dixie Café to buy a coke. He was standing at the counter when a large, red-faced man, dressed in overalls with no shirt and long red hair all over his head, arms, and chest, said to him, "I understand that you're dating Sandy McCormick."

Being proud that a girl as beautiful and nice as Sandy deemed to date him, Jeremy replied with a huge smile, "Yes, sir!"

With a scowl, the barrel-chested man, who was at least twice Jeremy's age and size, reached into his overall pants pocket and pulled out a switchblade knife. With a quick motion, he popped the blade out and in a voice of hate that Jeremy had never heard before snarled, "Anyone who'll date one of them is no better than they are."

According to Jeremy, he left his Coke and money on the counter and ran as fast as he could to his car, jumped in, locked the door and started the engine. As Jeremy sped away, he saw the man and two of his buddies falling out laughing at the terrified teenager.

That evening when Jeremy told the story to their family, Dad said he knew the man. His name was Bilbo and he had a bad reputation. Then with a combined look of fear and worry, their dad added, "Boys, there are some mean people in this town who will hurt you. You have to stay away from them."

Both Mom and Dad remained firm that Jeremy could never date Sandy again. He never did, because the following week someone or several people ambushed Rev. McCormick and, after beating him with some pipes, pushed a large section of their church's partially built cinder block wall on top of him—perhaps in an effort to make it look like an accident. He remained unconscious in the hospital for over a month. When he was released from the hospital, the family moved and was never heard from again. No one was ever arrested for the crime. In fact, the "accident" was never even investigated by the sheriff.

These memories of his early days in Niceville bothered John as he now shifted around in the waiting room of the Sunset Funeral Home. In the years since he had left Niceville, he had come to view such a cultural system as bad, but now that he was perhaps only a few moments away from meeting God, he realized how horrible it had actually been, not only for black people but also for white people who had tried to change the system. In fact, he concluded that the system was so horrible that God had to view it as not just a sin, but a major sin against God's people.

There has to be a message in here for me, John thought. But while he was wondering what the message was, his mind went to another question. If the segregated cultural and legal system that kept millions of blacks in both poverty and a subservient role with no hope of escape was such a terrible sin, what were God's people and churches doing during those days to change it?

John realized that he didn't know what pastors were saying in black churches back then, but he did know what was being preached in his childhood years at the Rock Bottom Baptist Church in Niceville.

Rock Bottom was a completely committed Southern Baptist church. It had had the same pastor, Brother Calvin Averett, for seventeen years. He was an avid segregationist. That fact was illustrated in many ways, including the racist jokes that he told. John still remembered one of Brother Averett's jokes told during the time he had served as a monitor at the polling station for a local election. Only a very few blacks could vote back then, and most of them could not read. So, as Brother Averett told it to the deacons (and as John's father later repeated to John), Brother Averett had claimed that he had helped an elderly black lady who could not read fill out her ballot, which listed strong segregationist candidates like Darrell Evans. Brother Averett jokingly said that he said to the lady, "You don't want to vote for Darrel Evans, do you?" The lady responded, "No, sir." So, Brother Averett said, "Okay, we'll put an X by his name." The deacons loved the joke.

John, in his reflecting spiritual state of mind, decided, *Tell me what types of jokes you tell and I will tell you what type of a person you are.* Clearly, that joke told God and everyone else exactly what type of person Brother Averett was. Then, for a moment, John wondered about his own jokes, particularly his welfare queen jokes, and what those jokes told God about him. They weren't vulgar jokes, but they did belittle other people, especially black people. He wondered if his welfare queen jokes were a holdover from his early years in Niceville. Was he, himself, still a bit racist even though he had accepted racial integration a long time ago? Was his own racism the reason God had him in this waiting room, giving him time to find the message? Maybe that was it.

But jokes were not the only way that Brother Averett demonstrated that he was a firm segregationist. John remembered Brother Averett once telling his dad that it would be a cold day in July (actually, he used another word, but "July" is okay for this recall) when blacks attended his church. In fact, John now thought of the time that Brother Averett heard that some blacks were going to try to attend a Rock Bottom Baptist Sunday service. He called John's father, and the deacons held an emergency meeting, at which it was decided that some of the deacons would guard the doors with shotguns.

John still remembered riding to church in his father's 1957 Chevrolet with a shotgun in the trunk. At the church, his father and Rob Coles stationed themselves at the front entrance with their shotguns boldly displayed to show God's love and grace to all who approached the door. Inside the church, Brother Averett's sermon topic was "Showing the Love of Christ to our Neighbors in Africa," after which a special Southern Baptist foreign missions offering was taken.

On the Sunday following the gun-toting guards, John remembered that Brother Averett even more clearly stated what God's churches—well, at least Rock Bottom Baptist—would do to eliminate all the hurt that racial segregation placed on Blacks in Niceville and the rest of our nation, and that was absolutely nothing. No criticism or objection was ever voiced by Bro. Averett or any church member regarding Rev. McCormick being beaten or the dogs and fire hoses being used against the Selma marchers or the murder of the Black teenagers in Mississippi or the Alabama bombing of a Black church with little children inside. His church and all its members gave their approval of these events by being stone silent, choosing instead to preach about things that happened thousands of years ago, not those happening right now.

Instead of speaking out against all the hurt being placed on their black brothers and sister, they did everything they could to perpetuate the hurt, while bald-facedly proclaiming to spread the love of God to all.

In fact, Brother Averett's sermon that following Sunday was so strongly worded against racial integration that John could still hear the words. Brother Averett started by looking out at his congregation with exasperation. He said, "Y'all know that just a few years ago, our nation's Supreme Court ruled that our schools must be integrated and now our Congress, led by left-wing liberals, has mandated that our churches and businesses, including our restaurants and hotels, must serve people of all races.

"Our own government has turned on us, threatening the most sacred part of our national constitution, our freedom of religion. I have news for our Supreme Court and the left-wing liberals: they cannot overrule God's laws that have stood the test of time over hundreds of generations. Every thinking Christian knows that the integration of our schools, our churches, and our playgrounds will lead to interracial marriages which are strictly forbidden by God."

John remembered that, as a boy, he accepted every morsel of such pronouncements as if they were direct messages from God. He now wondered if that wasn't the greatest sin of all, brainwashing young minds that could not yet defend themselves in the name of God. But he could not figure out what to do with that thought because, surely, Christians must teach their children.

Brother Averett continued, "In the Bible, Noah was saved because he was pure blooded, while those around him, who were mongrelized, were drowned by our Lord so that the races would remain pure. And in Deuteronomy 23:2, God says, 'A bastard shall not enter into the Congregation of the Lord: even to his tenth generation shall he not enter into the Congregation of the Lord.'" John remembered thinking at the time that Brother Averett had just used a curse word in church. But Brother Averett quickly explained the word by saying, "The Hebrew word for 'bastard' in this scripture does not refer to the married status of one's parents, but rather it refers to a mixed breed or mongrel. It refers to the forbidden intermixture of races. That's why the penalty extends for ten generations, and it shows how seriously God views this sin. If a black person and white person have a child, then it's a mongrel—that child and its children for nine more generations shall not enter the house of God. Can you imagine the hurt that one must feel when they're prevented from entering God's house by God's own law? As Christians, we cannot ever let this happen to a child."

John tried to think back if he felt any pity for those children who already existed as such in the world, but he couldn't remember even thinking about such children at the time. The memory simply consisted of the awful power of the preacher's words.

Brother Averett continued, "It's clear from the Bible that God intended for the races to stay apart and to stay pure. And make no mistake about it—integration of our schools and churches will quickly lead to interracial marriages. Can you imagine what would happen if we allow white and black children to be together in our schools and Sunday school classes? At their young ages, children don't understand God's laws against interracial mixing. They must be taught how to be discriminating in their social interactions. If we allow them to be together as children, we will quickly have black and white kids becoming friends, and the next thing you know they will be dating and then, before you know it, we will have interracial marriages, which is a sin against both God and the children born from those marriages."

John remembered that Sunday thinking that Brother Averett was right. Of course, he did. No intellectual room had been left to think anything else, not for an impressionable child. The white people in Niceville would never tolerate a mixed marriage in their town. The couple would be run out of town on a rail, if the KKK did not beat them to a pulp beforehand.

With his next comment, Brother Averett reinforced John's thoughts that every effort had to be made to prevent such marriages. "God is calling us as Christians to take a strong stand against this sin and we have done just that," he declared. "Our church has a policy against accepting Blacks as members, and in obedience to God's laws, we will maintain that policy no matter what our corrupt government does to try to force us to change. Some churches, like the Episcopal Church, may acquiesce, but we Southern Baptists will never acquiesce. We'll stand strong against this violation of God's interracial marriage laws."

Brother Averett paused to catch his breath, looked around at his audience with dead seriousness, and, after a few more moments, went on. "Fortunately, we don't stand alone," he said. "Already, God has called great Christian leaders like Bob Jones, George Wallace, Lester Maddox, and Orval Faubus to lead us. And we at Rock Bottom Baptist Church must support them by saying 'no' to the integration of our schools and churches. I don't know where you stand today, but as for me and my house, we choose to abide by God's laws, not man's laws." He paused for what seemed like eternity to let the congregation ponder his total commitment to God and then, in almost a whisper, asked "What do you and *your* house choose?" Still almost whispering but with even more seriousness, he called for a commitment: "If you join me today in standing firm against this sin being forced on God's churches, I invite you to join me down front at God's altar. If you choose to side with the devil, then you may stay in your seat or leave.

John remembered looking back to see if he could see Clint and Jeremy, who were home from Clemson and N.C. State, but could not find them. He did, however, see other members rising and heading down toward the altar. Turning back around, John saw his father rise, step out into the aisle and wait for John and his mom to join him. Initially neither did. John's father motioned to his mom, but she still did not stand. He then reached, softly grabbed her arm, and gave a gentle pull. To his father's obvious relief, she stood. He pulled again, and she walked toward him with tears flowing from her eyes.

Together, he, his dad, and his mother slowly made their way down to the front with about a hundred other people. Without saying a word, his mother gave his dad a look that said *This walk will change our lives forever.* As they reached the altar and turned around to face the congregation, John noticed Clint and Jeremy walking out the back door.

After the church service, John was not sure what he had just committed to, but it had to be big, he thought. In fact, now, almost sixty years later looking back on that day, it was far bigger and meaner than he realized at the time.

When the family got home from church, their father was irate at Clint and Jeremy for having walked out. Dad did not know then that both Clint and Jeremy had participated in Martin Luther King's Civil Rights marches. If he had known, he would probably have disowned them right then and there rather than waiting several months. Mom, however, did know about their marches, and John was sure that was why she was crying as they walked down front. She knew that this event could destroy her family, perhaps forever.

Their dad addressed Clint and Jeremy directly. "Why in the world would you embarrass me and our family by walking out during the commitment to God's laws and our Niceville way of life? Now, the whole church knows that my sons are nigger lovers."

Clint was the first to respond, with a pent-up anger that surprised everyone, including himself. "And God and the whole church knows that you're a racial bigot," he said. "You've been a bigot ever since you fired Joe and took away my friend Ben. You didn't even have the decency to go see Joe after he was beaten by those thugs! It's bad enough that you're a bigot, but you're more, you're a Christian bigot using the Bible to justify your bigotry. All you care about is making sure that your raciest friends and fellow church members know that you are one of them. You don't care how many people you have to hurt to protect that reputation."

Their dad looked both stunned and hurt but said nothing. Although no one knew it at the time, their dad could have mentioned the personal KKK threats that he feared, but he didn't. He could have mentioned that his Dixie Truck and Car lot was totally dependent on a line of credit from the bank owned by Rob Coles, the KKK Grand Dragon, but he didn't. He could have mentioned that if the

KKK targeted him, his business would go bankrupt in only weeks, but he didn't. He just sat there stunned and hurt.

Finally, their dad said, "Boys, I'm just worried about your safety." Turning toward Jeremy, he said, "Remember what happened to you a couple of years ago when Bilbo pulled his knife on you? Well, he and his buddies are the same people who whipped Joe. And the same people who beat Rev. McCormick. There are some really mean people in this town, and none of us are safe if they think you're siding with the niggers."

Clint responded, "Dad, these are exactly the people that we have to stand up to if Blacks are ever to get equal rights."

After that, there was nothing but silence until Mom intervened. "These are trying times for all of us and for all families, black and white," she said wearily. "We have to try and understand each person's views and feelings." With that, the discussion ended.

Only four months later, their father learned from Rob Coles that Clint and Jeremy had participated in the Selma and Washington, DC Civil Rights marches.

Rob had pictures to prove it. Dad looked at the pictures, not with disbelief because he knew his two sons' feelings about the horrible way blacks were treated in the South, but with sickening fear because he knew what he had to do to protect his business and his ability to support his family.

Clint did not help the situation any by bringing a surprise friend home with him from college a few weeks later. On the Selma March, Clint had been beaten by a deputy, who snarled, "What's a nice white boy like you doing with a bunch of niggers on this bridge?" He then smashed his Billy club on to Clint's head. As the deputy swung his arm back to strike Clint again, however, a young black man stepped in front to try to deflect the blow. Unfortunately, his attempt did not fully work, and the young man took a deflected Billy blow to his own head. The blow knocked him to the pavement, blood seeping from the wound.

Both young men were placed in a paddy wagon for a trip to the jail. On the way to the jail, Clint's newfound friend asked him where he was from. Clint responded that he was from Niceville, South Carolina, to which his new friend said, "No joke? I used to live there. My dad worked at the Dixie Truck and Car Lot."

Then the two simultaneously recognized each other. "Ben!" Clint shouted. "Clint!" shouted Ben. The two embraced with a love that only the best of friends know.

Clint learned that Ben's father had used the six months' salary that Clint's father had sent to him to move to Boston, where he had family. After a few months, Joe's back had healed, and he got a job as a cook in the Coastal Seafood restaurant. Over the next few years, Joe learned that he had a real talent for cooking. Within two years, he was the head chef at the restaurant. Four years later, with some financial help from friends, Joe opened the now famous Boston Joe's Soul Food restaurant. The restaurant had been a huge success and was now nationally recognized.

Ben and Hank were among the first blacks to enroll in previously all white colleges, Ben at the pre-med program in Clemson and Hank in engineering at N.C. State.

As they caught up on old times, Clint and Ben both said that when they heard that Martin Luther King, Jr. had organized the Selma March, their memory of the Claude Stoner episode at the truck and car lot and Joe's KKK beating required that they be there. From that point on, Ben and Clint were almost inseparable, picking up where they had left off at the Dixie Truck and Car Lot ten years earlier.

Clint should have known better. Things had not changed in Niceville and, in fact, had gotten worse since the freedom marches in Alabama and Washington, DC had begun. But he was so happy to have reunited with his friend Ben that he wanted to share that excitement with John and his parents. Perhaps, more importantly, he wanted to stand up to the barrel-chested segregationists in Niceville.

When Clint drove up, John remembered that he and his father and mother ran to the car. They had hoped that this visit proved to be a healing reunion with their son after their last confrontation. When they approached the car, however, they gasped when they saw that Clint's surprise friend was black. It didn't matter that the friend was Ben, the young boy who had played at the Dixie Truck and Car lot way back when. It didn't matter that Ben's father, Joe, had volunteered to quit his job to save their father's business, that their father had hugged Joe when they departed, that Joe had been beaten for no reason, that their father had felt so bad that he sent Joe six months' salary when Joe voluntarily left, or that Joe had gone on to become a huge success in Boston. It didn't even matter that Ben was now an honor student in the pre-med program at Clemson.

All that mattered in Niceville, South Carolina, at that moment was that Ben was black and Clint and his family were white.

If John's father let Ben sleep in his house, eat at his table, and use his bathroom, it would be the end of everything he had worked for all his life. First and foremost, he would be violating God's law, which he had just a few months ago committed to uphold, in front of God and everybody. Beyond that, he would lose his business. The powers-that-be would strip him of his position as a deacon and Sunday school teacher. The local Southern Baptist Association might even demand his excommunication. They certainly could not tolerate having an integrationist in their ranks. They would start losing members and the money that those members produced. And how could they send missionaries to take the love of God to the people of Africa if they lost their funds?

In a spirit of finding a compromise, their father offered to pay for a hotel, but suddenly realized that Niceville had no hotels for Blacks. So, he offered to call some black people he knew and see if they would let Ben spend the night with them.

Clint did not back down. He had come to stand up to bigotry and intended to do so at all costs. It was either Ben stayed with the family in their house, or Clint and Ben would leave.

So, Dad did what he had to do. He told Clint and Ben to leave. They never made it into the house.

Clint said that if they left, he would never come back.

Dad responded, "Fine."

John never forgot the sadness in his father's eyes and the tears running down his mom's face as Clint and Ben drove away, not even turning to wave goodbye.

His father had just been forced to choose between his son and God's laws and the Niceville way of life.

John was sure that he heard his mother, under her breath, curse the Southern Baptist Convention and call Brother Averett a bastard; in fact, she may have called both bastards—as the three of them walked back into the house.

John remembered the horror of that day in their front yard and thought the message had to be in there, somewhere.

Was it that one should never force their family to choose between God's laws and their children?

Or was it that one must be willing to sacrifice family to uphold God's laws?

Or was it that when it comes to ridding a town of corrupt sin, the church will be the last to speak up—if it ever speaks up at all?

Or, maybe, the message was even worse: the church will do its best to perpetuate and reinforce the sin—even to the extent of demonizing any members who violate the church culture, no matter how cruel the culture is to other people.

John was totally confused now and hoped that no one came right then to take him to heaven. He would never be able to pass any sort of test. He needed more time.

As he hovered near the ceiling of the waiting room, all those memories from more than fifty years ago continued to run through his soul. Although he had not seen it at the time, he now realized that the Civil Rights movement, while critical to abolishing the horrible written and unwritten laws of segregation, was also difficult for many white individuals and families who were torn between maintaining their historical way of life and showing God's love to their black brothers and sisters. Some, like Clint and Jeremy, were willing to brave the dangers and pay whatever price came their way. Others, like the KKK, flying their Confederate flags with brazen pride, were willing to demand a high price from any who threatened its way of life. Both groups claimed to have God on their side. Still others, like his parents, got snared in a situation where everything they had worked for all their lives could be taken away at a moment's notice—even by the actions of their children.

Then John thought about the man who had chased Jeremy with the knife, who whipped Joe and who beat Rev. McCormick until he was unconscious. What happened to him when he died? Did he go directly to hell? Or did God reward him for trying to protect Niceville's way of life and enforce God's laws? After all, racial integration can lead, and has led over the past several decades, to interracial marriages, which the Bible and Brother Averett clearly stated was against God's law.

Then, for the first time since he had begun to reminisce about his childhood years in Niceville, John thought of the similarity of the civil rights movement and today's gay rights movement, asking himself, *Is equality for gays not the same thing? It can lead to gay marriages, which according to Pastor Flake is against God's laws. Maybe we need more barrel-chested men with switchblades and whips today to help Pastor Flake protect us from gay marriages.*

Maybe that was the message. Even though it seemed wrong when Bilbo, the KKK "whupper," pulled the switchblade knife on Jeremy and when he whipped Joe, maybe it was not wrong. Maybe there comes a time when we must be strong men and women with switchblade knives and whips for our God.

But what if these men and women in churches are just bullies and it turns out that Christian bullying is not the path to heaven as Pastor Flake had claimed? *So, which is the way to heaven?* He wondered.

Then it dawned on him. He didn't have a choice. His record had been closed and it was one of being a barrel-chested enforcer of God's rules. That was it. That was his only choice. That was the case that he would have to present to God as soon as someone came for him. *Sure hope that it works*, he weakly concluded.

Soon after, John remembered the biggest crisis that his family ever experienced, although the boys did not know it at the time. Their mother arrived unexpectedly at their father's car lot and found him embracing Charlene, the woman who had replaced Joe. Well, they were doing more than embracing, and the scene was not completely unexpected on his mother's part.

What had started out as a little flirting between Charlene and their father had soon turned into more flirting, which turned into their dad putting his wedding ring in his pocket, which turned into a ride on some country roads, which turned into frequent late afternoon visits to Charlene's home where she lived alone since her mother had died.

Dad had started coming home later and later, claiming that he was really behind with his bookkeeping. After several weeks, one of mother's friends told her that when she took her maid home late one afternoon, she had seen Dad walking with a white woman into a home in the black neighborhood. Mom confronted their dad and Charlene right then and there, as they let go of their embrace. They both knew that what they were doing was wrong and begged for forgiveness.

Mom left immediately and moved in with her sister who lived in nearby Livingston. Dad drove over every night and begged her to come home, promising that nothing like that would ever happen again. After a week, Mom finally agreed, with the understanding that if it did ever happen again, she would perform serious surgery on him while he slept. Somehow, they were able to keep Dad's tryst a secret so that no one at church or even the community ever found out.

In fact, John did not learn about the affair until several years later when his cousin Robert told him about it. Robert had been living at home at the time of the affair and had heard John's mother describe the whole thing.

All the boys knew at the time that it happened was that Mom had gone to visit her sister, that Charlene had decided to move out of town, and that their dad had been able to get his backlog of work completed so that he could come home on time every afternoon. Mom and Dad had kept right on teaching Sunday school classes, and their dad continued to assert to his Sunday school class that interracial marriages and adultery were against God's laws. He was even asked to serve as the chair of the deacons, and in that capacity blocked the appointment of a divorced man who had remarried after his wife left him and his two small children for another man— because the Bible says that a divorced man cannot serve as a deacon.

He had never thought about it much before, but John now wondered if his father had gone to hell because of his adultery, or because of his hypocrisy, or neither. Maybe hypocrisy is okay if it is done in God's name. Maybe, he hoped, his father had sought forgiveness and had really gone to heaven. That works for sins that one knows one has committed, but what about sins that one does not know about—like, maybe, being a barrel-chested bully. Then he wondered if one can, just maybe, obtain forgiveness after death by saying, simply, "Please forgive me," every time another sin is read off. That just did not make sense, however. If that were the case, one could spend one's whole life in sin and just go to their judgment day with a million *please-forgive-me*s in his pocket—except he remembered again that spirits don't have pockets.

Chapter 7

Sunday — Time for Church

*God laid it on my heart, I had to preach His Word. When I finished, I realized that I had used God's word to preach **my** word.*

K. Boutwell

John had been waiting and thinking all night—searching his experiences back in Niceville—trying to decipher messages and explanations that would ensure his entry into heaven. It was now Sunday and he was still here.

What really amazed him was that, as a spirit, he had no need nor any desire for food or water. He could keep on going forever and ever and ever into eternity. And rain, snow, heat, storms, and wind—nothing bothered him, at least nothing except why he was still here rather than in heaven.

He began to think again of all the things that could be keeping him out. He had definitely done his share of fighting sin. Every time the minister had asked people to come down to God's altar to commit to taking our country back from the devil, he had enthusiastically volunteered. Maybe that was not enough. Even though he had sent a lot of emails, and truckloads of righteous hate had spewed from his mouth aimed at gays, lefties, immigrants, Muslims, and the devil's Supreme Court, he was certainly way behind Pastor Flake and probably the national saints. But, he had to be among the best in Columbia and had to rank at least in the top 100 in South Carolina, he concluded.

Because he had been so good at hating the violation of God's laws, that could not be the problem. It had to be something else. Maybe it was the lack of flowers at his funeral, or Rev. Love's lukewarm recommendation, or it could be JoAnn calling Pastor Flake a bastard, or it could even be, he was reluctant to admit, sins that he did not know he had committed.

Or it could be something else that he had not yet found. He now felt sure, however, that as soon as he found that crucial message or reason, he would be in heaven basking in all its glory. He had to keep searching.

Because it was Sunday, he decided that the Columbia churches would be good places to search. He initially decided to check out the early service at Christ Episcopal, but then chose a totally new church, the Broadstreet Methodist Church—new to him, at any rate, since the Broadstreet Church itself was over a hundred years old. Some say that John Wesley himself had worshiped there.

Clyde, his business partner, was a member at Broadstreet and often bragged that its pastor, Rev. Bill Young, was the best in Columbia at preaching God's love for all people regardless of race, gender, or ethnic background. Clyde had said, on more than one occasion, that every person who attends one of Rev. Young's services comes away feeling blessed and loved. But as great as Rev. Young was, his wife, Manci, was even better, because she practiced what he preached.

"Manci is a human dynamo in serving the least of these," Clyde often said. If she was not down at the church garden growing vegetables to help those in hunger, she was at the church clothes closet bundling clothes for families in need. In between those tasks, she managed visits to nursing home residents without families in town and even got Rev. Young to go with her on prison mission trips. Clyde said that just talking to Manci about all her good work made him exhausted.

It took John less than three seconds to arrive inside the Broadstreet sanctuary, where Rev. Young was just beginning to speak at the early service. John settled in near the ceiling at the back of the sanctuary and immediately noticed perhaps as many as two-thirds of the pews empty.

Rev. Young began, "As you may remember, I mentioned in a sermon about a month ago that as followers of our Lord, Jesus Christ, we need to pray long and hard about what we will do if the Supreme Court rules in favor of same-sex marriages. I mentioned that my own prayers and study of Jesus's ministry had led me to believe that I must accept gay marriage with the same love that Jesus extended to me when he gave His life so that I could have everlasting life. I went on to say that I was not asking that you adopt my position on gay marriage, but that I was asking you to join me in praying for God's guidance and that you study Jesus's ministry to see where you, yourself, are led."

John looked around the small congregation who seemed to be looking at the minister not with fear and awe but as if they were fully taking in what he was saying and trying to come to terms in their own thinking.

"I also promised you at that time that if the courts did, indeed, rule in favor of gay marriage, I would address the topic in detail," Rev. Young continued. "Well, they did rule in favor of gay marriage this past week, and I now stand before you to address this very sensitive subject.

"I must tell you that I received lots of phone calls, letters, emails, and visits after just mentioning where I felt God had led me a few weeks ago. After that, I found that I face one of the most difficult decisions of my life. It was made abundantly clear to me, beyond any doubt, that if I continue to endorse gay marriage, many members of our congregation will leave.

"If you look around this morning, you will see that we have lots of empty pews that would normally be filled with worshipers. In fact, one of our adult Sunday school departments informed me that they will never attend another Broadstreet Church service as long as I'm your pastor. I've been told that about forty-five members of that department are visiting Holly Hill Lutheran Church this morning. I know that if our church loses forty-five or more of our members, we will face major financial problems. And I could, almost certainly will, lose my job as your pastor. With two children in college and very limited savings, this will place a major hardship on my family. So, my dilemma: Do I say to you what God has placed in my heart? Or do I capitulate to save my job?"

John could not help but notice the hurt and pain in Rev. Young's face. After a long pause and a successful effort to fight back tears, Rev. Young answered his own question:

"After hours of prayer and thought, Manci and I've weighed the consequences and have jointly concluded that we, together, must do what both of us feel with all our heart God has called us to do and that's to stand on the side of love, respect, and equality for our gay brothers and sisters."

John looked at the audience and saw some tears quietly wiped away and then, suddenly, a little over half of the congregation stood and clapped with enthusiasm. The others sat there with looks of either disgust or fear on their faces.

For a moment, John himself wanted to join in the clapping, but then remembered that he had staked his entry into heaven on fighting to prevent the sin of gay lifestyles being forced on innocent victims. That was the path he had chosen, and he needed to stick to it. Left-wingers were intent on forcing this wicked lifestyle on the nation and its children. But Rev. Young did not seem like a left-wing liberal. Instead, he and his wife seemed like sincere people willing to make major personal sacrifices to help gay people have the same rights and privileges as other people. *What if the Rev. Youngs in our nation are really not left-wing liberals, after all, but just very concerned, decent people wanting to help?* John wondered.

After the clapping had ceased and those standing had taken their seats, Rev. Young continued.

"One of the Biblical passages that Manci and I read over and over was First Corinthians, chapter thirteen, with particular emphasis on verses twelve and thirteen," he said, opening his worn copy of the Living Bible. "I quote, 'In the same way, we can see and understand only a little about God now, as if we were peering at his reflection in a poor mirror; but someday we're going to see him in his completeness, face to face. Now all that I know is hazy and blurred, but then I will see everything clearly, just as clearly as God sees into my heart right now. There are three things that remain—faith, hope and love—and the greatest of these is love.'

"I know that many of us don't understand why people fall in love with people of their own sex because God did not wire us that way. But we can understand love and respect and dignity and equality. Our nation, in the fifties and sixties, faced this same dilemma regarding the treatment of our black brothers and sisters. It was a time when they suffered almost beyond belief under the unwritten, unfair, oppressive, and sinful rules of segregation. For the most part, God's white churches were active in enforcing those rules, not in recognizing and fighting the injustice. In too many of our white pulpits, pastors quoted scriptures to support the horrible treatment of blacks. Almost no white churches, especially in South Carolina, took a leadership position opposing such treatment. To our shame, the burden of throwing off the sinful yoke of racial segregation was passed on to our black Christian churches and the support that they received from white Christians from other parts of our nation. Our South Carolina white Christian churches fought them every step of the way. Ultimately, however, we as a nation and as God's people did what was right, although it took some of us a lot longer than others, and some of our white churches may still not be there, more than fifty years later."

"Our own church suffered greatly in those days when Rev. Saunders spoke from this very same pulpit in favor of equal rights for our black brothers and sisters. It was about this same time of the year in 1963 when Rev. Saunders delivered his sermon asking our members to join him in simply recognizing that all of God's children, of every race and ethnic group, needed to be treated with respect, dignity, and equality. He asked our members in 1963 to do the right thing."

"The following Sunday, almost half of our members chose to attend other churches and never came back. Our church's giving immediately dropped by more than half, and the church was unable to meet its financial obligations. Two weeks later, our trustees fired Rev. Saunders. The Methodist conference could not find another pastoral job for him in South Carolina. After going for over a year without a job, he chose to leave the ministerial profession and remained, for years, a broken man."

There was a long pause, as if Rev. Young were allowing anyone who had missed it to make the connections to the current situation.

Then he continued, "There comes a time in every society when God's people must do what is right, and often this splits families and friends and congregations and calls for personal sacrifice. We were at that point in the 1960s in the treatment of our black brothers and sisters, and we're at that point today in the treatment of our gay brothers and sisters. This time, God's people need to be out front leading instead of mounting counter attacks as the rest of our nation marches on in doing what is right and just."

"Manci and I fully understand what the Bible says in both the Old and New Testaments about the treatment of gay people. We also know that the Bible gives full permission to keep slaves. Yet as a society, we came to realize that slavery is not right and just and, in spite of what the Bible says, we now have laws that prevent it. We know that the Bible, in Exodus, demands that witches be put to death. But after years of killing innocent people accused of being witches, we came to understand that that biblical law must not only be absolutely ignored but also condemned. Today, one would most likely be executed if they killed a person accused of being a witch."

John noticed that even some in the congregation who had not stood up to clap nodded their heads in agreement.

Rev. Young went on, "We know that the Bible strictly prohibits people with mixed race heritage from entering God's house for ten generations, but we realized long ago that such a prohibition is not right and not just, so we also ignore that biblical law."

"We know that the Bible prohibits divorces, except in cases of adultery, and that our church culture has, over the years, viewed divorce as a sign of failure. We now understand that there are often valid reasons for divorce other than adultery and that divorce need not be thought as failure, necessarily. So today, we do what is right and just. Divorced people are treated just like anyone else. We know that the Bible strictly prohibits women from speaking in church. Yet, we—at least we Methodists—now recognize that women have the full right to speak in our churches. We ignore that biblical law, too."

"We know that, in Deuteronomy, the bible requires a rape victim to marry her rapist. We would never even think of obeying that cruel and indecent biblical law today."

All this seemed to make a lot of sense, although John knew full well that in many other churches such broad condemnation of the scriptures would be considered blasphemy.

"There comes a time when God's people must prayerfully go beyond the cultural laws of the Bible to apply love—the kind of love that Paul called the greatest of the three fundamentals---and do what is right and just," Rev. Young argued passionately. "Manci and I feel that that time for us is now. We understand, however, as I mentioned a moment ago, that many of you don't fully comprehend why some people fall in love with other people of the same sex. Paul says in our passage today that there are lots of things that we don't know or understand."

"One day when we see God face to face, however, we, who are not ourselves gay, will know and understand. For now, we must have faith that that which God has made is exactly what He intended to make. None of us are mistakes. Although on occasion, Manci has wondered if I was a mistake."

The joke did little to relieve the tension in the air, so Rev. Young pushed on.

"None of us, including our gay brothers and sisters, is a mistake. We're exactly who God intended for us to be. Falling in love is not a mistake. Wanting to marry the person whom we love is not a mistake. Manci and I have wonderful gay friends who have been with their partners for years but have been denied the same benefits and privileges of marriage other people enjoy. They're asking for no more or no less than the same treatment under our nation's laws that Manci and I enjoy, or you and your spouses enjoy. They've been struggling for equal treatment for a long time. Manci and I are so glad that they have finally achieved it—at least to some degree."

"I'm very ashamed to admit, that it has been us, God's people, who have been and still are most vocal in denying them those benefits. Paul says that of these three—faith, hope, and love—the greatest is love. And it has been that love that we, God's people, have not given freely. But it's never too late to give God's love."

He's wrong on that point, John thought. *It may not be too late for the rest of these people, but it's too late for me. My record is fully closed, and it's not a record of showing love and respect for gays. It's a record of hating the sin and doing what I could to prevent those sins from being forced on others.*

John wondered, just for a moment, however, what his life would have been like if he had chosen to show such love and respect. Maybe, if he had, he would now be in heaven instead of still on earth frantically searching for a message, or at least an explanation.

Rev. Young continued, "Felix Frankfurter, a Supreme Court Justice, once said, 'Wisdom too often never comes, and so one ought not to reject it merely because it comes later.' We should have given our gay sons and daughters and brothers and sisters our love along with respect, dignity, and equality many years ago. But we didn't—some of us because we believed that being gay was a chosen sin, others because we were afraid of what our friends and neighbors would say, others because we feared what our fellow church members would say, and still others because we simply didn't want to get involved."

"Thank God, there were those who have been willing to speak out over the past few decades so that gay couples can now enjoy the same marriage privileges as others. Wisdom on what is right on this issue was late in coming to Manci and me, but now that it has come, we cannot reject it. The time has come that we must join those who are speaking out on the side of respect, dignity, equality, and the greatest of these, love, for gay people. And we, humbly, ask that you consider joining us."

"I'm not sure what the future holds for us. I may be looking for a new job next week. But Manci and I have faith that when we stand before our God, He will say, 'Well done, my good and faithful servants. When it was time for you to do what was right and just, you did just that.'"

Rev. Young paused and anxiously looked over at Manci, who was sitting on the front row with prideful tears sliding down her cheeks. She smiled that big smile that said "You did a great job. I am so proud to be your wife!" Rev Young smiled back and with the boost of confidence that she had just sent his way raised his head to look his audience squarely in their eyes as he closed with "Please join me in our closing prayer?"

"Our God, we know that these are troubling times for all of us. So, we pray for wisdom and the ability to give love to all. We ask that you guide our thinking as each of us wrestles with our own decision as to where we stand on same-sex marriages. Grant us grace, grant us compassion, and grant us understanding, wherever we stand. Amen."

John had to admit feeling moved by the words Rev. Young had spoken, thinking that doing what is right and just might be the message he was looking for, but he knew that he and Rev. Young had taken different paths toward heaven. *What is right and just for Rev. Young was granting love, justice, and equality to gay people and what is right for me is full discrimination because sin must always be discriminated against.*

But he couldn't get out of his mind that here is a pastor and his wife willing to risk everything for the rights of gays to marry. And here I am, only moments away from my final judgment, risking my very entrance into heaven, dead set against the sinful lifestyles of gay people.

I sure hope that Pastor Flake and Franklin Graham and Pat Robertson and that Southern Baptist guy, Ronnie Floyd, are right, he thought.

Rather than leaving immediately, John decided to wait a few minutes to try to hear some of the individual congregation conversations.

One lady said to the person walking out with her, "Surely God was with us today and was pleased with what He heard."

Her friend responded, "I agree. What courage! That was one of the most wonderful, loving messages I've ever heard. Our country and our church have come a long way."

Then John noticed two gentlemen huddling in the corner of the sanctuary with determined looks on their faces. To say that they were angry would be an understatement. John shifted toward them and took a hovering position just over their heads so that he could clearly hear their conversation. By their body language, John thought that they must be members of the church board and, it turned out, he was right.

The younger man said in disgust, "This was his swan song today." To which the older gentleman replied, "He will be gone as soon as I can call a board meeting, a week, at most."

John fully agreed with the two gentlemen, but somehow wished that he didn't.

He then gave one last thought as to whether the message he was seeking was in there somewhere, but he was sure that sacrificing one's future to support sin was not the message he was searching for.

John was fortunate that Holly Hill Lutheran Church had a 10 a.m. service. That way he would be able to hear three sermons today, Broadstreet Methodist at 9 a.m., Holly Hill Lutheran at 10 a.m. and Zealot Baptist at 11 a.m. He reasoned, *Hearing three sermons in one day ought to significantly increase my chances of finding that missing key message.*

His initial feeling of peace immediately after he had died had now been replaced by anxiety. He had to find the missing message or, at least, the explanation that would get him into heaven. He was becoming more and more desperate.

In this state, John zoomed to Holly Hill and settled into his favorite spot near the ceiling at the back of the sanctuary. He continued to be amazed that he did not need a seat in a pew. In his aerial pew, he had an unobstructed view, except for that one chandelier that hung down in the middle. So, he moved a little to the left and he could now see everything clearly.

The church was full. Clearly, the forty-five visitors from Broadstreet Methodist had added significantly to today's attendance.

He watched as the choir filled the choir loft and opened the service with a beautiful and enthusiastic rendition of "When the Saints Go Marching In."

Rev. Len Kowell, Holly Hill's pastor, took a seat in one of the large chairs behind the pulpit. Though he was smiling, he looked a little worried and stressed, as if he were about to deliver a very difficult sermon to a very difficult congregation.

What John didn't know was that Rev. Kowell and his wife, Zeanie, had fretted over this sermon all week. They both knew that Rev. Kowell faced one of the largest dilemmas of his ministerial career.

Just this past Friday night, Rev. Kowell had explained his dilemma to Zeanie, as if she didn't remember their dinner conversation every previous night for the past week. "Zeanie," he said, "I've been getting messages from everywhere for the past six weeks on the gay marriage issue. Since the Supreme Court decision, I must have received at least a hundred calls, maybe two. Twenty from Klink Cummings, who left no doubt that he will leave our church and never darken its doors again if I don't absolutely condemn same-sex marriages on Sunday. He said he would take a hundred members with him. That we already have too many gay people in our church and that if we didn't draw the line somewhere, we would be overrun with them. I got him to agree that the gay people who are members of our church are wonderful, loving Christians. But he said, 'Enough is enough. Let them go somewhere else'."

Len added tensely, "Zeanie, if I don't condemn the Supreme Court decision on Sunday, Klink and his supporters may very well move their membership to another church. But that's not all. I received a call today from Claude Sanders, a Sunday school department leader at Broadstreet Methodist Church. He said that his entire Sunday school department of about forty-five people is looking for a new church home and will be visiting us on Sunday. If I say the right words tomorrow, we could pick up forty-five new members. We could then build that new homeless shelter—including the expanded kitchen we have been dreaming about! This would give Holly Hill its best service to the least of these in our church's history."

"But Len," Zeanie responded, "You know that you're your brother Kale's only family now that your parents have disowned him. You told him that you will always be there for him—that he would always have your love and support. He will be devastated if you say anything that even appears to be anti-gay."

"I know. I know," Len shook his head.

Zeanie continued, "And Judy and Mary Lou will be crushed. Holly Hill has been their sanctuary after they got kicked out of Flathead Baptist by that deacon who told them that they and their two children were no longer welcome there."

"Judy also called me this past week," Len said. "She was the only one who seemed to understand the situation that we're in. She said she and Mary Lou understood the pressure that I was under from Klink and his crowd and asked only that I not demonize gay marriages in front of their two children."

"You know that you have an obligation to honor Judy and Mary Lou's request, Zeanie quickly responded.

"I know. But this is Holly Hill's opportunity to really extend the love of Christ to those who are at the bottom rung of life. If we can get those Broadstreet members to join us, I'm telling you, we really can build that new homeless shelter!"

Zeanie, with a sudden look of hope said, "Let's each pray for God's guidance tonight. We can cancel our trip to the arts festival and you can prepare your sermon tomorrow."

Early Saturday morning, Len walked into the kitchen where Zeanie sat drinking her cup of coffee and reading her morning devotion.

"Honey, I'm not sure whether God gave me this idea or whether it came from my own feeble brain, but I'm going to try to straddle the fence Sunday and preach a sermon on reconciliation."

"If you do, babes, you had better wear two pairs of Depends because that fence is made of very sharp barbed wire," Zeanie responded.

"I know," Len responded, "but I'm going to make some telephone calls to Kale and Judy this morning and let them know that I'm under a lot of pressure from Klink and his friends to deliver a strong anti-gay sermon but am not going to do so. I am, however, going to recognize their rights to their beliefs. I'm going to ask Judy and Kale to make some calls to a few of their friends, telling them to listen very carefully to what I say about gay marriages."

Len then went to his study, made the telephone calls and started writing his sermon.

The choir finished "When the Saints Go Marching In" and John watched as Rev. Kowell made his way to the pulpit.

He smiled broadly as he began with a welcome. "We're absolutely delighted to have so many visitors joining us this morning to worship our God and our Savior, Jesus Christ," he said warmly.

"We hope that you will find that we're a loving church who follows Christ's commands that we love our neighbors and serve the least of these in our community. We ask that our visitors please stand just for a moment so that we can give you the warm welcome that we want you to have."

John watched as the large group of visitors from Broadstreet Methodist stood. He quickly counted and got to about forty-two before Rev. Kowell said, "Now I ask that our members stand and greet each other and our visitors with the love of Christ and a good old fashion Holly Hill welcome."

The rest of the congregation stood and enthusiastically greeted the visitors and each other with handshakes and even hugs. The sanctuary was filled with smiles and "welcome" and "so good to see you" greetings.

Rev. Kowell let the greetings continue for almost five minutes—about three minutes longer than usual—to make sure that the Broadstreet visitors felt totally welcome. Based upon what John saw, they almost certainly did. Many Holly Hill members recognized some of the Broadstreet visitors as friends and acquaintances and made a special effort to cross over pews to give them big hugs and handshakes. It was like a good old-fashioned South Carolina home-week gathering, John concluded.

Rev. Kowell finally interrupted the happy greetings. "Thank you so much. Thank you. Please be seated. Thank you."

He then started his message.

"As we all know," he began, "a lot has happened this past week that will have a profound impact on our nation and, probably, on the world. Zeanie and I have spent a lot of time discussing and praying as to what I should say to you this morning."

After a long pause, he said, "So I speak to you this morning from what God has laid on my heart for me to say."

Then another long pause...which told John that there was trouble in the pastor's heart. Somehow, John seemed to sense such trouble easier as a spirit than he had been able to as a human being.

Rev. Kowell continued, "First and foremost, I feel that God wants us to continue to be a warm and friendly congregation, dedicated to serving Him and His people. So, I hope that you see how warm and friendly our church family is. We try our very best to both preach and practice the love of Christ at Holly Hill. In fact, we have two mottos at Holly Hill."

"Our first motto is: 'In all that we do, we will show the love of Christ.'

"And our second motto, 'We recognize, respect and will not denigrate each member's personal beliefs.'

"Our first motto, of course, is based on Jesus's commandment in Mark 12:31: 'Thou shalt love thy neighbor as thyself.'"

"And our second motto is based on our strong belief that each of us is directly responsible to our God. We believe that, ultimately, when each of us stands before our Maker on our judgment day, we will stand alone—each of us solely responsible for our thoughts and actions as well as lack of actions while we're on this Earth. We cannot blame anyone else for what we thought or did or did not do. We will be completely on our own."

Rats! John thought. *That just shot my plan to blame Pastor Flake if I've any problems getting into heaven.* But the belief made sense. What would happen to any kind of judgment, if every person could escape personal responsibility by blaming his or her actions on someone else?

John wondered if either or maybe both of these mottos were the message that he was looking for. *If they are, I may be in deep trouble*, he thought. Then he remembered Pastor Flake's strongly held position that one serves Christ by being aggressive in condemning sin, even when it requires showing tough love toward the sinner. So, John concluded that neither of the mottos were the message and settled back to hear more of the minister's sermon.

Rev. Kowell continued, "Through our personal beliefs motto, each of us is allowed, in fact encouraged, to pray and study God's word to discover what God expects each of us, individually, to believe and practice. We fully recognize that this may, in fact almost certainly will, lead to each of us having different beliefs. That's fine with us, because we respect each member's right and responsibility to determine his or her own beliefs—even when those beliefs differ from ours. Perhaps even more importantly, we can learn from each other and all grow in our relationship with our Lord."

"Different beliefs are not a problem for us because of our love motto: 'In all that we do, we will show the love of Christ.' Through this motto, we remain a unified church, loving and respecting one another and all growing in our knowledge of and service to our Lord."

"We sometimes discuss our different beliefs and, even sometimes kid each other about our beliefs, but we don't denigrate those beliefs."

"Our respect for and tolerance of different beliefs brings me to the topic that's on the minds of many, in fact, maybe on all of our minds this morning. And that topic is the Supreme Court's decision this past week recognizing that gay people have the same rights to marriage as heterosexual people."

"To some of us, who have gay family members for whom we care deeply, or who are, ourselves, gay, that decision is welcomed with great joy. To others of us, who feel that being gay is a sinful choice made by an individual and that allowing gays to marry actually threatens the morality of our nation, that decision is an affront to God."

John shouted *Amen* to that statement, but no one heard him.

"This is a large divide in beliefs," said Pastor Kowell. "In many churches, such a divide will lead to major battles, with friendships lost, pastors fired, and families and churches split. Those are things that we, here at Holly Hill, hope will never happen because of our commitment to our two mottos, which, as a reminder are: We recognize, respect and will not denigrate each member's personal beliefs; and, in all that we do, we will show the love of Christ."

The love of Christ. The love of Christ. That phrase kept bouncing around in John's head like a loose rubber ball. *Did that have anything to do with the message that he was seeking?*

Pastor Kowell continued, "So you may ask—and you have the right to know—'Where does Holly Hill stand on the issue of gay marriage?' Our answer is, 'We recognize that our members have vastly different beliefs on this issue and we, each, humbly respect those differences.' Your belief may be totally different from the person sitting in the pew next to you, and their belief may be totally different from mine. But you don't condemn the person sitting next to you and they, hopefully, don't condemn either you or me."

"We will, each, in due time stand before God and, at that time, learn whether our belief was right or wrong. In the meantime, we believe, and do as we feel guided by God, and we allow our fellow church members to do the same."

Sounds good to me, John thought. But then he remembered Bro. Averett's and Pastor Flake's condemnations of those who sit silently in the face of evil—they're just as guilty as those who perform the evil. He decided to go with Bro. Averett and Pastor Flake and again felt confident that his history of speaking out against this evil was his best option.

Rev. Kowell now addressed another tough question. He said, "Many of you have called me asking and many of you in our sanctuary today may be asking, 'Will Holly Hill allow gay couples to be married in its sanctuary or any other part of its facilities?'"

Smiling and turning to his left, as if to address a specific person in the audience, Rev. Kowell said, "In fact, Klink and I have had several conversations on this topic this past week and lots of others of you on both sides of the issue have also called."

"The answer to the marriage question that's of concern to many of you is, 'No, we will not permit same-sex marriage ceremonies in our church because our current church policy prohibits such ceremonies'."

"Your follow-up question may be, 'Will Holly Hill ever change its policy to permit same-sex marriages in its facilities?' The answer is that our church policy is determined by our membership through a majority vote. So, will our membership ever change its same-sex marriage prohibition policy? Any church policy will change only if our membership wants it to change, and I've been here, as your pastor, long enough to know that I can never predict what our members will do."

Wise. John would have liked to have nodded, although he disagreed with the failure to take a strong stand.

Rev. Kowell continued, "Now, going against all protocols, I've waited until the end of this message from God to read its scriptural basis. So, as we close, I invite you to take your Bibles and turn to Paul's letter to the Ephesians in which he calls for all of us to be reconciled to one another. Paul says, 'And be ye kind one to another, tenderhearted, forgiving one another, even as God for Christ's sake hath forgiven you.' In the spirit of our being reconciled one to another and respecting each other's beliefs, please join me in our closing prayer."

"Our Lord and Savior, our church, we, who are here today and, indeed, our nation, face huge differences of opinion on the issue of gay marriage. In fact, this issue is so huge that it threatens the unity of our families, churches, and friendships—even the unity of our nation. So, we come to you this day to humbly—even anxiously—ask that you guide us as we try to remain true to our own beliefs while at the same time respecting the beliefs of others. We thank you for our visitors today and pray your special blessings on them. To be totally honest with you, Father, we would love to have these wonderful people join our church and walk arm in arm with us as we try, individually and as a church, to serve you and our fellow man."

"Please help us to remember Paul's admonition to be reconciled one to another in tenderheartedness. For it's in your holy name we pray. Amen."

Immediately upon ending his prayer, Rev. Kowell looked anxiously first at Kale, Judy, and Mary Lou and then at the Broadstreet visitors to see their reactions. His answers came quickly; Kale, Judy, and Mary Lou had smiles on their faces and were making their way to the front to talk to him. The visitors had turned immediately and were walking out of the church, murmuring to each other.

John, himself, had mixed emotions about the sermon. One part of him agreed: we need to be reconciled to each other. Perhaps, this issue was not so big that it had to split churches and families and friendships. Maybe, there was a message for him in here somewhere that he had failed to see.

While still wondering if he had found or was in the process of finding the message, John noticed a couple of the visitors talking as they walked out of the church. He shifted closer so that he could hear their conversation. The first comment that he heard shocked him—not because of the comment itself but because of the choice of words. With a look of almost anger, one of the visitors said, "Reconcile, forgive? —Hell, I don't give a damn about what Paul or Kowell or anybody else says. I will never reconcile with these gay loving sinners."

"I wholeheartedly agree," responded his friend. "We need to visit Zealot Baptist next Sunday. Klink told me that they will never reconcile with the Devil. That's where we belong!"

John then noticed a man who he was sure must be Klink with several other people talking near the back corner of the sanctuary. So, he shifted closer. The man who he was sure was Klink was speaking. "I told Kowell," he said, refusing to call him Reverend any longer, "this past week in no uncertain terms that if he did not come out strongly against gay marriages today, I would leave and take at least a hundred members of this church with me. I could not have made it any clearer. Instead, he came out with all that namby-pamby junk today about love and reconciliation and toleration. What does he take me for—an idiot? Franklin Graham is right. Our nation is in moral decline and Kowell is part of that decline. I know a libbie when I see one and Kowell is one! I'm out of here. You guys coming with me?"

John was totally surprised to hear the response. "Klink, don't be in such a hurry. We've always been a church of love and tolerance, and we can continue to be on this issue—even as big as it is. Each one of us needs to stop and pray and seek God's guidance."

Noticeably gasping, Klink was obviously startled that he did not have the strong support that he had expected and responded with a confused and almost angry look "What do you mean seek God's guidance? The bible gives us all of the guidance that we need."

He gasped a second time when another member of the group chimed in, "I agree with Syble. Let's give Rev. Kowell's message a chance before we split the church."

"I also agree," said another member of the group. "Klink, what if gay marriage is the right thing to do and you're wrong? I would hate to see you get to your judgment day and find out you're wrong on this issue. Let's give love a chance before we do anything else."

Looking rather sheepish now, perhaps realizing that he did not have the wide support that he had thought, and maybe thinking about his own judgment day, Klink stared off into space for a minute, almost like he was waiting for a message from God. To John's absolute surprise, he responded "Okay. Maybe I got too angry too fast. It's just that Mike Huckabee and Pat Robertson have me so worked up on this issue. I guess that they, too, could be in for a big surprise on their judgment day! If I were honest with myself, I would have to admit: I don't really know that gay marriage is a sin. So, maybe, I do need to stay around a little longer and be a little more tolerant. I'm sure that tolerance will get me more points on my judgment day than intolerance."

John was astounded. He had never, in his whole life, seen such a quick turnaround. It was almost like Klink had been "born again" to a new relationship with God. It came so quickly and so easily, it seemed fake. Perhaps this was an example of what Rev. Love used to say was the planting of a few chosen words when God was already working on an individual's soul.

But Klink's quick conversion really bothered John. Maybe, just maybe, love and tolerance was the message that God was revealing to him. *Unfortunately, if it is,* he realized again, *it's too late for me because, unlike Klink, the record of my life has already been written. Even if I wanted to do so, I cannot change it now.*

Which Path to Heaven?

John looked at Klink's watch and realized that the Zealot Baptist church service would be starting in just a couple of minutes. He needed to zoom over there. As he prepared to zoom, he noticed a long line of Holly Hill church members waiting to shake Rev. Kowell's hand. The smiles on their faces told him that they all felt that Rev. Kowell had just delivered a message directly from God.

Still thinking about the fact that his own record being closed but his still being here instead of heaven, John zoomed to Zealot Baptist, which took him nanoseconds.

As he entered Zealot Baptist, the choir was just finishing singing "Lord, I'm Coming Home," which John was sure had been chosen in his memory since they probably thought that he was already in his heavenly home—where he wished he were.

Taking his favorite aerial pew in the back of the sanctuary near the ceiling, John noticed that, unlike at Broadstreet Methodist church, almost every seat was taken. Clearly, Pastor Flake had a message that many people wanted to hear. *This alone proves that I'm on the right path to heaven*, he thought.

John looked down front and saw Deacon Fred with a bandage on his head. Apparently, Billy had given him a nice little knot yesterday at the graveside service. John noticed that Deacon Fred's wife was not with him. Instead he was holding hands with a new, younger woman, who was quite attractive in her sheer purple dress. Clyde, who was in the same civic club as Fred, had told him just last week that Fred's third wife, just like his two previous wives, had caught him fornicating and moved out.

As the choir finished singing "Lord, I'm Coming Home," the music director asked all to stand and join the choir in singing "When the Roll is Called Up Yonder." *Perhaps this is also to honor me*, John thought.

As the congregation continued to sing, Pastor Flake, dressed in the long white robe that he wore every Sunday, walked down to stand in front of the altar on which three large lighted candles stood, representing the Trinity.

As they did at the beginning of every Sunday service while the congregation sang its opening hymn, three deacons approached down the center aisle, each carrying a large flag in an act of worship and commitment. As Pastor Flake had explained when the flag ceremony was first adopted three years ago, the first flag was the Christian flag representing Zealot's total commitment to God's Bible and the laws that it lays down. Next came the Confederate flag, which represented Zealot's commitment to fight against the devil and his liberal companions who are trying to take away our right to serve our God. And finally, the American flag, which represented Zealot's constant prayer for God to protect our nation from its enemies, both foreign and domestic.

As the choir continued its rendition of "When the Roll is Called Up Yonder," the three deacons marched slowly down the aisle to the stage where, John knew, they would reverently place the flags in their holders. The Christian flag would be placed in the center part of the stage, representing that Christ is to occupy center stage in our lives. The Confederate flag would be placed on the left part of the stage representing Zealot's fight against left-wing liberals. Then the American flag would be positioned on the right, representing Zealot's commitment to tried-and-true conservative views.

John noticed that Deacon Don Gravendale carried the Christian flag, Deacon Henry the Confederate flag, and Deacon Jerry the American flag. Deacons Henry and Jerry looked like they had survived yesterday's graveside service confrontation with Clint and Jeremy in reasonably good condition. Neither limped or had any bandages.

The ceremony was being beautifully performed as the flags approached the altar. Deacon Don bowed reverently with his Christian flag when he approached Pastor Flake and the altar, and then turned the corner and placed the Christian flag in its center stage holder. Deacon Henry now approached Pastor Flake and the altar with his Confederate flag.

Unfortunately, Deacon Henry turned to get a good look at Deacon Fred's new girlfriend sitting on the second row. Before he could turn back around, he stumbled and hit Pastor Flake upside the head with the Confederate flagpole, knocking him down. That might have not been so bad had his flagpole not also knocked two of the candles off the altar onto Pastor Flake's nice white robe. And that might have still been okay had the robe not caught on fire. This, too, might have been manageable, had Deacon Henry not tried to put the fire out by beating Pastor Flake's robe with his Confederate flagpole. Things became a little less manageable, however, when the Confederate flag caught fire and Deacon Henry threw it up on the stage just under the Christian flag. Recognizing the danger of the situation, Deacon Jerry ran up on stage and started beating the burning Confederate flag with his American flag, which turned out to be a big mistake because the moving air fanned the flame and caused the Christian flag to catch on fire. So now, Deacon Jerry attempted to extinguish both fires by beating both flags. That turned out to be an even bigger mistake because the American flag caught fire as well.

From that point, things just plain went downhill. Pastor Flake struggled to extinguish his own fire by frantically running around the stage doing stops, drops, and rolls. Unfortunately, it was not working, and the bottom of his robe was now a full-blown, but fortunately not yet large, flame.

Realizing the dangerous situation that had evolved over the past forty-five seconds, Deacon Fred jumped from his pew to help. As he approached him, Pastor Flake tried to stand up, so he could do another stop, drop, and roll. But Deacon Fred knocked him back down and started stomping both the robe and Pastor Flake. Deacon Henry decided to leave Deacon Jerry in charge of the three burning flags on the stage and turned his attention back to helping stomp Pastor Flake.

John did not know how, but somehow with all the stomping and all the stopping, dropping, and rolling, Deacons Fred and Henry, with Pastor Flake's frantic zipper pulling, were able to strip the burning robe off Pastor Flake to reveal that all he was wearing under his robe was a pair of yellow teddy-bear boxer shorts.

This is not a pretty sight, John thought. He then remembered to check and, sure enough, JoAnn was right. Pastor Flake's belly was yellow. *And big and saggy, too,*

The congregation must have agreed with John, because the sight of Pastor Flake mostly in his birthday suit led to a loud, church-wide gasp.

At this point, everyone who had just been sitting in their pews— well not really sitting but standing on their pews so that they could see all the commotion—realized that the church's fire alarm system wasn't working. But that was okay, because the fun was ending. Pastor Flake ran from the stage in his teddy bear boxer shorts, the burning robe had been thrown into the baptismal pool, and the three flags were now only smoldering ashes.

Recognizing the need to restore calm, the minister of music stepped forward and asked the congregation to remain standing and turn to page 212 in their hymnal and sing "Come, Jesus, Lord, with Holy Fire."

As the congregation began to sing, John, having witnessed everything from his unobstructed vantage position up near the ceiling, tried to decipher a message from what he had just witnessed. He had just seen Pastor Flake striped down to his teddy bear underwear and the Confederate flag destroy both the Christian flag and the American flag and, in the process, destroy itself. *There absolutely has to be a message here,* he thought, but he couldn't find it.

As John continued to search and the congregation continued to sing, Pastor Flake returned in a new robe and took his pastoral seat on the stage.

Almost as if nothing had happened, when the last verse was sung, and the congregation had reseated themselves, Pastor Flake walked to the pulpit, glanced out at his congregation, gave a long pause, then with a broad grin said, "I hope that everyone enjoyed the opening flag ceremony." After another pause and a bigger grin, he added, "That's as close to burning in hell as I ever want to get."

He then began his sermon, "We have a very serious topic to address today and that's not the start that we had planned. But maybe it's a good sendoff, after all, because sin can destroy our nation and us as individuals, just as surely as the fires destroyed our flags today. Because of the moral decline in our nation, I spent this entire past week thinking and praying about what I should say to you today. Finally, God laid it on my heart. I simply had to speak his Word."

"Like Jonah, who ran from God to avoid going to Nineveh to tell them of their sins, I too wanted to run. But God would not let me run from my responsibility to speak out against the terrible sin that our Supreme Court forced on our nation this past week."

Looking out at his audience and pausing again for a moment, he continued, "As the world now knows, this past week our court ruled that our nation's states and counties must extend to same-sex couples the same rights of marriage as heterosexuals now enjoy. But I must tell you that *the* Supreme Court, above all supreme courts, has already issued the final decision on gay marriages. As I've spoken to you many times from this pulpit, God's law, as laid out so clearly in the Bible, absolutely forbids homosexuality and that biblical law cannot be overturned by any man or group of men."

"Under the leadership of our Lord and Savior Jesus Christ, this nation was founded as a Christian nation. But it has now turned on God and His people. We're no longer allowed by our own government to follow the laws that God laid before us thousands of years ago. Somehow, this group of five lawyers thinks that it's now superior to our God, the God of Abraham and Isaac. If we follow God's law, we now risk being incarcerated by our own government."

John now shifted back and forth along the back ceiling of the church, excited to hear the message that he was sure would get him into heaven, even if it was delivered by a messenger who wore teddy bear boxer shorts and had a saggy, yellow belly.

Pastor Flake continued, "Just yesterday, when your deacons and I spoke about the evils of same-sex marriages at John Willis' funeral, we were arrested. That's right. You heard me right! We were arrested by our own government for speaking out against the moral decline of our nation."

"Well, I want you to know that I'll wear my mug shot as a badge of honor, knowing that it signifies my total commitment to God's laws. And when my trial comes, I'll proudly carry my Bible into the courtroom and tell the judge that I answer to a higher power, God's law. He can send me to prison forever, but I must and will always serve my God and abide by his laws—every one of them!"

Pausing for a moment to let his last statement sink in, Pastor Flake continued in an even more determined voice, "I know that many people, especially liberals, choose to ignore God's laws regarding homosexual lifestyles. In fact, they choose to ignore lots of God's laws by simply 'cherry-picking' only those that they want to obey, as if the Bible were a buffet. But that's not an option that God's people have. The Bible is either true or it's nothing. As I spoke last week, it's not there for us to choose a little of this and a little of that and then ignore other parts, as liberals do."

Yes, John thought. *Pastor Flake is absolutely right. Liberals are just a bunch of pseudo-Christian hypocrites believing only what they want to believe.* But he could still not get the image of the teddy bear undies and all the burning flags out of his mind. Was his message hidden in here?

"I said it yesterday at John's funeral and I say it again today," Pastor Flake went on. "We at Zealot Baptist will obey every law in the Bible and, in doing so, we will never, ever let God's house be used for a gay marriage."

"There comes a time, my Uncle Bilbo used to say, when God's people must take a stand and hold firmly against sin, or as he used to say, 'we must be barrel-chested defenders of God's word.' I used to spend lots of time in the summer with Uncle Bilbo down in Niceville, South Carolina. Even though I have a seminary degree, I think that I may have learned more theology from Uncle Bilbo than I did from all my seminary professors."

"Uncle Bilbo was a big, barrel-chested Irish man with red hair, even on his chest and arms, as was my father, his brother. Uncle Bilbo felt strongly during the fifties and sixties that God was calling him and his Southern Baptist friends at Mudbottom Baptist church to stand up in defense of God's word. "Or, as he used to say, 'our nation will go into moral decline and never recover.' And that same moral decline is happening again today. My uncle used to say--figuratively, I hope--that we must be barrel-chested and, if necessary, be willing to use our switchblade knives and cattle whips to defend God's word against the sinners who are attacking it."

John was astounded. Pastor Flake's uncle was the man who threatened Jeremy with his switchblade knife at the Dixie Café. He was the KKK "Whupper" who beat Joe with the whip. John remembered his father saying that the man who distributed the pamphlets calling him the "father of nigger lovers" was the same man who threatened Jeremy with the knife. *Pastor Flake's Uncle Bilbo was the man who destroyed my father's career! And here is Pastor Flake holding him up as a model for us to follow! How can this be? This can't be! There has got to be a mistake. This is so crazy, there must be a message in here somewhere!*

Pastor Flake continued, with what he must have intended as a little humor. "You may ask, if your father was a red-haired Irishman, why, Pastor Flake, is your skin so dark? Well, that came from my mother's side of the family. My mother was from South Florida and was half Native American. Her mother was a full-blooded Seminole. So, I've ties all the way back to the beginning of our nation, even before the Europeans came, when it was a Christian nation true to our God and His laws."

John was now doubly flabbergasted, as the thoughts of what he had just learned raced through his radio-signal mind. *Not only has Pastor Flake held his KKK criminal uncle out as a Christian role model, I now find out Pastor Flake is a bastard. He's one of those 'mongrels' that Brother Averett, back at Rock Bottom Baptist church, said would happen if our government forced racial integration on our nation. The Bible says in Deuteronomy that he cannot enter the house of God for eight more generations. And here he is, not only in God's house, but standing in the pulpit. JoAnn was right when she called him a yellow-bellied bastard yesterday.*

Now my chances of getting into heaven are totally shot, John concluded. *God is going to ask me who my pastor was and I'm going to have to say JoAnn was right, he really was a yellow-bellied bastard. How is that going to sound?*

John paused for a second, surprised by his thoughts about Pastor Flake's mixed-race heritage. As a college-educated man with a highly successful career, he knew that a person having a mixed heritage should not bother him, even though the Bible indisputably says that a bastard cannot enter the house of God for ten generations. He knew, intellectually, that this was another one of the biblical laws that needed to be ignored. But when one is only moments away from being judged, one cannot be too careful.

Then, John remembered. He remembered something terrible---a horrible remembrance---in fact, a dooming remembrance. He, himself, was a bastard and not only a bastard, but exactly the type of bad bastard mentioned in Deuteronomy—a mongrel child from a Jew marrying outside his religion. He remembered his mother telling him that his great grandfather was a Jew who migrated from Germany in 1873 with his Catholic wife. *This means that I'm a fourth-generation bastard and should not even be in God's house myself and, most especially, not in God's house listening to a bastard preacher. I'm doubly doomed,* he concluded.

Pastor Flake, apparently, was not concerned in the least that he had just confessed to being a bastard and continued, "But it's not just you and me and the God-fearing members of our Zealot Baptist Church who are speaking out against our being bullied by the gay communities and their left-wing liberal supporters into accepting the sinful act of gay marriage as the law of the land."

"When we speak out, we're joining strong Christian leaders like Roy Moore, Pat Robertson, Mike Huckabee, Ted Cruz, our own Southern Baptist Convention and, of course, Franklin Graham, whom I frequently quote. I did some Googling this past week and let me give you some of the quotes that I found from these wonderful God-fearing leaders. By the way, you may want to also Google what these devoted men of God say about gay marriages yourself when you get home today."

"Roy Moore, that great Christian Alabama Supreme Court leader said this about gay marriage when he spoke at a church's God and Country Day: 'Is there such a thing as morality anymore? Sodomy for centuries was declared to be against the laws of nature and nature's God. And now if you say that in public, and I guess I am, am I violating somebody's civil rights? Have we elevated morality to immorality? Do we call good, bad? What are we Christians to do?'"

John loved the quote because it showed how sinful a homosexual life was, and it confirmed in his own mind the wisdom of his commitment to fighting this terrible sin. John already knew that Roy Moore was one of the most caring, loving, devout Christians in the country, who was fully committed to obeying every law in the Bible. He also recalled that Judge Moore had previously shown his commitment to God by calling for the criminalization of homosexuality. *What a wonderful, strong, loving Christian!* John thought. *Following his example should get me into heaven.*

Pastor Flake moved on to the next quote: "Ted Cruz, who is one of the strongest Christians serving in the U.S. Senate, has warned us of the threat to our freedom of religion in this country by the Supreme Court's decision. He just recently said, 'Because of their partisan desire to mandate gay marriage everywhere in this country, they also want to persecute anyone who has a good faith religious belief that marriage is a holy sacrament, the union of one man and one woman, and ordained as a covenant by God'."

John had never thought about it before, but he now saw that the liberals were using the Supreme Court to force their hidden agenda of preventing people from practicing their religious beliefs. This was not about gay rights at all. It was a subversive movement to deny Christians the right to worship God at all. Fortunately, he now realized, God had blessed Ted Cruz with a brilliant mind that could see these hidden agendas long before they're seen by anybody else. For a moment, John forgot that he was dead and concluded that Cruz was right: *we have to stand up to these hidden conspiracies now or it will be too late.*

His conclusion was confirmed by Pastor Flake's next quote: "Another strong Christian saint, Mike Huckabee, is showing us how we have to stand up to this tyranny. Again, according to the internet, our brother in Christ has said, 'The Supreme Court has spoken with a very divided voice on something only the Supreme Being can do—redefine marriage. I will not acquiesce to an imperial court any more than our Founders acquiesced to an imperial British monarch. We must resist and reject judicial tyranny, not retreat.......This ruling is not about marriage equality, it's about marriage redefinition. This irrational, unconstitutional rejection of the expressed will of the people in over thirty states will prove to be one of the court's most disastrous decisions.'"

Pastor Flake paused for a moment, looked out at his congregation, and then with a full-blown sense of confidence that everything that he had been saying about gay marriages was confirmed by Huckabee, declared, "How fortunate our God is to have a totally dedicated saint like Mike Huckabee in His corner fighting to protect His biblical laws. I can't tell you this for sure, but if I were a betting man, I would bet that there is not a single biblical law that Mike Huckabee will not fight to save from being overruled by the devil and his Supreme Court minions. He probably doesn't even eat shrimp."

That's all the proof that I need that I'm on the right path to heaven, John thought. If Mike Huckabee says it, it's true. Then John thought about how much he loved shrimp cocktail and lobster and hoped that Mike might get God to grant an exemption for that law.

To show that he and the Zealot members were definitely right on their condemnation of gay marriages, Pastor Flake moved on to his next quote saying, with another look of full confidence, "Perhaps the greatest Christian leader of our generation, the Rev. Pat Robertson, has given us his Godly thoughts about gay marriages and gay lifestyles. Rev. Robertson has said, 'I don't really believe homosexuals want to get married; what they want to do is destroy marriage and some of the other things we have in our society.' On another occasion, he has warned us, 'Some of these radical gay groups are willing to do anything in the world to have their way of doing sex legitimized by this country. They'll tear down any institution, the church—the Episcopal Church, for example—in order to have their way, and it's basically wrong'."

On a roll now, and confident that the congregation had forgotten all about his undies, Pastor Flake raised his voice to a tone of defiance almost as if to dare anyone to disagree with him and continued. "And joining Rev. Robertson in his warning about gay marriages is that great Christian leader Franklin Graham who I consider to be my role model. Rev. Graham is calling the gay movement what it is: a threat against our nation, our churches, and you and me, who are just trying to serve our God without interference from our government. Rev. Graham just recently gave us these dire warnings after the Supreme Court ruling: 'I'm disappointed because the government is recognizing sin. This court is recognizing sin. That's what homosexuality is—a sin against God......The Supreme Court's decision means gay rights now trump religious liberty. And if you think the cultural purging of the Southern States has been breathtaking, wait until you see what LGBT activists are about to unleash on American Christians. .... Pastors who refuse to perform gay marriages and preach from the Bible should prepare for hate crime charges. All dissent will be silenced by the government and the activists.'"

"And there is more," Pastor Flake added, as if he were making the closing arguments in a court case. "Our very own Southern Baptist Convention President Ronnie Floyd has taken a very strong stand against gay marriages. I discovered on the Internet that in a recent address to SBC delegates, he said, 'While some evangelicals may be bowing down to the deception of the inclusiveness of same-sex marriage in their churches, we will not bow down, nor will we be silent.' He went on to say, 'I want to remind everyone today, humbly, the Supreme Court of the United States is not the final authority, nor is the culture itself, but the Bible is God's final authority about marriage and on this book we stand.'"

With a look of total satisfaction that he was delivering his best sermon ever, Pastor Flake raised his voice still another pitch and announced, "As I've done many times before from this sacred pulpit, I want to again state unequivocally here today before you and the God whom we serve: we at Zealot Baptist join these great national Christian saints in opposing the imposition of this sinful law on our nation. To show our full defiance, we, at Zealot Baptist will never, ever, allow God's house to be used for a same-sex marriage. We remain as firmly opposed to same-sex marriage as we are to the ordination of women. Neither will ever happen in our great Southern Baptist church!"

Getting carried away in the heat of the moment--no pun intended given the previous events of the service--and for no apparent reason whatsoever, Pastor Flake added with an even louder voice, "The Bible says in 1 Corinthians 14:34, 'Women should be silent during church meetings. They're not to take part in the discussion for they are subordinate to men'."

John noticed that as soon as Pastor Flake had completed that quote, he glanced over at Lucretia with a sick look on his face, wishing that he had kept his fat mouth shut, because she was discretely giving him the finger.

Pastor Flake must have taken Lucretia's gesture as a signal that he should close his sermon.

"Although what God laid on my heart to say today may sound harsh, I want to close by letting all our gay brothers and sisters and friends and family know that we love you," he said smarmily. "We're devoted servants of our God, who commands that we love our neighbor as ourselves. To show our love, we're proud to announce today the establishment of three new programs designed to show the love of God to our Columbia gay community. The first is our Deacon Don Homosexual Recovery Counseling Center, named after our own Deacon Don, the first to think of founding our wonderful Zealot Baptist church as a force in fighting the attempts of homosexuals to recruit our children and grandchildren into their sinful lifestyle. This center will help our gay brothers and sisters repent for the sinful lifestyle they have chosen and, in so doing, join the rest of us in heaven when they die."

Which Path to Heaven?

"The second program is our 'Getta' Divorce Counseling Center. This center will help gay married couples understand the sinful relationship they have established and advise them on how to get a divorce. I'm proud to add that the Gunk & Stench law firm has agreed to provide free legal counseling. Upon being divorced, gays can then join Zealot Baptist as full-fledged members and save their souls from hell."

"Our third program is, perhaps, the most important program to show our love and help our gay friends. It's our Eyes of Love Monitoring Program. This program will be made up of volunteer Zealot Baptist members who, out of their love, will monitor all reformed gay members to make sure that they don't slip back into their sinful ways and become doomed to eternal damnation. This means that all of our former gay members, as well as any we suspect of being gay, can have the comfort of knowing that their every move is being watched with loving eyes."

Suddenly, the entire congregation rose in loud applause. John had never seen or heard such excitement and concluded that everyone must be really pleased that Zealot Baptist was going to do more than just protest gay marriages. It was going to go further to show the love of God to the gay community. They could all leave today with a real sense of pride.................... Or could they?..................... Something just did not seem to be right.

But John needed for it to be right, so he gave himself a little pep talk. *Beyond any doubt, God must be pleased with the commitment of His people to keeping their gay brothers and sisters out of hell--no man has more love for his fellow man,* he thought.

When the clapping and hollering had finally stopped, Pastor Flake spoke to end the service. "Let's remain standing for our closing prayer. Before we pray, however, I want to remind the deacons of our regularly scheduled meeting right after the service."

"Pray with me, please. Our God, we know that our nation faces major differences in beliefs about gay marriages. Surveys show that over half of our citizens now support gay marriages. We wonder how such a moral decline can occur and know that we, your people, have failed You. We have failed to speak out against the devil and his minions who are forcing this evil law on Your people. So, we pray that You will give us the courage to say what needs to be said and to do what needs to be done. Help us to be barrel-chested defenders of your Biblical laws, every last one of them. We pray especially for our three new programs designed to show Your love to our gay brothers and sisters. These things, we humbly ask in the name of Christ, our Savior. Amen."

John remained befuddled, feeling as lost as ever since the moment his spirit first left his flesh. Today he had heard Rev. Young say that he and his wife were willing to sacrifice their careers to show the love of Christ by supporting the rights of their gay brothers and sisters to marry the persons they loved. He had heard Rev. Kowell ask his congregation to show the love of Christ by loving all people, gays as well as anti-gays, and being tolerant of other people's beliefs. And he had now heard Pastor Flake ask--no, command--his congregation to show the love of Christ by being barrel-chested enforcers of God's laws condemning gay relationships.

All three pastors had said that they had prayed for God's guidance in preparing their sermons, and each said that he had received that guidance. *How could that be?* Why would God give each pastor a different message—messages that were totally different from each other?

John wondered, *Could God be giving me these different messages to force me to think and choose the right message?* If so, he was still not sure what the message was. But he did feel that if someone were to put a gun to his spiritual head and force him to choose, he would have to choose either the message from Rev. Young or the one from Rev. Kowell. And that was not good, because his life record had already been closed and it was a barrel-chested A. Reel Flake record—well, for the last four years it had been—as barrel-chested a record as any. Before that he and JoAnn had been caring, loving, and tolerant Christians helping those in need.

While he was thinking all these confusing thoughts, John noticed his fellow deacons walking out the side door to attend the meeting after the 11 a.m. service. The meetings were for the sole purpose of giving Pastor Flake feedback on his sermon, and they usually consisted of everyone telling him what a great sermon he had just preached. The meetings usually lasted only about five minutes, so they could beat the Methodist to the local restaurants for lunch.

As John shifted into the room, Deacon Don, looking very disturbed, stood and angrily asked, "Has anyone read this stupid letter to the editor that was in this morning's paper?" Without giving any opportunity for a response, he continued, "Let me read it." He ruffled through the day's paper.

"The headline is, 'The Hypocrisy of Zealot Baptists,' and it's written by some left-wing liberal named Chris who attended our church last week when Pastor Flake preached that wonderful sermon about God not letting us cherry-pick his Biblical laws."

John then remembered. Chris had said in his email the other day that he had attended Zealot Baptist church last Sunday and had written a letter to the editor to be published today. He knew immediately what his letter was going to say and wondered if he was going to, again, end it with "so I shot the pastor" to emphasize his point. *Bet he shoots someone in there somewhere,* John mused.

Deacon Don, in a voice that sounded like a snarling dog, continued "Let me read what this triple idiot said: *'Last Sunday, I was in the need for some spiritual uplifting and guidance during these troubled times, so I attended the church service at Zealot Baptist church.*

However, the only uplifting I received was walking away totally disheartened about how cruel, heartless, and misguided our Christian faith has become. No wonder young people are turned off. The service started with a parade of flags in which the Confederate flag, along with the Christian and American flags, was honored. From that weird beginning, it was clear that the service was not going to be one of worshiping God, but one of worshiping carefully selected words printed in the Bible. The title of the sermon was 'No Cherry-Picking.' The pastor hammered away at Zealot's total commitment to obeying every last one of God's biblical laws. Then, with condescending hatred, he flat-out ignored all other biblical laws and cherry-picked those laws regarding same-sex marriages and used them to lambast liberals who support same-gender marriages. The hypocrisy was overwhelming. Here was a pastor telling his flock that same-gender marriages had to be condemned because every law and every word in the Bible had to be obeyed. Yet, unless he is an ignorant Bible scholar, the pastor had to know that neither he nor anyone else of sound mind obeys, or even should seek to obey, all of the laws in the Bible."

"Only a fool would attempt to obey God's law laid down in Exodus 35:2 which says that 'Six days shall work be done, but on the seventh day there shall be to you an holy day, a Sabbath of rest to the Lord: **whosoever doeth work therein shall be put to death.**'"

The deacon paused for a moment to let the stupidity of the letter sink in and then continued reading with even more anger:

"'Have we here in Columbia come to the point where we must worry about Zealot Baptist members coming to our shopping malls with automatic weapons every Sunday to 'put to death' all who are working that day so that they can obey the Bible? Or do we conclude that the pastor was intentionally lying to his congregation when he said that Christians must obey every law and every word in the Bible as a way of justifying his homophobic hatred?

"'I came away from the Zealot Baptist service sick to my stomach. I had just heard a hypocrite stand in God's pulpit and lie to his congregation. And the sad thing is, as I looked around the congregation, I'm convinced that they believed his lies.

"'If that is Christianity, I want no part of it.'"

When Deacon Don finished, the room was deafeningly quiet. Even the houseflies felt the tension in the room and hid in dark corners. Everyone just looked at each other in disbelief.

Finally, Pastor Flake, looking like he wished he had hidden with the flies, spoke. "This is what I've been talking about. This letter shows exactly what's happening. The liberals are taking our country from us. They'll say and do whatever they can to force their gay agenda on our nation. We must fight them every step of the way. We must redouble our efforts, or we will lose our ability to even speak God's word from our pulpits. My suggestion is that we not dignify the letter with a response. Instead, we must continue to serve our God by obeying his every law, especially the laws prohibiting same-sex marriages."

Deacon Jerry looked perplexed and addressed Pastor Flake directly. "I've got two questions. First, is the letter right that the Bible calls for people to be put to death for working on Sunday?"

Pastor Flake, looking like he had been stripped down to his skivvies again, responded, "Well, uh…uh, yes, that's, uh…that's correct."

Looking much more perplexed, Deacon Jerry asked his second question: "Is this law included in all of the biblical laws that you have been saying that we must obey?" Without giving Pastor Flake a chance to respond, he also asked, "Does this mean that we must establish death squads to put all of those who work on Sundays to death, as the letter writer says?"

Pastor Flake, now desperately searching for an honorable way out of the hypocritical box that he was trapped in, rose to the occasion and responded with clear logic that any fool could understand. "Some of God's laws have…. uh…have…. uh…changed over the years and that's one of them. Most Christians no longer consider working on the Sabbath a sin. However, that does not mean that we can cherry-pick God's laws. We must still obey every one of them. It's just that we now know that some of them are no longer in effect and working on the Sabbath is one of those."

Then, in a tone that left no doubt that he was speaking on behalf of God Himself he added: "When we pray, God reveals to us which laws are still in effect and He has revealed to us that we no longer have to put people who work on Sundays to death. At the same time, however, He has revealed to us that His laws prohibiting gay relationships must be enforced to prevent the moral decline of our nation. This is not cherry-picking. This is praying, listening carefully to what God says, and then obeying His revelations to us."

Deacon Jerry seemed to not buy the convoluted explanation and responded, "That's not what you've been saying. You've been saying that we must obey every one of God's laws. I think that the letter writer is right. I think that we absolutely have to organize death squads to obey God's law about putting all who work on Sundays to death." He started thinking how such a plan would work, and a troubled look crossed his face.

Deacon Gary, a local attorney, was not so sure about all of this because he and his wife had planned to go out for lunch right after the meeting. So, he turned to Jerry and with a somewhat dry grin, said, "Sylvia and I are going to Billie Jean's for lunch today. Would it be okay if we waited until after we finished eating to put the cook and waitresses to death?"

"This is not a joke, Gary," Jerry quickly and emphatically responded. "The Bible is God's inerrant word. We either obey all its laws or admit that it is not God's word at all. You are a deacon in this church. Which are you choosing?"

Obviously disturbed, Deacon Henry quickly jumped in: "Jerry, you can't put these people to death. You will be arrested and sent to prison, maybe executed."

Being a true and literal believer in God's word, Jerry retorted, "That's man's law, not God's law. Pastor Flake has told us many times; the Bible is not a buffet. We cannot pick and choose which parts we obey. Just as Roy Moore defied man's laws by refusing to remove the Ten Commandments from public property in Alabama, we must obey God's law and defy man's law. I know that we can get support from lots of great political and religious leaders. Once we have killed a few of these Sunday-working sinners and get arrested, I know that some of the national saints will immediately stand up with us against our corrupt government's attempt to take away our freedom to obey God's laws. They would never miss such a great opportunity to have their pictures taken with us standing beside the bodies of dead sinners in their support of our religious freedom."

Apparently, God also spoke to Deacon Don, who also didn't like where the conversation was going and interjected a much clearer explanation. "Now, Jerry," he admonished. "What Alex said a few moments ago makes perfect sense. God has revealed to us that His Sabbath law is sometimes in effect and sometimes not. Right now, God has told us that it's not. So, you don't have to put these sinners to death because they're no longer sinning. They used to be sinning and might be sinning in the future if we decide – I mean – if God decides that they are, but right now, are not sinning. You've nothing to worry about. But, just to be clear, God's homosexual laws are still binding. This is where people are still sinning and where we need to stand up for God. It's that simple."

Not totally convinced, Deacon Jerry responded, "Well, you better be right. If I end up in hell because I disobeyed God's law by not killing all these Sunday-working sinners, I'm borrowing the devil's pitchfork and coming after every one of you."

While Pastor Flake and the deacons desperately tried to get out of the trap that they had talked themselves into, John was in his own deep thought, not hearing a thing that Pastor Flake or anyone else was saying. The more he thought, the more worried he had become. He had had no idea that there was a law in the Bible that called for people to be put to death for working on Sunday. During tax season, he had worked lots of Sunday afternoons and evenings. *Why had Pastor Flake never told him about this specific law? Why hadn't the national saints made a big deal out of it? They could have at least mentioned it.* It seemed just as important or even more important than the laws about homosexuality, especially since so many people work on the Sabbath and the punishment is death.

John was sure that he finally had the message and it was not a good one for him—not good at all. In fact, it was terrible. There was no way that he could hide the fact that he had worked on lots of Sunday afternoons over the years. He now understood why God had not yet called him to heaven. He was not going to heaven. He was going down below. Not only was he a fourth-generation bastard, he was a Sunday-working sinner!

Now in a deep funk, John hadn't even noticed until just now that all the deacons had left and the room was completely empty. So, he just shifted around the room and thought and then thought some more. After an hour or so of shifting and thinking—well, worrying---his desperation led to his latching on to a more positive thought--like a drowning man grabbing a straw. *The fact that I'm not already in hell must mean something because there is no doubt that I disobeyed God's Sabbath law. Maybe there is another reason that I'm waiting. Maybe, the biblical law prohibiting working on Sunday is not the message. In fact, maybe obeying all of God's biblical laws is not the message either. Maybe the message is more profound than all of those. I need to keep searching.*

While he was still pondering that thought, he suddenly felt the need to visit with Martha. *That's it! In all those years that Martha was in my Christ Episcopal Sunday school class, she always looked like she had something that she wanted to tell me. Even when she came to my visitation, she just stood there looking at my old body, looking like she wished that she had told me something.* He remembered that she had leaned over and whispered something into his old ear. *That has to be it! Martha has the message that God wants me to find. Maybe a visit to her home can help me sort through everything and find the real message.*

First, however, he needed to check back at his waiting room at the Sunset Funeral Home to see if Jesus or someone else sent by God had stopped by to take him to heaven. After all, he had been gone for almost four hours. He did not want to be absent when God's servant came for him and have to spend all eternity shifting around on earth. He immediately zoomed back to the funeral home and cemetery. Everything was quiet there. No waiting chariots or angels or even a note that said "We came by, but you weren't here. Sorry that we missed you."

His grave was in good shape except that a deer had stepped on the loose soil overnight. But that would be covered as soon as they put the new sod over the bare dirt.

Remembering that he wanted to visit Martha, he decided to take a chance and be gone for just another little while.

Chapter 8

A Visit with Martha

"You must receive something of heaven into the soul, before the soul can be received in heaven."

John Thornton

John realized that he did not know where Martha lived. In fact, he did not even know her last name. He couldn't believe that in all those years that she had been in his Sunday school class, he had never even bothered to learn her last name. *What kind of a Sunday school teacher does not know the last names of his class members? Maybe that's what she wanted to tell me—just her last name, so that she would be a real person to me.*

John felt terrible. *I can't blame her if she hides the message when I visit her—if I can ever find out where she lives.*

He then remembered that he was a spirit and decided to test his ability to travel without an address. So, he thought, *I want to visit with Martha in her home,* and immediately he was there in her family room hovering near the ceiling, resting comfortably in his aerial easy chair. Death did have some advantages—he had his own built-in advanced GPS that could operate without an address.

Martha was not in the room, but he could hear her rattling some pots and pans in the kitchen. So, she was home.

John looked around the family room. It was nice and neat with all the appearances of a loving home. There was a La-Z-Boy recliner facing a large-screen TV slightly to the right. Facing the recliner from across the room was a comfortable-looking couch with pillows embroidered with the saying "In all things Love" placed in the corners. On the wall behind the couch, there were some carefully hung, smaller framed sayings grouped around a large framed quote. John shifted closer to read the sayings. On the upper right, above the larger framed quote, was an embroidered, "Do unto others as you would have them do unto you." Another frame held Rudyard

Kipling's "If" poem, a copy of which John's mother had given him when he graduated from high school. John always loved the first part of the opening stanza "If you can keep your head when all about you are losing theirs . . ."

Then he wondered which of the church services he had just attended were "losing their heads" or whether he had long ago lost his. Based on the conflicting messages, someone had surely lost a head.

John now looked at the larger, center quote. He noted that it was in a child's handwriting and must be from the Bible because it said, at the end of the quote, "Martha 1:1, My Version." Then he realized that it was a quote that Martha must have written herself, when she was a child, in a form that made it look like it came from the Bible, a "bible" that Martha herself had written. That had to be the message that he was seeking! But it did not look like a message from God because it simply said, "There are no bigots in heaven."

In fact, it definitely was not a message from God because John 3:16 states, "Whosoever believeth in Him shall not perish, but have ever lasting life." So, that means that even bigots who feel that they have been chosen by God and given all the answers, making them superior to all others and having the authority to condemn---even murder-- others, will go to heaven. If they believe, they're automatically in heaven. It's very simple. *Believe and go to heaven, no matter what. Don't believe and go to hell, no matter what.*

So, what was Martha saying with such a misinformed quote? Did she know something that he didn't about John 3:16? Something that would keep some believers out of heaven? If she did, that might be the message he sought, because here he was a believer and still waiting to get into heaven!

Turning his attention to the rest of the room, he noticed a table about the size of a card table in the corner of the room next to the TV. Sitting on it was a vase full of beautiful white and purple lilies— just like the lilies that he had hoped someone would send to his funeral.

Next to the lilies stood some smaller framed pictures grouped around a larger picture of a very nice-looking woman. The woman looked a lot like Martha, except that she had slightly darker skin. At the bottom of the picture was written, "Mom, I will always love you." Next to her mom's picture on the right was a picture of an older couple. Looking closer, John was surprised to see that the couple was Sally and Aaron—the same Sally!

Why does Martha have a picture of Sally and Aaron next to the picture of her mom? he wondered. *How did she even know them? Sally must also be her maid.*

Then he noticed written at the bottom of the picture, "Thank you for your love and support." *Now what is that all about? You don't thank maids for support. You just pay them.*

Next to the picture of Sally and Aaron were some other pictures of kids, some black and some white, playing at a playground. He did not recognize any of the kids, but they looked like they might be playing at the Boys and Girls Club. He thought that he remembered Martha once saying that she volunteered for the Club.

Looking back to the left of Martha's mom's picture, he saw a photo of a man in his late fifties. John then did a double take, followed by a triple take, followed by a quadruple take. It was a picture of his father! What was a picture of his father doing in Martha's home?

As he pondered that question, he noticed an opened letter lying on the table addressed to Martha Grissett. Grissett? Grissett! That was the name of the black lady who took Joe's place when Claude Stoner, the owner of the logging company, demanded that Joe be fired. Looking back at and studying Martha's Mom's picture a moment longer, John realized that her mom was, for sure, the lady who worked for his dad back at Niceville. What a small world!

Then John noticed something written at the bottom of his dad's picture. Looking closer, he saw that it said, "Dad, I so wish that I could have met you before you died."

Suddenly, John came to the realization that Martha was his sister— well, half-sister—blood of his blood! To say that he was astounded would be an understatement. He had a sister and she was black.

Thank goodness, his fellow Zealot Baptist members never learned about Martha. He would have never been able to look them in the eyes again. Not only was she black, she was illegitimate, and his father was her father What a disgrace.

Right behind his dad's picture was a framed snapshot of another man. It was taken at a distance, but John instantly recognized it as his own picture, probably taken at a Christ Episcopal Sunday school picnic. Written at the bottom of his picture was, "John, I always wanted to tell you." Reading those words made his spiritual heart sink, so much so that he could feel it beating furiously as if it were still all flesh and blood, or a really believable spiritual version of it. He was sure that she always wanted to tell him that she was his sister, but never did. That must have been what she whispered to his body at his funeral.

He wondered how he would have reacted if she had told him while he was alive. Sadly, he knew the answer. He would have been totally humiliated. He would definitely have not believed her. More than likely, he would have called her a liar and ridiculed her, accused her of making the whole story up, hoping to get some of his money or maybe trying to improve her status in life by claiming to be part of a successful white family. For sure, he would have not welcomed an illegitimate, mixed race black woman into his family.

That is almost certainly what he would have done back then, but now that he was only moments away from his final judgement, his feelings were totally different. Amazing how being only a few moments away from one's final judgement changes one's perspective. Now he viewed things more from her point of view instead of his own or even what his fellow church members thought. Now he thought about what she might be feeling, how he might feel if he were her, how God might expect him to feel and behave. Now, he would be kind and considerate and loving.

Just then, something else caught his attention. On the coffee table, in front of the couch, were copies of five different children's Snow Rabbit books. There had been twelve different Snow Rabbit books published. He knew, because he had read every one of them to his grandchildren many times. Every book had a message for children about helping those who were less fortunate. They were books that every parent wanted for their children and had taken the nation by a storm. They were everywhere, in every bookstore, in every child's room, and on every parent's Kindle and iPad.

But why would Martha have copies? She had no children. Then he put two and two together. The author of the books was Martha Grissett. The author was *this* Martha Grissett! Nationally renowned authors always live somewhere else, not right here in Columbia, and they're never your sister, or at least your half-sister.

It never dawned on him, all those years that he read those books to his grandchildren, that they were written by *the* Martha who was in his Christ Episcopal Sunday School class—probably because he never bothered to learn Martha's last name.

But here he was—in the home of *the* Martha Grissett, nationally renowned author, who, in spite of her fame, was still just as humble and loving as she always was in his Sunday school class. *She does not need to claim to be a part of my family to upgrade her status in life. She is already successful.* He smiled. *I need to claim to be a part of her family to raise my status in life.* All of a sudden, he was proud that she was his sister and wished that he could tell her.

Just then the doorbell rang, and Martha came from the kitchen to the front door, which opened directly into the family room. Now that he knew that she was a nationally renowned author and his sister, she looked a lot more vibrant and intelligent and beautiful.

Opening the door, Martha exclaimed enthusiastically, "Aunt Sally! Uncle Aaron! It's so great to see you! Uncle Aaron, you look fit as a horse. No one would ever know that you had cancer."

The revelation of the relationships floored John. That meant that Sally and Aaron were almost part of his family. They were his sister's aunt and uncle.

Sally responded, "He got a clean bill of health from his doctor this past week and tomorrow will be the fifth year since his last treatment. We're so grateful to God for His answer to our prayers."

After quick hugs, Martha said, "Come on in. I was so hoping that you would drop by this weekend. I saw you at a distance at John's funeral, but you were gone by the time I finished talking to JoAnn and the family and a few friends from Christ Episcopal."

"Sorry," Sally said. "We didn't know you were there. We were wondering if you were going to go to the funeral and are glad that you did. Did you stay for both the funeral and the burial services?"

"Yes. Stayed for both services," responded Martha. "I simply could not let him go without telling him that I was his sister and that I loved him."

Starting to cry, Martha continued, "It may have seemed strange to the other people there, but I leaned in and whispered to him, 'John, I always wanted to tell you, but never could. I'm your sister and you're my brother. I've always admired you and always will. Please remember that forever.' I then kissed him, Aunt Sally. I just had to kiss him. He was my brother—my brother! I so wish that he could have just looked at me and smiled—he did not have to say anything-- just smile--smile like he was proud that I was his sister."

Tears, if he had had any, would have brimmed in John's eyes.

Sally, of course, knew and simply responded, "I'm glad that you told him even though it was at his funeral. That's something that you needed to do."

Now, even without tears, John cried. Not just for Martha but for himself. He knew that his earthly case was now closed, but he wished that he had done a lot of things differently! At the time, he did them, however, he thought that he was doing the right thing. He did think that, right? Now he wasn't sure. Maybe he did know, deep down, that some of the things he was doing and saying were not right but did them anyhow because he was seeking the approval of his fellow Christians. They seemed to love his putdowns of other people, especially welfare queens and gays--and, alright, immigrants and blacks and liberals and Muslims. The fact that he was now only moments away from his final judgment was definitely causing him to see things a lot differently. *Maybe*, he thought, *everybody ought to guide their life as if their final judgment were only moments away.*

Martha responded, "I know. I absolutely had to tell him, but it was difficult."

Sally rose and gave Martha a hug and said, "It has been a long haul, Martha, but you have every reason to be proud."

"I know," responded Martha. "I wish that mom had lived to see me now. Those early days were difficult, but quickly turned good because of some saintly Christian people. You remember, after the incident in Niceville, Mom moved here with almost no money, except that Mr. Willis continued to send her a small check every month—about $75, I think Mom said, for several years. She told me that she was scared to death. You do remember, right, Aunt Sally? You guys had spent your whole life in Niceville, which is as about as rural as you can get in South Carolina. Mom always said she suddenly found herself to be a single pregnant black woman in the big city of Columbia with no car, no job, no place to stay, and almost no money."

"I know," Sally said. "Our whole family tried to get her to not go, but she said that her child was going to amount to something great someday, and there was no way that could ever happen in Niceville. She said that she was dedicating her whole life to her child and would do whatever she had to do to help you become a success. And she was going to start by moving out of not so nice Niceville and never coming back. She said her child would never be subjected to the discrimination, hate, and cruelty of that Confederate flag capital of the world."

Martha continued with the story, which they often retold to each other to bolster themselves during difficult times. She described, "Mom said she took a bus here and spent the first week in the homeless shelter down on Hope Street. I think that she said the shelter was owned by the city but managed by volunteers. She said that one of the volunteers from Christ Episcopal Church told her that she knew a church family looking for a maid. The lady drove mom to meet the couple, who turned out to be Pat and Buddy Parker, who Mom claimed until her death were two of the nicest people to ever walk this earth. Mr. Parker owned the largest car dealership in Columbia where both he and Pat worked. Both were active members of Christ Episcopal Church.

"Mom remembered that after only a brief interview, Mrs. Parker hired her, paying her the unheard-of salary in those days of seventy-five dollars a week and let her start the next day."

Although they were older than he and JoAnn, John remembered the Parkers. Martha's mom was right. They were saints, dedicated Christian servants devoted to helping the least of these. They were also way ahead of their time in terms of racial relations—especially for South Carolina. They led an effort, which failed at the time, to get Christ Episcopal to integrate its membership—unheard of in Columbia in those days. A few years later, maybe because of this initial push, the church did quietly accept Blacks.

Martha said she remembered her mom saying that on the way back to the homeless shelter, the volunteer lady told her that she knew a good Christian black lady with a room for rent and took Mom by her home. "While the room was small," she said, "it was nice, and the price was only fifteen dollars a week. Just like that, Mom said she had a job and a place to stay—all because of good Christian people who were willing to show the love of God by giving of themselves.

"Mom was absolutely convinced that God had sent her to the right shelter with the right volunteer from the right church who knew the right family looking for a maid and to the right lady looking for the right renter.

Mom said that although Mrs. Parker tried to get her to take some time off, she worked up until the day that I was born—she worked until 5:30 p.m. and I was born at 10:30 p.m. Fortunately, the lady she was renting from was a midwife, and she delivered me for free. Mom took a week off and then went right back to work. Mrs. Parker told her that it was fine to bring the baby to work with her. Mom was so thankful. I remember her saying that both Mr. and Mrs. Parker took turns rocking me, treating me as if I were one of their grandchildren when they came home for lunch.

"Mom had now saved enough money to rent a one-bedroom apartment and felt that 'life was good'--at least far better than she had feared."

Aaron chimed in, "I remember getting a letter from her. She was so proud of her new apartment and most especially of you. As she said in her letter, 'God has blessed me with an angel.'"

"I know," Martha responded, laughing. "She called me 'Martha, my angel' so much I thought that was my name until I was in kindergarten and had to write my name. The teacher had to convince me that my name was just 'Martha,' not 'Martha, my angel.'"

"When I was about a year old, Mrs. Parker surprised Mom by telling her that the time had come for me to get enrolled in school so that I could get a good education. Mrs. Parker was a stern believer in 'the earlier you start, the more you can learn' philosophy. Mom explained that she could not afford to pay the tuition, to which Mrs. Parker responded, 'It's already paid.' Then Mom said that she had no way to get me to and from the daycare center every day, to which Mr. Parker responded, 'That 1963 Chevrolet in the driveway is yours. It's a little old but in good condition.'

"And just like that I became the first black girl to enroll in the Christ Episcopal Day School, and mom got her first car."

"They probably did not know that you were black, Martha, because your skin is so light," said Sally.

Laughing again, Martha responded, "Well, I never told them. I did not even know whether I was blue, green, or yellow in those days. And I didn't care."

Martha went on, "The next few years went by fast. I basically grew up at Christ Episcopal Day School, which went through the sixth grade. I made lots of wonderful friends, some with whom I'm still close.

"We had one major crisis, which almost destroyed Mom. One day when I was in the second or third grade, Mom was picking me up at school and a man who she recognized from Niceville, Claude Stoner, the logger who bought trucks from the Dixie Truck and Car lot, was visiting in Columbia and came by to pick up his grandson. He saw Mom and recognized her. He asked what she was doing there. Mom said that her first instinct was to lie and tell him that she was a maid at the school. But she felt that she could not lie, so she told him that she was there to pick up her daughter.

"Mom said that his eyes bugged out like a mad man and he shouted, 'What the hell do you mean 'here to pick up your daughter? Do they know that you're a nigger? No grandson of mine is going to school with a nigger, even if the nigger is a white nigger.'"

"Mom said that she begged him not to cause a problem, but all he said was, 'We'll see about this!' and stormed off.

"A few minutes later, she saw him talking to Mrs. Rosser, the school principal. Mom could not hear what he was saying, but it was obvious that he was very angry. He was waving his arms in all directions and talking a mile a minute. He finished in an extra loud voice that Mom did hear. 'And until that white nigger is out of here, you will never receive another penny from me!'

"Mrs. Rosser stood there in shock, not saying a thing. Then Mr. Stoner turned, grabbed his grandson by the arm, and stalked off. He shoved his grandson into the pickup truck, jumped in himself, cranked the motor, revved it a few times, and peeled off, slinging rocks at nearby cars.

"When Mom picked me up, I remember she was sobbing, a look of desperate fear was all over her face. She told me the whole story on our way home and, for the first time in my memory, I understood what it meant to be black in South Carolina. Mom was afraid that she would be forced to take me out of the school and I, in turn, was afraid that I would lose all my friends. We drove the rest of the way home with Mom crying and me scared to death.

"That night, there was a knock on our apartment door. Opening the door, Mom saw that it was both Mrs. Rosser and Christ Episcopal's pastor, Rev. Borders.

"Rev. Borders looked worried and asked if they could come in and talk. Mom was frozen with fear, but managed to invite them in. As all four of us sat down, I remember Mom saying, 'I can explain everything, Rev. Borders. Martha just has to stay in Christ Episcopal School. I know that you took a risk letting a black student in, but I will do whatever I have to do keep Martha there. Just let me know what I need to do.'"

"Rev. Borders interrupted, 'Ms. Grissett, we did not come here to ask for an explanation. We came here to apologize to you for the way you were treated today. We love having Martha at our school.'"

John was astounded. Would he, himself, have done what Rev. Borders did? He did not like his answer.

"Then Mrs. Rosser spoke, 'I wanted to apologize to you before you left, but you left before I could get to you. You and Martha are extremely important to our school, as are all our students and their parents. Mr. Stoner has been our largest donor for the past five years, but we do not treat people the way that he treated you this afternoon. We serve a God who respects and loves all people. We will never sell that for money, no matter how large the donation.'"

Hearing that, John wondered what Pastor Flake had sold to get the ten million dollars to build the Zealot Baptist church. He, of course, knew.

Martha continued, "Rev. Borders followed Mrs. Rosser, immediately with 'Please accept all our apologies. We want to make sure that you and Martha always feel welcome at our school and we would love to have both of you become members of our church.'

"Mom could not believe it. Rev. Borders was asking a black person to join their church. That was a no-no in most other white churches in Columbia in those days and a "Hell, no!" in Niceville.

"Mom asked to have more time to think about joining, telling him that we were really happy at Ebenezer Methodist. Rev. Borders responded, 'Fine, but we just want you to know that you're welcome and could really help us get our members to be more accepting of other races.' Mom was overcome with relief and started to cry again. She had thought that she had lost all that she was trying to achieve with my schooling and would have to start all over someplace else.

"When Mom started to cry, so did I, and then so did Rev. Borders and Mrs. Rosser. Spontaneously, all four of us stood and formed a big foursome-crying hug. Finally, Rev. Borders broke the spell with 'Let's say a prayer to our God.' Mom agreed, and he prayed, 'Father, thank you for Ms. Grissett and for Martha and for all that they mean to our school. We are so glad you sent them our way. Thank you for loving each of us just as we are. Please help us to extend that love to others—even to Mr. Stoner. We pray that the day will come when all your children are treated with respect, dignity, equality and love so that conversations like the one we just had will never have to take place again. Amen.'

"With that, we said our goodbyes, had another round of hugs, and they left. Closing the door, Mom cried uncontrollably for a while before saying, 'Martha, I love you. I was so afraid that they were going to tell me that I had to take you out of the school. They would have done just that back in Niceville, and the KKK might have burned a cross in our yard. But tonight, has given me hope that someday all races will treat each other with respect and dignity.

"Mom then wondered out loud if there were any bigots like Mr. Stoner in heaven. We both decided there couldn't be because then it would not be heaven. I went straight to my room and wrote that saying over there: 'There are no bigots in heaven,' and signed it, as if it came from the Bible, with Martha 1:1 My Version. I showed it to Mom, and we both laughed. A few days later, Mom framed it and it has hung somewhere in our home ever since. It became our relief valve every time someone tried to bully us or belittle us because of our race or our gender."

Martha said that the next day at school everyone acted as if nothing had happened the day before, except that the teacher told the class that Ronnie Stoner's parents had decided to enroll him in the Robert E. Lee School across town. One of the students asked if that was the school with the big Confederate flag flying from the top, and the teacher said, "Yes."

"That's all that was ever said at school about the incident," Martha said.

However, Martha remembered her mom saying that when she got to work the next morning, she told Mrs. Parker the whole story. Mrs. Parker initially reacted with anger at Claude Stoner, even calling him a few choice names, but then stood and gave Mom a hug and said that she was really pleased with the outcome.

"That afternoon, when Mom picked me up, Mrs. Rosser came out with a big smile on her face and told mom that Mrs. Parker had called and said that she was proud of how the church and school had responded to Mr. Stoner's bullying. She said that she and Buddy would replace any donations to the school that he withdrew."

John was overcome by the story that Martha had just told to Sally and Aaron and, though she did not know it, to him as well. He wondered again whether he would have done what Rev. Borders and Mrs. Rosser or what Pat and Buddy Parker did, or would he have caved in to Claude Stoner's bullying just as his dad had done years before? He was again too afraid to answer his own question. And this made him even more afraid about everything in his life, especially his record of what he had done and said. Although he could not see it clearly, he was definitely getting the feeling that his message was in here somewhere and he did not like what he was feeling.

Not knowing that John was anywhere around, Sally spoke up, "Then we showed up unannounced at your house one day with our two sons. Remember that? Your mom had gotten a second job at Christ Episcopal helping with late-hour printing and other office jobs. With the extra money, she had rented a two-bedroom house the week before we showed up. She thought that you would each have your own room, but we moved into the extra bedroom for about six months, I think."

"I remember," Martha said. "Mom was so proud that she had the extra bedroom that she could share with you. It was crowded, but we had a lot of fun. Every night was like a campout."

"You kids may have had fun, but your Uncle Aaron and I were scared stiff," Sally lamented. "We had no money and had to sponge off you and your mom who was working two jobs. Although we were grateful, we felt terrible. I was so happy when I got that job with the Willises. They were really wonderful people, despite Mr. Willis being a little racist. He loved to tell welfare jokes that belittled poor people, especially poor black people. JoAnn never criticized him for his jokes, but would sometimes roll her eyes as if saying, 'you can take the boy out of Niceville, but you can't take the Niceville out of the boy.'"

John felt terrible and tried to remember why he ever thought his belittling racist jokes were so funny. Now that he had seen things from Martha's and Sally's perspectives, they were not funny at all. He was now hoping that his jokes did not come up in his final judgment. How does one explain belittling jokes to God? He did not have an answer. And he was afraid to think one through.

Martha laughed and said, "John was a good person, but he did have that need to belittle poor people with his jokes. After I grew up and Mom told me that he was my brother, I joined his Sunday school class at Christ Episcopal to get to know him. He knew his bible and did a good job of teaching, except that he peppered his lessons with jokes about welfare queens and entitlement kings. He even called you and Uncle Aaron welfare queens one time when you had to borrow money to pay off that payday loan. Most of the class would laugh, but I never could, and he always looked uneasy when I didn't—like maybe I didn't understand his jokes. The problem was that I understood them far more than anyone else in the class, and they were not funny. They were humiliating.

"It seemed like every time I would go to church prepared to tell him that I was his sister, he would tell one of his racist jokes, and I would chicken out. I was afraid that if I told him that he had a fortysomething-year-old sister who was a quarter black, he would get angry and say hurtful things about my mother—that he would say that it was all Mom's fault and call her a whore and me a whore's daughter.

"Aunt Sally, you cannot imagine the horrible feeling that I've had all these years, especially after Mom died in the auto wreck when that drunk broadsided her car. Despite all that Mom had done for me, I felt that I was a second-class citizen who was never allowed to even meet her father. I never got to sit in his lap or walk with him in the park or hold his hand or sing songs with him or even have him just look down at me and say, "I love you". Instead, he disowned me, refusing to even admit that I was his daughter. Am I that bad, Aunt Sally---so bad that my own father refused to even meet me?"

"I thought that I could fill part of that huge hole in my heart if I could just tell John that I was his sister and have him be proud that we were brother and sister. Losing Mom made me want to tell him even more, but I never worked up the courage. I know that I should not have let it get to me, but I cried lots of nights, just wanting to tell John that I was his sister but terrified of how he would take it."

"And at John's funeral yesterday, all of that hurt came flooding back. I wanted to tell JoAnn and the rest of the family that I was John's sister. I wanted them to know that I was a part of their family and that I was hurting as much, maybe even more than they were. But, I couldn't, Aunt Sally, I just couldn't tell them. Do you know how much it hurt to be there with my family and not be able to tell them who I am? I'm sure they thought that I was just a distant friend from their days at Christ's Episcopal Church. Why did it have to be that way? Why could I not tell them? Why do I have to be an unknown outcast not worthy of being a part of my true family? Why, Aunt Sally, why?"

Sally rose, hugged Martha again while staring off into space as she pondered the question. She then quietly said, "I wish I had the answer. We live in a cruel world that too often lets cultural rules and peer pressure override decency and love. But I can tell you one thing, God knows who you are and has to be proud of what you and your mother accomplished in a world filled with so much hate and anger."

"Thank God, you and Uncle Aaron have been living here all of this time and could give me the support that I need," Martha said. "I am still just a second-class citizen not able to tell my family who I am. I really don't know what I would do without you. You are the only family I have."

Sally responded, "Martha, you were never a second-class citizen. If you ever were, then I pray that the whole world would be second-class citizens. The Bible says that God judges us by what we do for others. You and your mom were not only first-class citizens in helping others; you were role models. I know that God called your mother home early just to make heaven a better place."

That comment really worried John because he could not remember helping a lot of people, especially over the past four years. It was almost certain that if Sally was right in why God called Martha's mom home—this could be the reason that he was still waiting to be called home. What bothered him most, however, was the "Martha 1:1 My Version" quote. Was that the message that God wanted him to find? If so, he was only a few moments from being fried.

Sally continued, "Martha, I don't know what Uncle Aaron and I would have done if you and your mom had not taken us in again when Aaron came down with cancer and we lost our home. We would have been homeless. The money that our sons were sending us was not even enough to pay our doctor and hospital bills."

Martha reassured her, "We were delighted to do it, Aunt Sally. By that time, you remember, I had graduated from USC and was working as a social worker for the state. Mom was working full time for Christ Episcopal and helping the Parkers out whenever they needed help. We had bought this house and had plenty of money—

well, at least enough to pay all our bills and also help you. Those were not really fun times because of your cancer, Uncle Aaron. But they were heartwarming times as we came together as a family.

"We really hated to see you move back into your own apartment after Uncle Aaron regained his strength. Things got a little lonely around here, especially after Mom was killed."

"They may have been lonely, but they gave you time to write those great books," Sally replied. "I've always wanted to ask you, where did you ever come up with the idea of a snow rabbit?"

"Ah, Mom used to make up snow rabbit stories when I was young, and she didn't have enough money to buy me store bought books. She would make up the stories, and I loved them. Sometimes, she would even write them out to help me learn to read.

"I wrote the first story in remembrance of Mom. I showed it to Mrs. Parker one day and she said that I absolutely had to get it published. She even lined me up with an agent who loved the story. Everything then went at breakneck speed, and within five months, I had published my first book and had a contract for three more. Suddenly I had more money than I had ever dreamed about. But I was determined to use it like Mom would have wanted—to help other people. So, I give away almost three-quarters of my royalties to places like the homeless shelter that helped Mom when she first came to Columbia and the Christ Episcopal School for scholarships for children, whose parents, like mom, cannot afford the tuition."

With a big smile, Martha then turned to Uncle Aaron and Aunt Sally and said, "I have a surprise for you. I just finished my thirteenth book and signed the contract last week. Here is your copy of the contract. All the royalties will be sent to you. They have been running about seven thousand dollars per month for the first year and about four thousand per month after that."

Sally objected, "Martha, you can't do that. We're getting along just fine on what I get from my house cleaning jobs and what Uncle Aaron gets from his auto repair work."

Martha smiled and responded, "Sorry, already done and, as Mom used to say, 'end of discussion.' Aunt Sally, this is only money. What you and Uncle Aaron have given me over the years is far more valuable than any money that I may ever be able to give to you."

Martha then walked over to Aunt Sally and Uncle Aaron, who now had tears sliding down their own cheeks, and gave them big hugs. For the first time in their lives, in their late sixties, they would be financially secure.

John sat in his aerial chair mesmerized. He had never witnessed such love and generosity in his life. His mind kept comparing what he had just witnessed to the Zealot Baptist church service a few hours before. There was no comparison. One was filled with words of hate and the other with deeds of love and service. He wished he could kick himself.

John felt that he was finally getting God's message. He was right. God had given Martha, his sister, the message. Yet, it was too late for him. His record had been closed. Everything that he was ever going to do or not do was finished. *Why have I been so stupid?* he thought. *Even my jokes were stupid, but the things that I did were the most stupid. I don't belong in heaven, or anywhere near heaven.*

It was at that moment that he knew that he had to go to Washington, D.C. He had to go now. He did not even have time to go by his waiting room at the funeral home and cemetery. He had to go now- even if he missed his ride to heaven. In fact, he was already three and-a-half years late.

Chapter 9

A Visit to Washington, DC

"Never be too proud to say 'I'm sorry' to your child when you have made a mistake."

Unknown

In less time than it takes to say, "John Henry," John was hovering near the ceiling of the family room in a comfortable home on the outskirts of Washington, DC. No one was in the room, but he could hear the happy voices of adults and children in the kitchen.

At first, he did not recognize the voices, but then he heard a voice that made him sob deep within his soul. It was the voice of Danny, the son he had loved so much during his years growing up at home but whom he had disowned when he announced that he was gay. He had so willfully abandoned him that his spirit had not even seriously considered coming to him until now. How could that be? What kind of a father, man, or Christian did that make him?

Sorrow totally captured John's soul. *How could I have ever disowned my own son? How could I have forbidden anyone in the family from even speaking his name in my presence, as if he no longer existed? How could I have ever been so cruel and heartless? If only I could go back and do everything over.*

He knew, however, that his case was closed. What did any repentance matter now? Nothing could be done over again. His sobs became almost unbearable as he remembered the pain that he had inflicted on his son whom he had loved so much.

John remembered that day—really those two days—every word and every detail, as if it were yesterday. Danny had called and said that he was coming home from his new job with the World Bank and wanted to make sure that both his mom and he would be there. He had something that he wanted to talk to them about.

John remembered that both JoAnn and he were hoping that Danny was going to announce that he had found the girl of his dreams, and that they would be getting married. They waited with bated breath all week until Friday afternoon when Danny arrived. After lots of greeting hugs, and after Danny carried his luggage into his old room, JoAnn fixed some coffee and apple pie, and they went into the family room to talk.

At first, the conversation was about Danny's new job, which was a management-level job that few graduates right out of college ever get. But Danny had both a double major in economics and international affairs and excellent grades, graduating at the top of his class at USC.

Danny had been a late-in-life baby. John and JoAnn were both forty-four when he was born, Bo and Billy eight and nine at the time. So, in many ways, Danny was an only child by the time he was ten. JoAnn had let John pick the name and he had chosen Danny from the song "Oh, Danny Boy." He always loved that song and wanted to name one of his children Danny but thought that that would never happen until he and JoAnn found out that they were having another boy.

Danny came along when he and JoAnn had more time and money to spend on their children, but by then, Danny was the only one home. They did everything with Danny, and they loved every moment of it. They went to every ball game, every school play, every school cookout, every band concert—everything. Just perfect. They took special camping trips and spent long hours telling stories around campfires. They did a lot of fishing. Even though they seldom caught anything, they developed a close bond that few fathers and sons ever get a chance to develop.

Danny never got into any trouble. They never had any reason to think that he was smoking or drinking or doing drugs. He was active in church and chosen to serve as a youth leader, a true role model for younger children with parents who could not have been prouder.

In short, John kept thinking as they drank their coffee and ate their pie, *Danny has to be the best son a father could ever want.*

Then Danny looked serious, almost worried, and said, "Mom, Dad, I've something to tell you, but before I do, I have to stress I need your love and support on this. This is probably the most important conversation we will ever have. So please don't get upset with me. Just hear me and give me your love and support. Promise?"

John grew anxious, but he nodded. He assured his son that he would never be without their love and support.

Danny then said it. He said those words that John thought that he would never hear. He said, "Mom, Dad, I'm gay and have known that I was since I was in middle school. I knew it but did not want to admit it to either you or myself. There's nothing that I can do about it. It's the way that God made me, and I've finally become comfortable with who I am. And the great news is that I've found a partner who I love and want to spend the rest of my life with. He loves me and feels the same. We both want to adopt children and have already made some inquiries."

Then Danny asked the question that he hoped that they would answer with an enthusiastic "Yes." He asked, "I have your love and support, right?"

JoAnn responded immediately. "Yes, we love you. You are our son. We have always loved you and always will." John was frozen. He never expected to be put in this situation. His first thought was not of Danny and his feelings but "What will I tell my church friends?" He would never be able to look them in the face again if he endorsed his own son having a gay partner. This was something that happened in other families, not his own family.

His only response was "Are you sure?" And then, "Have you tried counseling?"

Danny responded, "Yes, Dad, I'm sure," and "No, I've not tried counseling because being gay is who I am, not something that counseling can change."

The conversation ended with John saying that he needed to pray and think about how he could give his support. Danny responded that he was tired from the drive and was going to bed but hoped that John could give his support by morning.

John and JoAnn cleaned up the dishes without saying a word, and then went to their bedroom. Finally, JoAnn said, "John, I know this is difficult for you, but you have to give Danny your love and support. He needs it more now than ever before and he needs it more than Bo and Billy ever did. You really need to do the right thing in the morning."

John remembers being confused and finally saying, "I'm going to call Pastor Flake. I have to talk to him." He distinctly remembered JoAnn begging him to not make the call, but he ignored her.

When Pastor Flake answered, John said, "I need to talk to you tonight. Can I meet you at the church office in fifteen minutes?"

Pastor Flake responded, "Lucretia and I are just getting ready to go to bed. Does it need to be tonight?"

John said, "Yes. Tonight. It cannot wait until morning."

"Okay, I'll be there in twenty," Pastor Flake said.

John remembered those being the longest twenty minutes of his life. Finally, Pastor Flake arrived, and they went immediately into his office. As soon as they sat down, John blurted out. "Alex, my son Danny just told JoAnn and me that he is gay and wants our love and support. What am I going to do? He wants an answer in the morning."

Pastor Flake sat there for a moment without speaking. John had expected that he would say something like, "I'm sorry, John. I know that this really saddens you and JoAnn. Danny has always been such a wonderful son. But, with God's guidance, we can work through this."

Instead, Pastor Flake said, with a scowl. "What a horrible thing for a son to do to a father! After all that you and JoAnn have done for him—it shows a complete lack of respect and appreciation for your support over the years. He has obviously been associating with these gay recruiters and bought their sinful lifestyle."

Pastor Flake continued, "John, you know that if you let him get away with this, he is going to hell. The Bible is very clear. This is a sin so horrible that the Bible calls for execution. But the Bible is not all, both Franklin Graham and Pat Robertson, two of God's great prophets of our time, have warned us over and over that this is what the gay communities want to do. They want to recruit our sons and daughters and then have them become recruiters, themselves, until they have destroyed the institution of marriage between a man and a woman. That is their goal and Danny has fallen into their trap. You and JoAnn must save him. You cannot even let him near your grandchildren or he may recruit them."

John was beside himself. Pastor Flake was absolutely right. The son he had loved so dearly had turned on him.

So, he asked the critical question, "What am I going to do, Alex?"

Pastor Flake had a ready answer. "John, you have to practice tough love. You cannot give in on this issue or you will live to regret it. If you fail to correct Danny's false sense of commitment to this terrible sin, you'll not only be condemning him to an entire life of sin and ultimately to burn in hell but condemning those who he recruits. Let me ask you this John: Does he have a partner and, if so, are they talking about adopting children?"

John, not able to speak, managed only to nod, "Yes."

"That's exactly what I thought, John. This is exactly what Franklin Graham has warned us about. Danny and his so-called partner are teaming up to recruit children for God knows what perversions. John, you have got to stop him at all cost, or the blood and suffering of those children will be on your hands."

"Here is what you have to do in the morning," Pastor Flake said in an emphatic tone as if his message were coming directly from God. "You have to give Danny the choice of getting counseling or leaving your home forever. I know that this will be tough, but you must do it for Danny as well as for your grandchildren and other children that he and his so-called partner will be recruiting. This is serious, John. If you love him at all, this is what you must do."

John remembers feeling sick to his stomach but nodding silently.

Then he remembered Pastor Flake saying, "Let's go to our Lord in prayer to ask that he give you strength in the morning to do what has to be done to nip this sinful chain in the bud."

They bowed their heads and Pastor Flake prayed, "Our God, you have told us in your holy word that you will be there for us in our time of need. John is in his deepest hour of need. His son, Danny, has betrayed his entire family by allowing himself to be captured by wicked sinners. Through your prophet, Pat Robertson, we fortunately understand how gross this sin really is. And these gross sinners have convinced Danny that he will enjoy their sinful lifestyle more than the life that you endowed him with. Danny has sinned against you and against his parents and, as your prophet Franklin Graham has reminded us, there is a grave danger that Danny will now sin against the weakest of your people, little children. Our gracious and loving God, we ask that you give John the strength in the morning, as he meets with Danny, to turn Danny's life around. Allow your sinner Danny to seek counseling so that he understands the wickedness of his sin. We pray that he will repent of his sins and seek your loving grace. Please, God, help John to be strong in the face of adversity and show his love for Danny by defeating this evil that has hold of him. We ask these things in the strong name of our Lord and Savior, Jesus Christ. Amen."

With that, John remembered, they walked toward the door and Pastor Flake placed his hand on his shoulder and said, "John, you know what you have to do. God will be there to help you do it. Good luck."

As John now hovered very uncomfortably in the corner of Danny's family room near the ceiling and heard the laughter of children in the kitchen, he again felt sick, exactly like he had felt that evening three-and-a-half years ago when he was driving back home from his meeting with Pastor Flake. This time, however, his sickness was different; it was the sickness of sorrow and regret, not the sickness of fear and hate that he had felt then.

John then remembered arriving back home to find JoAnn waiting up for him. As soon as he walked in, she asked, "Well?"

Pausing for a moment to find the right words, John remembered responding, "He said that we had to get Danny into counseling as soon as possible, and if he refuses, we have to apply tough love by refusing to communicate with him until he surrenders. He said that this is not something that Danny was born with, but something that he has chosen because he thinks that it's more fun than God's way. Danny has fallen into the wrong crowd, and we have to get him into counseling so that he understands what a terrible sin he is committing."

He then remembered JoAnn looking at him as if he were a complete idiot and asking, "So, what are you going to tell Danny tomorrow morning?"

"Just that," he responded with a fake confidence. "Except, I'm going to add that I love him, but not his sin."

JoAnn responded, "John, if you do that, you'll destroy your relationship with Danny and with me. You'll destroy our marriage and our family. I've known that Danny was gay for years. A mother knows these things, and I've loved him every moment of those years. That's the reason that I cried all the way down the aisle that day at Christ Episcopal when Pastor Flake invited all who were against ordaining gay priests to come down to God's altar. I knew then that this day was coming. We could not ask for a more caring, successful, and loving son who will do anything for us. And you're about to destroy every bit of that. Just so that you know, I will have no part of this. I'm perfectly content with who Danny is, and I will always love him. You can do what you want, but I'll not sever any ties with him. In fact, I'll strengthen those ties. I'll always be there for him."

With that, she got up and went to bed.

John sat down in his chair totally exhausted, struggling with what JoAnn had just said and what Pastor Flake had told him. How was he going to choose?

He then remembered thinking that God must have anticipated that these kinds of difficult situations would come up in life and there had to be some guidance in the Bible. So, he began a mental search for verses to help him during this crisis. Almost immediately he remembered Pastor Flake preaching a sermon on putting God ahead of family, and that the biblical reference for the sermon was Luke 14:26. So he reached for his Bible on the table near his chair and turned to Luke. He read, "If any man come to me and hate not his father and mother, and wife and children, and brethren and sisters, yea, and his own life also, he cannot be my disciple."

He never thought that he would have to make this choice, but he was at that point. He had to choose between serving God and serving his family. More importantly, he had to save his son from hell. And, maybe even more importantly, he had to save face with his church friends. His decision was made. He was ready to talk to Danny in the morning. With that, he got up and went to bed. When he got there, he found that JoAnn was not there. She was obviously sleeping in one of the guest rooms.

Early the next morning, John heard Danny and JoAnn in the kitchen laughing and talking about old times as if nothing had changed. *How could they be so cavalier in the face of this crisis?*

Postponing the inevitable as long as possible, John took a shower, shaved, and for some unexplainable reason, dressed as if he were going to work, even though it was Saturday. Finally, he remembered making his way into the kitchen and joining JoAnn and Danny for breakfast. They were now talking about Danny's new job at the World Bank and the business trip to Peru that he was taking next month.

They must have noticed his solemn mood, because they both stopped laughing when he entered the room—as if he had just thrown up all over them.

The conversation was stilted, to say the least, until Danny said, "Dad, do you have an answer for me? I prayed last night that today would be a wonderful day and that I would have your full support and love."

To his absolute regret and shame now, John remembered responding, "Let's go to my study and talk." He will never forget for all of eternity the pained look on both Danny's and JoAnn's faces as they glanced at each other.

Neither said a word as they walked to the study, with John leading the way. Inside, they took seats opposite each other and John started. "After our little talk yesterday afternoon, I called Pastor Flake and went to chat with him. I felt that I needed God's advice."

He remembered Danny saying quietly, almost under his breath, "Oh, no!"

But John continued, "Danny, what you're doing is a sin against God and against your fellow man. I love you, but I cannot love your sin."

He remembered Danny responding, "Dad, you cannot hate what I am and still love me. That's like my saying I hate your face and your heart, but I love you. Your face and your heart are part of who you are. I cannot hate them without also hating you. Being gay is part of who I am; you cannot hate that without also hating me."

John thought, as he now hovered in Danny's family room in DC, *Why does that make so much sense now and so little sense then? What a stupid fool I am!*

But John responded, "Danny, promise me this. Before you commit to this sinful lifestyle, please get counseling. I've heard that there are several really good counseling centers that have helped lots of gays realize their mistakes, and that they have repented of their sins and are now living happy, straight lives. Let's call them on Monday and get you in as soon as possible. What do you say?"

Danny replied, "Dad, there is nothing wrong with me. I'm who God made me to be. I'm not sinning, and I don't need counseling. Besides, those programs are frauds and have been condemned by medical experts, including the World Health Organization. I've heard that the suicide rate of gays who have gone through these counseling programs is far higher than the normal suicide rate. These programs are not only a farce, they kill people."

Danny, now crying, continued, "Dad, I don't need counseling. I just need your love and support. I've always admired you—almost worshiped you as my father. You always said to me when I was growing up that you would always be there for me. I now need for you to be there for me more than ever. Please, Dad, please."

What a fool I am! What a weak and inconsequential fool! John now kept thinking in the living room of his youngest son's home.

Back then, he had wanted very badly to say, "Okay, Danny, you have my love and support." He didn't because he remembered all the things that Pastor Flake and Franklin Graham and Pat Robertson had said about this being the grossest of all sins and the advice of Pastor Flake to be strong in the face of such pain. With these thoughts, he suddenly felt a surge of anger, which he attributed to God giving him the courage to say what had to be said—even though he did not want to say it.

So, he responded, "Danny, I've studied the Bible. I've listened to the advice of godly people like Franklin Graham, Pat Robertson, Roy Moore, Ronnie Floyd, Pastor Flake, Michelle Bachman, Mike Huckabee, and those in our own Southern Baptist church. They all say that you have fallen into a sinful life style and if you don't repent, Pastor Flake says that you will go to hell when you die. I could never live with myself if I did not speak up now to try to keep your soul out of hell."

Danny now sobbed, and John became convinced that his strength was causing Danny to realize that he had sinned and was on the verge of repenting—that his tears were tears of joy as he was being born again to God's holy way. So, he remembered thinking, *I need to now reaffirm his decision to repent.*

So, he said to Danny, "Son, I'm so happy that you understand the repulsiveness of your sin. Will you now agree to get counseling? I will pay for all of it, and we can put all of this behind us as if it never happened."

John remembered being surprised to hear Danny respond in the midst of his tears, "Dad, I'm not crying because I suddenly see the wisdom of your way. I'm crying because I've lost a father. I've lost a father whom I've always loved dearly. From this point forward, I will have to live knowing that I have a father who no longer loves and supports me. I'll try to remember the father I used to have—the father who was there to help when I scraped my knee, whom I could look up and see in the bleachers when I was playing ball and know that he was there just for me, who was always there for me, no matter what. I must now go forward without that father. I'll carry on, but there will always be a big hole in my heart."

John remembered that he almost caved in again. It was true; he had always loved Danny and been there for him. Not that they were not proud of Bo and Billy, but he and JoAnn had been especially proud of Danny and, until now, he had been a perfect son.

But then John remembered again all the things that the Bible said about gays and all the statements from Pastor Flake and the national godly saints. He was especially concerned about the statements issued by the Southern Baptist Church. How could he stand in front of his church having endorsed a sinful gay lifestyle in his own family? It would be the same as committing the sin itself. Wouldn't it? He remembered one of these godly men saying that to not speak out in the face of evil was the same as participating in the evil itself—something like that. He simply could not cave in now and risk sending both himself and his son to hell.

So, he responded, "Danny, I too remember those great times we had together. I loved you then, and I love you now, but I simply cannot love your sin. Let's discuss counseling one more time."

Realizing that there was no convincing his dad, Danny responded, "Dad, there'll be no counseling. You either accept me for who I am, or we part ways. This is not what I want or what I was praying I would receive. But I am who I am, and I will not let the likes of Pastor Flake and your national anti-gay heroes destroy my life. You and Mom were wonderful, loving people when you were members of Christ Episcopal Church. Those were wonderful times. But ever since you joined that Southern Baptist church, you–not Mom, but you--have lost the concept of being a loving Christian."

John remembered briefly thinking that Danny was right in all that he said, but he could not yield now. How could he ever face his fellow church members if he endorsed this devastating sin? Besides, Pastor Flake had told him that he had to apply tough love no matter how hard it became. That was the only way to save his son and others that his son would recruit. So, he responded, "Son, I'm so sad that it has come to this, but unless you get counseling and change your lifestyle, you're no longer my son and I want you out of my house. As far as I'm concerned, you never existed. I don't want you at any family events, not birthdays, not Christmas, not even at my funeral unless you reject this horrible sin."

At which, John will forever remember, Danny got up slowly with tears running down his cheeks and said, "Goodbye, Dad, I love you and will pray for you every day for the rest of my life."

He then turned and walked out of the room, gathered his things, got into his car and drove away.

That was the last time he had heard from Danny, except for the flowers that Danny had sent to his funeral with the message: "I still love you and am praying for you." He knew that the flowers had come from Danny. Even in his death, he just realized, he had still been disowning his son—that is, up until this very moment.

After Danny left, John remembered spending all afternoon at his computer Googling what the Bible and people like Franklin Graham, Pat Robertson, Mike Huckabee, Michelle Bachman, Ted Cruz, and his own Southern Baptist Church leaders said about gay marriages. Their every statement confirmed the strong stand that he had just taken. He felt confident that he had done what God and his fellow Christians expected of him.

But now he had doubts, in fact, lots of doubts about all the absolutely stupid stuff he had done back then. In fact, he concluded, *What a fool! What a rotten and heartless fool, I was!*

He just realized that he had not yet seen Danny but did still hear him laughing in the kitchen with some kids. So, he knew that he was okay, and apparently happy.

John wondered why JoAnn did not leave him then, but she didn't, and they never mentioned Danny again. Except he knew that she talked to him several times a week by telephone, and that she had flown to DC a couple of times with some friends for a "girls' weekend."

But the closeness that he and JoAnn had shared throughout their marriage was gone, never to return.

As John now hovered in Danny's living room, he noticed that it was requiring more and more effort to stay at the top of the room near the ceiling. *Perhaps radio signals do peter out,* he thought again. *Perhaps, I'm approaching the end of my existence.* Then he wondered if it was just the weight of his now very heavy spiritual heart as he confronted the sin that he had committed against his own son and his wife and even his God. How could he have treated his son in such a cruel and inhuman way? There was no way that he could get into heaven. *I don't deserve heaven*, he thought. Why would God even bother to speak to such a complete sinner as himself? No wonder God had not sent for him—He could not stomach being around such a cruel bigot— especially a bigot who was so cruel to his own son.

John felt utter depression invade his spiritual body as he realized for the umpteenth time that his case was closed. There was no way that he could undo all the cruel things that he had done to his son. He could not redo anything. *People ought to think a lot more about that than they do*, he thought.

Just then, a little girl and a little boy, about three and four years old, came running into the family room from the kitchen with Danny in full chase. The kids were squealing with laughter as Danny faked trying to catch them. That was the same game that he and Danny used to play, he remembered. Then, in walked another man about Danny's age who was saying, "Quick, run! Behind the couch! Don't let Daddy Dan catch you!"

Danny looked at his watch and said, "Uh oh, kids, it's bedtime. Kenny, will you read Joann a story and I'll read one to Johnny?" John was taken aback. Danny and Kenny had named their children after him and JoAnn. How in the world could Danny bring himself to do that after the way that he had treated him? *Obviously, Danny is a far better man and a far better Christian than I ever was,* he thought, wanting again to kick his own bottom.

Kenny asked, "What book is it tonight, kids?" Both shouted at the same time, "The Snow Rabbit book!"

John looked on the children's' bookshelf and saw that they had the complete set of Snow Rabbit books.

John watched the loving way that Kenny and Danny read the books to the kids. There was no question in his mind that this was a home full of love—wholesome, true love that comes from kindness and respect for each other.

Both fathers finished reading the books at about the same time and Kenny said, "Okay, kids, it's time for our evening prayers." All four of them immediately knelt around the coffee table, held hands, and bowed their heads.

Obviously, they did this every evening. Kenny prayed first, "God, thank you for bringing Joann and Johnny into our lives. They're the best kids ever. Please guide Daddy Dan and me as we do our very best to bring them up to be good, loving adults."

Then Johnny prayed, "I remember when we did not have a daddy and now we have two daddies. So, thank you God so much for sending them to us." Then Joann, the youngest, prayed, "Thank you God for loving our family and for giving us Snow Rabbit books."

Next it was Danny's time to pray. John looked and there were tears running down his face. There was a long pause while Danny composed himself and then he prayed, "God, as I pray every evening, please love my father, John Willis. He was the foundation of my life. I love him so much and miss him every day. He never got to see these wonderful kids or even meet Kenny. If he had, he would have understood. So please accept him into your heaven so that we may someday be together again." After a slight pause, all four said "amen" in unison and Danny said, "Off to bed now kids."

John felt the bottom drop out of his spiritual heart. How could his son, whom he disowned almost four years ago, still be praying for him every night? *How could he be so loving after I was so hateful? Not a fool, that's too kind,* he thought. *What a pile of crud I am.*

He wanted to go back and tell all fathers in the world what he had just experienced but realized that he couldn't.

Despite the bottom falling out of it, John's heart was now so heavy that his shifting spirit was touching the floor. Danny, unknowingly, stepped on him as he took Joann by the hand and walked toward her bedroom.

Realizing what had just happened, John thought, *how fitting, I'm not even worthy of having my son step on my very soul. Please God, forgive me for being a religious bigot—for that's exactly what I have been.*

He now had the message. He was sure that the message that Martha had written when she was nine years old was the message that God wanted him to find: "There are no bigots in heaven."

A nine-year-old understood God far better than he did at sixty-two when he walked down that aisle at Christ Episcopal to commit to a life of hate against homosexuals! No wonder his sister had walked out with that horribly sad look on her face. She had just witnessed a march of bigots.

John then started thinking about how he had become such a hate filled religious bigot that it culminated in his disowning his own son. He thought of all the sermons from Pastor Flake and then the statements issued by the Southern Baptists and then all the messages from the national saints whose opinions he greatly respected. But then he remembered the message from Rev. Kowell, "When we stand before God, we stand alone, solely responsible for our beliefs and actions or lack of beliefs and actions. We can blame no one except ourselves."

He now knew for sure that he would not make it into heaven and really did not want to face God with all his warts and blemishes. At least Pastor Flake had been right about that. He was covered with warts and blemishes big as mountains.

The more he thought about the horrible way that he had treated Danny, the worse he felt. He had to find a way to speak to him just one last time, to apologize and beg for his forgiveness. He just could not spend all eternity without letting Danny know how sorry he was and how much he really did love him. But he had no idea how to go about doing that. So, he did what lots of people do when all their earthly options have been exhausted. He prayed. *God, I confess that I don't know, at all, how my final judgment will be made or when it will be made, or even if it will be made. Nor do I even know if you hear the prayers of a dead person. But, God, I'm praying the sincerest prayer that I've ever prayed. I know that my earthly record has been completed. I confess that I was a religious bigot who thought that my Christian faith made me superior and that I had the right to judge and condemn other people who did not believe and act just as I thought they should. With this 'holier than thou' attitude, I disowned my own son, whom I loved and admired. I hurt him deeply and for the rest of his life he will have to live with that hurt.*

I know, God, that I don't belong in heaven. I understand that. But, I pray, with every part of my soul, that you will grant me one last chance to tell Danny how much I love him, how much I admire him, and how sorry I am for the way that I treated him. I want him to know through all eternity that I love him and am proud of him just the way that you made him.

God, I beg for just one last conversation with Danny. Just one short conversation. Please grant me just this one last chance to tell him that I love him. I don't care about me, God, but please don't let my son hurt anymore.

Chapter 10(a)

Final Judgment

We tell the world the god we worship not by how often we pray and quote the bible, but by how we treat other people.

K. Boutwell

As John ended his prayer, he was startled. He thought he heard someone call his name. He heard it again. "John!" And he instantly knew—he did not know how he knew, but he knew. It was Jesus calling his name. So, he answered, "I'm down here, on the floor, Lord, where I belong."

Jesus responded, "John, get up off the floor. With the strong, obedient Christian life that you led, you belong on a throne at the top of the mountain, not down on the floor. I've come to escort you to your welcome-to-heaven banquet. Remember that in the Bible, John the Disciple wrote in chapter 14, verse 6, 'Jesus answered, "I'm the way and the truth and the life. No one comes to the Father except through me."' I'm sure that you remember that verse, don't you?"

Given that he was on his way to his welcome banquet, John decided to answer "Yes," so that Jesus would think he knew his Bible inside and out. At this point, a little lie wouldn't matter and, in fact, might even help.

"Good," Jesus said, satisfied that John did know his Bible. "Well, as that verse says, it's now your time to be escorted to the Father by me. I escort all who are welcomed with a banquet. It's a real honor for me to be around such great Christians like you. It's time for you to personally meet God. Let's go!"

With that, John found himself facing God in all His radiance. The beauty was overwhelming, the feeling even more so. In fact, it was the most wonderful and exciting feeling that he had ever had.

Despite the feeling of awe and what Jesus had said about his strong, obedient Christian life, however, John was not yet sure that a bigot who had disowned his own son deserved to even be in God's presence—much less have God throw a welcome banquet in his honor.

Then God spoke, "John, welcome to heaven. Sorry that we had to delay your trip, but we had not expected you so quickly. So, we had to scramble to get the invitations out and prepare your welcome banquet. We are still running a little behind. Things can sometimes seem as complicated here as where you just came from. But in about an hour the guests will start arriving and the food and drink will be on the tables. That gives us a little time to just visit and get to know each other a little more—although, I already know that you led one of the most obedient Christian lives ever lived on earth. I'm so proud of you........ and for you."

John loved what he was hearing but could not get out of his mind the hurt that he had caused Danny. So, he got right to the point and pleaded, "God, please forgive me for the way that I treated my son, Danny. I am just crushed and want to apologize to him. I would be so grateful if I could have just one moment with him to apologize and tell him that I love him. Just one short moment. Please."

"John, you don't need to ask for forgiveness or apologize to anyone," God responded. "You did exactly what you should have done. A lot of preachers preach about the love of God, but they forget about the wrath of God. And I don't mind using that wrath when people do sinful things like living in homosexual relationships. So, you did exactly what I wanted you to do when you kicked your sinful son out of your family. I was actually very proud of you. When it came time for you to stand up against sin, you did just that—even when it destroyed your whole family."

"But God, you don't understand. I was a total religious bigot and treated my son like dirt. I disowned him, kicked him out of my home and he is hurting. I just need one moment to apologize to him. That's all that I am asking---just one moment to tell him how sorry I am for what I did."

God glared at John with an exasperated look for a few moments and then asked "John, what's wrong? Have those gay loving liberals gotten to you? I repeat: you did exactly what my biblical laws demand when you disowned your son. You do not need to let those gay lovers convince you otherwise."

John looked around as if someone might be playing some cosmic practical joke on him. But God seemed deadly serious. Not only was He not condemning him for the way he treated Danny, He was complimenting him.

A train load of confusing thoughts raced through John's spiritual mind. *So maybe Pastor Flake and all my church friends were right all along that being gay is a horrible sin that absolutely must be punished. When I thought that I was being a religious bigot a little while ago, I was really being a devoted Christian, doing what God expected of me. This must mean that God loves religious bigots who stand up for Him and obey His biblical laws. So, Martha's quote was not the message after all. Heaven is full of religious bigots!*

Despite John's new-found confidence that his bigotry would go a long way towards getting him into heaven, he was still worried that his entry might be blocked when God reviewed his service to the least of these. After all, Mathew 25 is as clear as a bell about where the sheep and goats go after death and John's sheep record was sketchy, at best. So, just in case, he volunteered "God, I really appreciate your compliments on the way that I stood up for you against the homosexual sins that are destroying our Christian nation, but when you review my records you will find that I could have done a lot more to feed the hungry, take in strangers, clothe the naked, and visit the sick and those in prison. I was going to do that but died before I could get to it. Please forgive me.

God interrupted, "John, you did help the least of these far more than you know. By refusing to give them food and clothing handouts, you forced them to get their lazy bodies to work to earn their own food and clothes. And all those prisoners? Why do you think they were in prison in the first place? Because they committed crimes—that's why. Even more of those thugs need to be in prisons and they do not need visits that will make their punishment less severe. And the sick, they did not need you hanging around bothering them when they were trying to rest. So, by not visiting them, you actually helped them get well faster. And when it comes to strangers, especially immigrant strangers, no loving Christian in their right mind in todays' world should ever take them in, no matter how impoverished and desperate they are. They should be reported to federal agents who will take their children away from them and send the parents back to the slop hole countries they came from."

John, now even more befuddled and still not fully convinced that what he was hearing was true, started to ask another question, but God continued, "One of the stupidest things I've seen on earth has been the governmental handout programs to the poor. I can understand handouts to the rich, but there is nothing Christian about handout programs to the poor. All they do is make people dependent on even more handouts. The programs remove all incentives to work and create large classes of welfare queens and entitlement kings. Any idiot should know that no society can function with huge groups of lazy welfare bums.

"And for those who are too old to work or who are invalids, their families should be taking care of them, not hard-working taxpayers. If an invalid has no family, people need to just let them die and we will take care of them, either here or there. Everyone has to die sooner or later and earlier is no real problem in the bigger scheme of things."

John looked around again to see if God was playing a joke on him. But, there were no winks of the eye or devious grins on God's spiritual face. He was still deadly serious. This was not a joke. Pastor Flake, the national saints and his Baptist friends were right after all. *God really does view the world the same way we do! This means that not only will I get to spend all eternity in heaven, but may even be given special privileges—because, after all, I told lots of welfare queen and entitlement king jokes in my Sunday School lessons. I fought hard against every governmental handout program for the poor ever proposed and I have a documented record of forwarding hundreds of emails, Facebook posts and texts that condemned Muslims, immigrants, gays, welfare bums and those ungrateful athletes who refused to stand for our holy national anthem. And, oh yeah, those left-wing liberals who supported them. This is looking good.*

John's confidence grew even more when God added, "And I loved the way that you walked out of Christ Episcopal Church when they endorsed gay pastors. When a church endorses sin, it's no longer my church and I expect strong Christians to have the courage to walk out and either join another sin-fighting church or form a new one—which you did. I'm so proud of the Zealot Baptist Church that you helped build. In its fight against equality for gays, it has done more good in my name than almost any church in earth's history. Only the churches killing witches did better. And I mean that. In fact, every time I look at that beautiful Zealot Baptist building, I think again 'What a fantastic I-hate-gays monument'."

Feeling even prouder of himself, John decided he would look even better if he showed some humility. So, he said, "Well, I cannot take all of the credit. I could not have done all of that without the help of Pastor Flake and the guidance of the great national saints."

"I know," God said. "I'm also proud of them. They're real warriors, not afraid to call a sin a sin—even when it makes them look like babbling fools. I'm so pleased with the Decision America tour that Franklin is conducting. He is a dedicated Christian, who clearly sees America's moral descent and is not afraid to shout it from the steps of every state capital in the nation. Others may see America as one of the most caring and respectful nations in the world. But not Franklin, he sees the sin, especially Muslims and gays, almost everywhere he looks. I am so proud of him."

Then God abruptly paused for a moment and looked around to see if anyone was listening. No one was close by, but He still motioned for John to come a little closer, lowered His voice and almost whispered "I would not say this to just anybody, John, but because of the almost perfect Christian life that you led on earth, I know that I can trust you."

John was beside himself. He was in God's presence and God was about to share His inner most thoughts. He pinched himself to see if this were all just a dream and it wasn't. It was real.

God leaned in even closer and did whisper this time "John, I knew it was going to happen. The morality of America has been going to the dogs ever since the white Christian men lost control. Look at what is happening today: women have control over their own bodies and are doing despicable things, immigrants are flooding the nation taking good jobs away from whites, women are demanding equal pay for equal work like any woman could ever do work equal to a man, half of the country is on governmental welfare, Blacks are shouting Black Lives matter like all lives don't matter, black and white people are getting married to each other every time I turn around, and the supreme court just ruled that gays can marry each other. A very sad day for America. And……….. this makes me want to throw up………….. The Christian nation that I so carefully created as a beacon to the world is welcoming Muslims."

Obviously ticked off, God's voice got a little louder, "I can't believe it. Franklin is exactly right, America is in such a state of moral decay, a moral sewer, really, to get my honest opinion, that something drastic has to be done. We have got to get white Christians back in control even if it requires finding a new strong leader who never goes to church, owns casinos, cheated on his wives, has been divorced several times, brags about assaulting women, ridicules Muslims and Mexicans and has a long history of lying. I hate to say this, but sometimes, just as it was with King David in the bible, it becomes necessary to find a real man who is willing to thumb his nose at religious values to provide the strength that is required to lead during difficult times. And this is one of those difficult times when Christians are losing control of the nation. In fact, if we don't move fast to find such a leader, control will be lost, and the government will start persecuting Christians, forcing them to do things that are strictly prohibited by My Holy Bible."

God then hesitated for a moment and stared off into space as if He were working through a really difficult problem. Finally, He said, "Right now, however, I have no idea where such a saint can be found in America's current cesspool. But we absolutely must find him because this may be our last hope to save America."

"As soon as we find him, however, I am ready to go. I already have a ten-point plan that all he has to do is follow."

With a broad smile that indicated He was very proud of His plan, God handed his electronic note pad to John and said, "Here, you want to read it?"

John began reading:

TEN-POINT PLAN TO RETURN AMERICA TO ITS CHRISTIAN ROOTS

God

March 13, 2015

Background. *I intentionally founded America in 1776 as a Christian nation to be controlled by rich white Christian men. All the founding fathers were white Christian men and they, wisely, established laws that limited voting to only rich white men. No voting by the inferior Native Americans, Blacks, women and poor white men who did not own property—just good, intelligent rich white Christian men. These are the white Christian roots to which we must return if we are to save America.*

With its solid democratic foundation and the nation's adopted capitalistic economy, my new Christian government moved methodically to confiscate the lands and properties of the Native Americans and redistribute ownership to white men. Those natives who objected were killed. Some people may call this socialism, but it wasn't. Socialism is when you take from the rich and give to the poor. When you take from the poor and give to the rich, it is democracy and capitalism working arm in arm. A beautiful example of this cooperation was the Trail of Tears that my Christian men forced on the native people to confiscate their lands. Jesus, Lucifer and I, especially Lucifer, were so proud when over 100,000 of the native men, women and children were rounded up and forced to march over a thousand miles to Oklahoma. We were even prouder when several thousand died on the march. After all, most of them were nothing more than brown heathens who couldn't even speak English. Lucifer was afraid that our white Christian churches would speak out against such treatment. But I assured him we had nothing to fear. My white Christians have a long history of remaining stone silent about how other people are treated. Instead, their members celebrated by quickly grabbing the vacated lands and showing their gratitude by using part of their newly gained wealth to support my causes.

To create even more wealth, thousands and thousands of African men and women were captured and sold as slaves to the wonderful white Christian men in the southern states. Slavery, of course, was nothing new to me. From the very beginning of the world back in biblical times, I saw the value of slaves and was so pleased when my new American state governments endorsed slavery as a way of building even more white Christian wealth to send missionaries to spread my gospel to a heathen world.

Everything was perfect until the socialists created their underground railroads in the 1840s to help runaway slaves reach freedom in the northern states. These freed slaves and their left-wing liberal supporters started spreading false rumors about the ways that slave owners were raping and beating their slaves, about how children were stripped from their parents and sold to other slave owners and about how states passed laws that criminalized the education of slaves. That was absolutely not true. Well, not always true. I know for certain that some slave owners sometimes let their slaves go to their churches as long as they sat in separate sections away from the white women and children. But all these false rumors led first to the division of the nation and then to one of the bloodiest wars in the history of the world. I was so pleased, however, when the slave owning states passed laws that prohibited slave owners from having to fight in the war. There was no reason for these fine wealthy white Christian men to have to risk their lives. I was even prouder when my white Baptist and Methodist men created their own church associations to support slavery. What a blessing the Southern Baptist churches have been in my fight, since those horrible years, to keep Blacks in their subservient roles, where they belong.

Losing the war was a major set-back, not only because innocent slave owners lost most of their wealth, but also because Blacks were given the right to vote. But I knew that my white Christian men would not let me down. They quickly rigged the criminal justice system to keep thousands of innocent young black men in slavery for almost fifty years after the civil war ended. Just as importantly, they *immediately passed state segregation laws that kept Blacks out of their churches, restaurant's, schools, hotels and waiting rooms of any sort. To make sure that the laws applied to all deserving Black people, their laws defined a Black person as anyone having one-eighth or more Black heritage. I could not have been prouder of my white Christian men, especially when they went even further to organize a national network of Ku Klux Klan Orders to keep black men from stealing everything white people had and raping their women. What a great patriotic Christian group the KKK was (and still is today) as evidenced by the commitment adopted by all their Orders: "We, the Order of the ---, reverentially acknowledge the majesty and supremacy of the Divine Being and recognize the goodness and providence of the same. And we recognize our relation to the United States government, the supremacy of the Constitution, the constitutional laws thereof, and the Union of states thereunder." Their Christian values were demonstrated time after time after time as they burned Jesus' cross in the yards of black families all over the South and lynched thousands of black men, leaving their bodies hanging in the trees as a warning to other Blacks.*

Lucifer got concerned again that the white Christian churches might say something about the way Blacks were being treated, but I assured him that would never happen and it didn't. I can always depend of my white Christen men preachers.

In fact, everything was fine until the left-wing liberals raised their ugly heads again and started a national movement to give women the right to vote. Everyone, who knows anything at all about my Bible, knows that I intended, from the very beginning, that women be subservient to men. I was really pleased when many of my Southern Baptist churches fought the constitutional amendment that would allow women to vote. Unfortunately, however, the left-wing liberals also won that battle and America is now suffering under the curse of women voters. But my Southern Baptist and Catholic men have not given up. They continue, to this very day, to keep their women in subservient roles…. absolutely no ordained women priests, preachers and deacons in Southern Baptist and Catholic churches. Lots of women now serve as business and governmental leaders, but not in the Southern Baptist and Catholic churches. I am so proud of these men and have reserved a special place for them when they die.

Then it happened. Martin Luther King, Jr. and his left-wing liberal supporters came along and unraveled everything that my KKK Orders, White Citizens' Council and Southern Baptist and Methodist churches had been able to accomplish. Over just as few short years, Black Americans and their heathen left-wing supporters persuaded congress to pass the American Civil Rights act in 1964 that ended my biblically ordained racial segregation and abolished the laws and processes that my devoted white Christian men had put in place to keep Blacks from voting---even my very legitimate poll tax was eliminated.

But that is not all. The left-wing liberals did not stop in their efforts to take over America and replace its capitalistic economy with their brand of socialism. Under their heathen leadership, they opened the borders of the nation to immigrants from all over the world, especially victims of wars who had lost everything and people suffering from poverty and crime in their home countries. The liberals knew full well that these unworthy people would have American-born children who will become eligible to vote. And everyone knows how these people vote.

And as if things were not bad enough, the left-wing liberals have now started this whole man-made global warming hoax that is killing the competitiveness of America's businesses by burying them with stupid environmental regulations. Duh! I have been naturally warming the earth ever since the ice age. This hoax is nothing more than an attempt by the off-color sinners and their socialist supporters to strip wealth from rich white Christian businesses. They will stop at nothing to force their communistic ideals on America.

All of this has led to the devastating condition that American now faces. The liberals have let so many of these rabbit-breeding off-color people in our country that **for the first time in America's history, white evangelical Christians no longer represent the majority of voters.** This fact was brought home loud and clear when the nation elected a black president and then nominated a woman to take his place. What a disgrace Never Again!! If our country is to remain under the control of white Christian men as I originally designed it to be, its form of government where all voters (including the left-wing liberals, Blacks, Jews, Muslims, Mexicans, Puerto Ricans, Homosexuals, women, former prisoners and socialists) determine the laws of the land has got to be abolished. White Christians have no choice but to take control of the nation and re-establish my ordained white Christian men government.

This is my ten-point plan to do just that:

1. We must replace America's democracy with one party rule similar to what China and lots of other nations enjoy today.
The very first step must be to place America under the control of a strongly

united white Christian party ordained by me. (I don't have a party name yet, but am thinking maybe the Love, Grace and Biblical Truth party. I am also thinking that we don't have to start from scratch. It will be much easier to simply convert one of the existing parties. We can rename it later.) To build this party, however, white Christians must start first by praying and then by significantly reducing the ability of these off-color dregs of our society and their left-wing socialist supporters to win elections. This will be easy with the following nine-step approach:

- <u>Step one:</u> Immediately appoint both federal and state voter integrity task forces to spread the word that voter fraud is rampant among the inferior, socialistic off-color people. This will build the needed foundation for the voter cleansing steps below.

- <u>Step two:</u> Wherever white Christians already have control or get control of state governments, the absolutely next order of business must be to gerrymander the voting districts so that white Christians are the majority in almost all districts. Our people have already made great progress in over ten states, including North Carolina, Georgia, Ohio, Pennsylvania, Louisiana, Texas and Arkansas. We need to just build on what these fine Christians have already accomplished. Other states, like Kentucky, West Virginia and Utah are ready to be harvested.

- <u>Step three:</u> Voter rolls must be purged to eliminate as many off-color and socialistic voters as possible. Rolls must be purged routinely anyhow to remove those who have died or moved to another voting district. Under the cover of these routine purges, our people must introduce other criteria, such as recent voting record, unknown address, and arrest records, to remove the names of thousands of off-color and socialist voters. Again, our people have already made great progress in states like Ohio, Georgia, Kansas, Florida and Texas. So, it can be done. I am betting that we can remove at least 6 million, hopefully more, off-color people from the eligible voter rolls in only a few years.

- <u>Step four:</u> In addition to purging the voter rolls, we must launch programs to reduce the number of eligible off-color voters actually voting. I used to rely on the poll tax to do this, but as I just pointed out, the left-wing liberals killed that idea. However, we can do the same thing through voter ID laws that require that every voter must have a photo ID and then making it very difficult for off-color people to get the IDs---things like a limited number of inconveniently located (e.g., 100 miles or so away) offices issuing IDs and then the requirement for extensive documentation to qualify for an ID---documentation like original copy of birth certificate and extensive written verifications of all historical places of residence since birth (e.g., copies of home deeds, rental agreements and utility bills).

- *Step five:* The voting rights of all prisoners and former prisoners need to be taken away forever. These people lost their rights to vote when they committed their crimes. Lots of sins can be forgiven, but not these. Besides, they are almost all off-color people.

- *Step six:* Immediately and absolutely stop the flow of immigrants into America, no matter how desperate they are or how cruel our government has to be to stop them. These people are not white Christians and their children will grow up to be voters threatening the very foundations of our Christianity. No more immigrants, period.

- *Step seven:* Even after all the above steps have been taken, there will still be some off-color citizens eligible to vote. So, we are not finished. We have to keep as many of these people as possible from actually casting their votes. We can do this through my "make it easy for us and hard for them to vote" program. To do this, the number and location of voting polls must be carefully designed to place a lot of conveniently located polls in white Christian neighborhoods and as few as possible and inconveniently located polls in the off-color neighborhoods. Voting hours need to carefully set so that the polls are only open when most off-color people are working. Additionally, staffing in the off-color neighborhood polls must be severely limited so as reduce the number of people allowed to vote per hour and there is nothing wrong with closing a poll at the set time even if long lines of voters waiting to vote still exist. And, absolutely no voting polls on college campuses, especially Historically Black College and Universities campuses.

- *Step eight:* Remove all regulations and laws that limit financial contributions to political campaigns and then make such contributions tax deductible for all people making more than $500,000 per year in taxable income. We need lots of wealthy white Christians pouring money into our white Christian party's coffers. Money is key to our political victory.

- *Step nine:* Once our people are in full control, the final step must be to pass laws that limit voting to only those holding a photo ID issued by a white Christian church showing the voter being baptized like Jesus was baptized.

2. As soon as our people gain legislative and executive control at both the state and federal levels, we must move quickly to fill local, state and federal courts with white judges who fully support white Christian values. This is critical both to make sure that laws that favor white Christians and their churches are not ruled unconstitutional and to ensure that off-color people receive the punishment they deserve. This is especially true for our voter integrity, immigration and freedom of religion laws as well as the laws keeping off-color people in their place. I cannot overemphasize how important this is to our control of the nation. It must be achieved at all costs. **Once we have our white Christian judges in place, we will be fixed for several decades and can then start ruling by executive order without fear that those orders will be overruled.**

(Word of caution here: appointed judges must be fully vetted. Not all white Christians support our Christian values. Some are WCINOs.)

3. Also, as soon as white Christians gain control of the legislative and executive branches, we must quickly get full control of all law enforcement agencies. The attorney general and all top management of the US Department of Justice and FBI must be immediately replaced with white Christian loyalists who will make sure that white Christians are not accused of crimes like violating election laws, insider trading, money laundering, tax evasion, racial and religious discrimination and sexual assaults, especially sexual assaults. Just as importantly, this will enable our Christian governmental officials to use the DOJ and FBI as tools to enforce our control of the nation. All opponents to our white Christian cause must be imprisoned and the key thrown away---just like other nations do to their political opponents.

That is what all good white Christians want. Just check their emails, text, twitter and Facebook postings and listen to their chants.

But we cannot stop at the federal level, the control must extend to all state and local law enforcement agencies to protect local white Christians and keep all these off-color people under control, especially if they start protesting their so-called unequal treatment and oppression. Killing one of these off-color people every now and then will send the message that our people are in control. We don't need to give them any slack here, like kneeling during our holy national anthem, or we will live to regret it.

4. Governments must absolutely maintain and improve the ability of our nation's capitalistic economic system to reward the hard work and innovative ideas of white Christians with well-earned wealth. *Wealth is critical to maintaining white Christians' long-term control of the nation. Most importantly, wealth produces huge political donations to support white Christian laws, values and control. What's left over, if any, can be used to send missionaries to take my message to the off-color people living in those foreign slop-hole countries.*

Wealth also enables our people to control the free enterprise economy—who gets what jobs (hint, hint), what the wages and benefits are, who gets what contracts, what is produced, where it is produced and who gets and who does not get access to investment capital. We already have a wide wealth gap in America and need that gap to expand, not contract. Designed properly, a good capitalist system can do just that by keeping most of the off-color people in the labor, not business owner or management, pools, preventing them from ever attaining any political or economic clout.

All of this can be easily accomplished by:

- Reducing the taxes that the wealthy pay. (Easily sold by claiming that making the rich richer also makes the poor richer. I love that one!)
- Pumping huge amounts of borrowed government money (I'm talking a trillion dollars or more per year.) into the economy to produce rapid economic growth for the owners of businesses. This is a really neat trick and works every time. Sure, the huge additions to the nation's debt may, very well, bankrupt the nation in a few years causing an economic depression like the world has never before seen. But that risk is worth

taking to gain control of the nation. Besides, the debt is for future generations to worry about. If we are lucky, the borrowed money will quickly produce rapid economic inflation making it possible to repay the debt with inflated dollars that are worth only fifty cents. And, I might point out, as a side benefit, inflation always rewards the rich and punishes the poor.

- Privatizing governmental operations and then awarding huge governmental contracts to politically supportive white Christian businesses---great way to get big bribes---I mean, political contributions.
- Providing public financial subsidies to large white Christian businesses.
- Abolishing public set aside programs for women and minority owned businesses. This will help ensure that minority business owners never accumulate enough wealth to become politically influential. And women owned businesses should never exist in the first place. Good Christian women always rely on their men for financial security as my Bible clearly states.
- Abolishing all consumer regulations that prevent businesses from developing new and innovative ideas for producing revenue—great ideas like secretly opening bank accounts in the name of unsuspecting customers and 285 percent annual interests on payday loans. Consumers are smart enough to make their own choices. They don't need governments making their choices for them. Every thinking Christian knows that consumer regulations are nothing more than socialistic ideas designed to prevent businesses from making money.
- Abolishing all federal regulations requiring that banks provide equal opportunity lending to all people. We all know that most off-color people never intend to repay loans.
- Blocking all political attempts to raise minimum wages because higher wages mean less income for white Christian businesses---I mean, hurt poor people by reducing the number of low wage jobs.
- Passing laws that not only prohibit labor unions but also criminalize labor strikes and protests of any kind. Organized labor is nothing more than attempts by socialists to confiscate and redistribute the wealth of white Christians.

5. An invincible white Christian voter support base must be established by convincing white Christians that the off-color liberals are evil enemies intent on taking over our nation and

destroying our Christian values---*just like the Jews were trying to do in Germany and like the Jews, Muslims, Blacks, Mexicans, WCINOs. immigrants, homosexuals and left-wing socialists are trying to do in America today.*

To help America's white Christian voters fully understand what is happening and commit their souls to returning America to its white Christian roots, a program must be established to remind our people, on a daily basis, that immigrants and their MS-13 gangs will rape and kill our people, Jews already control our economy, Muslims are committed to replacing our civil laws with their Sharia laws, Blacks are drug dealers who will steal everything we have and homosexuals are intent on recruiting our children into their sinful life styles. And if that were not bad enough, the left-wing socialists are committed to taking over our government, confiscating the wealth of white Christians and redistributing it to the lazy off-color parasites. The message everyday must be "They're out to get us"! "They're out to get us"! "They're out to get us"! We must defeat them at all costs---even if those costs include sacrificing all moral values.

My devoted servants Ann Coulter, Rush Limbaugh and Bill O'Reilly have already prepared the way. We must build and build and build on the solid foundation these wonderful Christian leaders have already constructed, until every true white Christian is so committed that they are willing to go to war, if necessary.

We will know that we are successful when white Christians start shouting at political rallies "Lock'em up, Lock'em up, Lock'em up"; "He's a Muslim, He's a Muslim, He's a Muslim"; "Jews will not replace us, Jews will not replace us"; "Send'm home", Send'm home", Send'm home". When we start to hear these wonderful chants of Christian love, we will know that we have at least 80 percent of the white Christian voters' support "come hell or high water" ... maybe 100 percent of the <u>true</u> white Christians.

6. The free press must be replaced with a white state-controlled press. The one thing that has kept democracy in place in America, over the past several hundred years, has been the free press. If we white Christians are to replace democracy with our one-party rule, the free press has got to go. This will be difficult in America; but can be done. I have done it before in nations like Russia, China, North Korea, Germany and Italy and am doing it right now in Poland and Hungary. With my three-phase plan we can do it in America in a very short time:

- <u>Phase one:</u> We must destroy the credibility of the free press by constantly accusing the press of publishing untrue fake news to support their own anti-white Christian agenda. The accusations do not need to be true, but do need to be constant, week after week after week, until people, especially white Christians, start to believe it. And I am pleased to note that we are almost there as I write this plan. Every thinking white Christian already knows that CNN, MSNBC, the New York Times and the Washington Post "suck."

- <u>Phase two:</u> Once we get buy-in from voters that the free press is publishing fake news to support its own left-wing socialist agenda, we can move to the next phase by having our leaders brand the free press as "enemies of the people." This may result in some reporters being threatened or even murdered by extremists, but that is a small price to pay to rid America of the one barrier that is preventing white Christians from taking over the nation.

- <u>Phase three:</u> Once we have convinced white Christians that the free press is the "enemy of the people," national leaders can easily move to replace the free press with state-controlled media which will publish only true facts furnished by the government. This can easily be done by requiring that all media have government issued licenses to publish anything and then requiring adherence to strong white Christian regulations to keep their licenses. Violations must be punishable by imprisonment. I won't mention the name now, but we already have one very good white Christian TV network that is already adhering to our standards. I am so proud of that network. It shows what can be accomplished when we have control of the media.

7. White Christian churches and pastors must be released from the current un-Christian political restriction laws.

White Christian churches are a ready-made political machine just waiting to be tapped to give our people control of the nation. We need every pastor, every lay leader and every bible study teacher speaking out week after week after week in support of white Christian values--- and laws--- and political candidates. Just as importantly, we need them vehemently condemning the Jews, Muslims, Blacks, immigrants, Puerta Ricans, homosexuals and left-wing socialists who are persecuting Christians on a daily basis. And the good news is that these wonderful white Christian leaders are sitting on ready. All we have to do is call them to the White House, kneel together in prayer, remind them that they are being persecuted every day and tell them that, with our control over the DOJ, they are free, at last, to preach my word---and we all know what words I am talking about here.

8. Gun rights must be maintained at all costs. *There is always a possibility that the unworthy, off-color sinners will rise up in revolt. If this happens, white Christians will need their guns to both defend themselves and keep control of the nation. For this reason, white Christians must never, ever stop supporting the NRA's Christian efforts to keep left wing socialists from taking our guns away from us. In fact, "I will give you my gun when you pry it from my cold, dead hands" needs to be the oath of every white Christian.*

I understand that we may have to pay for these rights with the lives of thousands of school children and other innocent victims. I really don't care how many innocent lives are lost as long as white Christians are able to accumulate large arsenals of automatic weapons. In the long-range scheme of things, the loss of lives is a small price to pay for our beloved guns.... unless you are one of the victims or their families, of course...but white Christians can always sooth our conscience---I mean the victims' grief----by announcing that "Our thoughts and prayers are with you and your family." The point is to keep guns in the hands of white Christians, whatever the cost.

9. Public funds must be used to finance private white Christian schools. *Public schools are corrupting our children. They don't teach from the Bible. They question my sovereignty by teaching evolution and they prohibit praying in their schools. They even have our children in classes with off-color students and provide teenage students with information about birth control. We have got to get our white students out of these left-wing schools and into our own white Christian schools where my truths are taught. To do this, white Christians must exercise their religious freedom by demanding that governments fund our private schools where Christian values can be instilled in every child and teenagers kept from learning about birth control.*

To produce a steady supply of cheap labor for white Christian businesses, however, public schools should still serve off-color children, but there is no need to go overboard in funding them. The big money needs to go to our private schools. Public school students need to learn only enough to be good laborers. So, costs can be kept low. Besides, most public-school teachers are women who don't need a lot of money to live.

10. Finally, white supremacists must be recognized as the good people they are. *White extremist groups have been falsely accused by the Southern Poverty Law Center and the left-wing media as "hate groups". Nothing could be further from the truth. I have, personally, guided the formation of these fine Christian organizations over the past several decades, preparing for this very day when white Christians will return America to its Christian roots.*

I know what I am doing here. I have worked with strong white Christians before- -wonderful people like my servant Martin Luther---in combating the attempts of off-color people to destroy Christian values. Luther was exactly right when he wrote about how to deal with Jews in his book <u>On the Jews and Their Lies</u>. *His very first advice was: "First to set fire to their synagogues or schools and to bury and cover with dirt whatever will not burn, so that no man will ever again see a stone or cinder of them. This is to be done in honor of our Lord and of Christendom, so that God might see that we are Christians, and do not condone or knowingly tolerate such public lying, cursing, and blaspheming of his Son and of his Christians."*

It only takes one look at organizations like ACT for America, Patriot Prayer, Proud boys, Freedom Center, Identity Evropa and almost a hundred more to know that they are strong Christians dedicated to following Martin Luther's advice in ridding America of the Jews, Arabs, Blacks, immigrants, Mexicans, homosexuals, Puerto Ricans, WCINOs, and socialists who are destroying our nation. These are MY organizations. Check their web sites and you will see that they recognize my deity. Instead of being denigrated, they need to be recognized for their courage in standing up for America's white Christian values and warning the world that those values are under attack day in and day out. Their memberships need to be expanded and we need to encourage them to become much more aggressive in preventing my confederate flags and statues from being removed and in vandalizing mosques, synagogues and black churches. We must act now or lose everything that we have been building since that beautiful day in 1776 when I created this great Christian nation. And we need to elect these dedicated patriots to public offices throughout our nation. Once that happens, we will have drained the swamp and it will be a downhill slide to victory.

This is what we did in Germany and it worked like a charm. In no time at all, we had about six million Jews and deformed people rounded up and out of there. We can do the same with the immigrants in America and then move on to the Muslims and homosexuals. Hopefully, the Blacks, Mexicans and Jews will see what is happening and leave on their own. We will then have a dry swamp owned and controlled by white Christian men. What a glorious day that will be.

Summary. *The time has come for white Christians to stick together like super glue. Failure to act quickly and decisively now to implement my plan will result in America being hopelessly locked in a democracy controlled by a majority of **all** voters for years to come. This is not what America's founding fathers intended and we white Christians cannot let it happen now. We either make a blood oath now to defeat these off-color sinners and return America to its Christian roots or line up to drink our own cool-aid.*

John should not have been, but was, totally surprised that God had such a good understanding of the persecutions that white Christian Americans are enduring every day. And he loved the plan. He wondered, however, if it would really work, so he complimented God on the plan and then asked, "But, will it really work?"

God responded quickly, "It will require prayer, fasting and sacrifices, but we can do it. As stated in my plan, with the strong support of white Christians, we pulled it off in Germany and I am doing it right now in Poland and Hungary. You just have to have the right setting where a group of people are so hungry for power and control they are willing to trade their moral values for that power and control. And we have that right setting now in America where every real white Christian is filled with dogged determination to defeat the devil and his off-color, left-wing minions who are destroying our nation. So, we have the right setting and the right plan, all we need now is a committed leader…someone like my servant Jim Jones…who is so charismatic that his supporters will vote for him even if he murdered someone in broad daylight in downtown New York city."

With a worried look, God said, "So, the big question is where can we find such a great leader? Lucifer says that we will recognize him by his small hands, but I don't see any candidates right now with hands that small." John admitted that he didn't either.

Then, after a few moments of puzzled thought, God smiled and said, "I have an idea. If my people who are called by my name will show that they really want to change by fasting and praying, I will work with the Association of Sin Searching Saints to raise up such a godly leader to put white Christian men back in charge, return the nation to its Christian roots and make America great again.

Now forgetting all about Danny, John was really pleased, in fact, excited, to hear God's commitment and to see his plan for putting white Christians in charge of America again.

That is exactly what I have been saying in the emails and texts that I have been forwarding. Everything was great when the white Christian men were in control. And the Association of Sin Searching Saints is the exact organization to help put them back in control.

John knew all about the ASSS. It and the national saints have been major forces in calling attention to both the nation's sins and the dire consequences of those sins for almost a decade now. They have strongly supported prayers in public schools and the display of the ten commandments in public buildings and parks. They have fought all programs to teach teenagers about birth control and even went to the supreme court to avoid providing birth control insurance coverage for women. The Association, of course, is not just against things. It did strongly support Viagra insurance coverage for men…a coverage that the deacons at Zealot Baptist, especially Deacon Fred, really appreciated. On other fronts, they have been very aggressive in sounding the alarm about the sinful practice of admitting immigrants into our country and were the only ones to see that God sent hurricane Katrina to destroy New Orleans because of all the gay people living there. In fact, his Zealot Baptist Church had been a longtime member and Pastor Flake had served as the national chair just last year.

Even with the full support of the ASSS, however, John still wondered if God could pull this off. After all, America has been a democracy governed by laws, not rulers, ever since it gained its independence almost 250 years ago. Replacing that democracy with a single party ruler will be a huge change. So, he again asked, "You really think that white Christians can pull this off?"

"Sure," God responded. "The only thing that could possibly stop us is if the WCINOs and women cross over and vote with the off-color dregs. My biggest fear is the women. I knew that giving them the right to vote was a mistake. But I'm betting that most of the white Christian women will vote the way their men tell them to vote and that the WCINOs will never have the courage to speak out. But even if we get a few setbacks, I still think that, with my plan and the right leader, we have this in the bag. We just have to control the women and label the WCINOs as left-wing socialists."

John loved God's reassurance and thought *This is looking better and better for me*, as God, now with a proud look of confidence, continued, "We are very fortunate that we have the full support of the national saints. But they are not the only ones stepping up to support my causes. I'm especially proud of what the Southern Baptists are doing and know that we can rely on them to support our white Christian agenda. And the good thing is they have their women under control, just like the Catholics and Muslims. None of these fine Baptist, Catholic and Muslim men will ever let their women think on their own. They know that women are not as smart as men and are much quicker to yield to temptation. Just look at what Eve did to Adam…and I ask you, 'Did Jesus have any women disciples? No! Absolutely not! Not a single one! Even Jesus knew that they are inferior."

John was a little bit surprised about God's lack of trust in women, especially when God added: "And you want to know what really ticks me off? It's all these no-name women falsely accusing good Christian men of sexual assaults. It's a sad day in America. We have reached the point where every man is living in fear that his life will be destroyed by some vengeful woman falsely accusing him of sexual assault or harassment. That is no way for these poor, innocent men to have to live."

"You can tell these poor little women are lying by the tears flowing from their eyes and the pain on their faces. Never have figured out, however, why when one accuser comes out, a whole bunch of others come out with the same accusations—like an organized scheme, funded by some rich left-wing liberal, to destroy the public image of these innocent men. I never intended for my men to be treated this way."

"Besides, even if these men did what the women claimed, there is nothing wrong with good Christian men having a little locker room fun every now and then. Men will be men, you know. In fact, these strong Christian men should be appointed to judgeships and given standing ovations when they enter my houses of worship."

"And the women---we need our white Christian men to smear their names with hog-pen mud every time one of them comes come out with their vengeful accusations. They should be publicly ridiculed and their lives threatened so that all women will know what will happen to them if they make their ridiculous claims. Fortunately, we still have some strong white Christian women who admire men who assault women and love to join the men in smearing the names of accusers. The smears of fellow women send an even stronger message to the victims, particularly young girls, that they have shamed their families. I am so proud of these strong women to whom power and control far outweigh empathy and compassion. Once we have a smear campaign started, we can use my Christian TV network to flood the airways with the smears, ridicule and shame. This will send an even stronger message to all young girls and women that their hoaxes will not be believed and that their lives will be destroyed if they report anything---big or small. Their best bet for a half-decent life is to keep their wimpy little mouths shut and do their little cry-baby acting in silence. Besides, that's why I put women on earth in the first place—to give men a little companionship and pleasure. These women should just thank me for briefly sending these wonderful Christian men into their lives, enjoy their moment of special attention, keep their mouths shut and vote the way they are told to vote. That is what most white Christians want---just listen to their cheers and chants at political rallies and what their male preachers are saying and not saying."

John clearly got the message that God did not trust women, but God, seeming to be almost totally consumed, at the moment, by his distrust in women, was not finished and continued: "In fact, Paul was exactly right when he wrote in the Bible that you can't let women speak out in church. Paul knew full well that if we let women start speaking out, we will wake up one day and find these Eves running for public offices. That would be a disaster. In fact, the women already have this left-wing thing they call the League of Women Voters that is causing all kinds of problems with my voting district designs. I am afraid that if we don't do something, the League will destroy our whole movement. I may have to call the pope and have him, once again, publicly reinforce the church's historic policy that women always have been and always will be in the church's lowest class, really trash class---dominated by men. I know that he will do it because the Cardinals will eat his lunch if he doesn't. There is no way that these fine Christian men will ever treat women with respect, dignity and equality."

"When it comes to the Southern Baptist men, we don't need to announce anything to them. They will never let a woman preach in one of their churches. I loved it when the male students at that Baptist seminary a few weeks ago walked out when that misguided woman tried to preach at one of their weekly assemblies. Who did she think she was, anyhow---a preacher? That's a good one. And just yesterday, I overheard one of the leaders at a Tallahassee, Florida Baptist Church say, "It's not going to happen," when asked about women deacons. He did agree, however, that women can serve on the flower committee. Always need to let them eat a few crumbs from the floor. What a blessing that church is to my cause to keep women in their place. So, we are safe with the Southern Baptists, but as a safety valve, we need to start some rumors that the League of Women Voters is made up of a bunch of left-wing socialists."

Hmmm, John thought as he remembered Lucretia, Pastor Flake's wife, *So Pastor Flake was doing exactly what God wanted him to do when he told Lucretia to not talk in a church meeting. Boy, is she ever going to be in for a surprise when she gets to heaven—that is, if she gets to heaven—which she won't, if she doesn't keep her big mouth shut at church meetings.*

God was obviously proud of what the Southern Baptists were doing to support white Christian values by keeping their women under control. But John did not know how proud until God, now speaking in his normal tone, said, "You know, don't you, that the Southern

Baptists have the contract to determine who goes to heaven and who goes to hell. In fact, they've had the contract since 1915 and it's a two-hundred-year contract. Good deal I worked out, saves me so many headaches."

John, of course, did not know but was very pleased because that should dramatically improve his heavenly privileges. Out of curiosity, he asked, "How did they get the contract?" God responded, "At the beginning of the twentieth century, the daily judgment day processing workload was getting bigger and bigger as the number of daily deaths grew. By 1915, when we were processing almost twenty-seven relocating souls per minute, I told Jesus and Lucifer that we had to do something. We were not even able to rest on the Sabbath. So, Lucifer came up with the idea of contracting the decision-making to one of the earthly religions. We knew that it might not be the best solution, but our projections showed that by 2015, we would be processing over a hundred per minute, so something had to be done—even if it were not an optimum solution. "We prepared a request for proposals and sent it to all of the earthly religious groups. We were surprised that we did not receive more and better responses. The Catholics, Muslims and Jews did not even respond because they thought that they were already in charge. The Mormons missed the deadline even though we gave everyone six months to respond, because they could not get their proposal processed through their bureaucracy. You remember it took them over a hundred years to decide whether to ordain blacks. Anyhow, we ended up with proposals from only four groups: The Southern Baptists, Methodists, Jehovah's Witnesses, and the Episcopalians."

"We immediately rejected the Jehovah's Witnesses proposal because they said that they would only admit 144,000 into heaven and we reached that limit about a million years ago. So, we ended up evaluating the proposals from the Southern Baptists, Methodists, and Episcopalians. Lucifer did not like the Methodist and Episcopalian proposals because they proposed the use of 'showing the love of God' as the major criterion for admission into heaven. He convinced Jesus and me that that was just not an appropriate criterion. Fortunately, the criterion proposed by the Southern Baptists had nothing to do with 'showing the love of God and was based totally on 'showing the wrath of God' toward sin and sinners. Lucifer particularly liked the Baptist criteria of sending all practicing gays and preaching women to hell."

"Anyhow," God continued with a sense of pride, "the Southern Baptists have had the contract for the past 100 years and we have been really pleased with their services. They know their stuff and have no hesitation about sending lots of people to hell. In fact, they have trained most of their members to be good judges. You can ask almost any good Southern Baptist today and they can immediately tell you who is going to hell and who's on the path to heaven. They have taken their responsibility very seriously. We like that. We could have never gotten that high level of service from the Episcopalians and Methodists, who, by their nature, are just too, well, just too lenient on and forgiving of sin."

"And I am so proud that the Baptist have gone further to teach the subordination of women, hatred of homosexual relationships and damnation of other religions in their seminaries. Religious hatred and discrimination do not come naturally. They have to be taught and there is no better group at doing that than the Southern Baptist seminaries, who teach from my inerrant holy bible. And their graduates are one of the keys to our eventual dominance of the nation…I mean, to our return of America to its Christian roots when it was governed by white Christian men. I am so proud of these seminaries. Can't figure out, for the life of me, however, why, with the strong loving Christian leadership coming out of their seminaries, the Southern Baptist have lost almost a million members over the past ten years."

In spite of their declining membership, however, John was now even more pleased that he, himself, was a Southern Baptist. *That should definitely get me some extra privileges*, he thought.

His confidence was boosted even higher when God, seeming to also ignore the loss of membership, continued, "Those new Baptist guys are doing a really great job. They certainly are. As of last week, they were letting into heaven all who say that they believe that Jesus is my son, just as stated in John 3:16---except gays and women who preach from my sacred pulpits."

"I say all but am not really sure that's right—a spokesman said last week that they were not yet sure about Mormons and Seventh Day Adventists and have been keeping them in a holding pen since 1915 until they decide. Then there are all those believing teachers who tell teenagers about birth controls, they're all condemned to hell. And those believers who are not reporting illegal immigrants to ICE, they're not making it to heaven either. So, come to think about it, I guess that not all people who believe are getting into heaven. But I'm confident that the Baptists have it all under control."

With a little concern, John asked "So, my son Danny, who has prayed for me every day since I disowned him, will the Baptists send him to hell when he dies even though he believes with all of his heart that Jesus is your son?"

God responded, "Yep, Danny's on his way to hell, no doubt about that one. He could have repented when you gave him the chance.

You tried. You tried as a good Christian father. No one can say that you didn't. So, yes, Danny's destined for hell unless he puts his children up for adoption, gets a divorce, repents, and goes back into the closet—no matter what John 3:16 says. That's the Baptist rule and both the ASSS and I support it."

John had one more burning question but knew the answer because Pastor Flake had told him many times. Still, he wanted God's verification and asked, "So where do all of the people in other religions go when they die?"

God responded, "Right now, straight to hell. This has not always been the case, however. Up until we gave the contract to the Southern Baptists in 1915, we let all people who cared for the least of these, regardless of religious faith, into heaven, but the Southern Baptists, with advice from the ASSS, put a stop to that. With the Baptist now in charge, they all go directly to hell."

"During the contract negotiations back in 1915, we had some concerns about excluding people from other religions but finally negotiated a compromise with the Baptists. We agreed to exclude people of other religions from heaven on the condition that the Baptists would establish strong foreign mission programs to convert those people to become Baptist. That program has not worked very well, and we recently discussed, again, the wisdom of excluding people from other religions, but the ASSS and some of the national saints convinced us that other religions are still evil. So, we continue with that policy right now."

"This non-Christian exclusion policy has been hard on my chosen people, the Jews. They were being admitted to heaven on a regular basis until 1915. Since then, the Baptists have allowed only the few who converted to Christianity. So, John, at your banquet in a few moments, you will see a lot of old Jews, but very few young ones. We just don't get many anymore since the Baptists are in charge.

Just then Jesus returned and said, "The guests are starting to arrive. We should be ready for the guest of honor in about five minutes. By the way, have you told John about his new home?"

God said, "Nope, Son, but I will." and then turned toward John and said, "We were so pleased with your welfare queen jokes, your hundreds of anti-gay, anti-Muslim, and anti-liberal emails and Facebook postings, your fight against governmental welfare programs, your splitting out of that sinful Episcopal church to form that God-fearing, sin-hating Zealot Baptist Church of love and, most of all, your willingness to sacrifice your whole family to enforce my biblical gay laws, we have given you one of the biggest mansions up on Golden Avenue."

I knew it! I knew it! John was overjoyed. He had hit pay dirt and it would be for all eternity.

"In fact," God continued, "your new home is at the corner of Golden Avenue and National Saints Boulevard. The boulevard is the new street of large mansions that we're just now building and will hold vacant until the ASSS members who are fighting gay marriage arrive. So, you will be blessed with kind, compassionate and loving neighbors--just like you."

"In the same neighborhood, we have started a large new housing development just for strong Christians who remain committed to protecting our confederate flags and statues, vandalizing mosques, synagogues and Black churches, prohibiting birth control insurance for women, stripping young children from immigrant parents, not telling teenagers about birth control and keeping women in their place."

"It's a fantastic community that we have named the Zealot Community in your honor. So that it remains a loving, wholesome place to spend eternity, only white Christians will be allowed to spend their eternity there. To keep the riffraff out, the community is fully gated, and the beautiful main Pastor A. Reel Flake gate is guarded by Christian KKK guards, not with whips and switchblade knives, but with automatic weapons donated by the NRA, who, out of their love for their fellow man, recognizes heaven as a fantastic, untapped market. Above the gate is the Claude Stoner Golden Archway with Confederate flags flying high on each side of the arch. The gate opens directly onto the beautifully landscaped "Love and Grace for All" Boulevard. All houses are mansions and the community has several really nice clubhouses with swimming pools and banquet rooms that are always filled with food. Each clubhouse also has a really nice Uncle Bilbo Sin Shooting Range, also donated by the NRA, where members can practice shooting sinners to keep their skills up."

"Down in the mudflats on the other side of the track, we're building some small prefab houses for Blacks, Mexicans, Orientals, and other Christians who sit silently by and don't condemn same-sex marriages. To keep them out of the upscale white Christian neighborhoods, we are building a big, tall wall on this side of the track. It will be one of the most beautiful walls ever built in heaven. We will let just enough of these off-color people come through the guarded gates to do the dirty work that the white Christians don't want to do."

John loved what he was hearing. Now totally forgetting about Danny, he wondered if he could get some of the mudflat residents to clean his mansion, do his laundry, run his bath water, and prepare his food. If they were really nice to him, to show his appreciation, he might let them eat some of his leftovers. But he would definitely not let them swim in his pool.

Just then, the doors swung open, the band began to play, and the guests started to shout, "John! John! John!" With that, God said, "Welcome to your eternal home, John."

With God on one side and Jesus on the other, John walked through the doors into his eternal home of glory—all well-earned because he had disowned his gay son, told humiliating racists jokes, forwarded hundreds of hate emails, split out of that sinful Episcopal church, helped erect a beautiful anti-gay church monument, and fought governmental handout programs to the poor.

What a wonderful God, John thought. *And, just think, from the back porch of my mansion, I will have a bird's eye view as God leads white Christians to take over America and return it to its Christian roots...that is, if the WCINOs and women don't screw the whole plan up!*

"I see the confusion of politics and religion as one of the greatest barriers to grace. C. S. Lewis observed that almost all crimes of Christian history have come about when religion is confused with politics. Politics, which always runs by the rules of ungrace, allures us to trade away grace for power, a temptation the church has often been unable to resist."

- Philip Yancey

Author's Confession

The problem is, many of the people in need of saving are in churches, and at least part of what they need saving from is the idea that God sees the world the same way they do.

Barbara Brown Taylor

Reggie apologizes. The final judgment chapter that you just read is not what happened at all. But he is confident that you picked up on that very early in the chapter. What you read was how John, prior to his death, had always envisioned God and his final interview with God. He had envisioned that God would share his same values and beliefs and would spend most of John's interview time complimenting him on both his high moral standards and on his condemnation of sin and sinners. In the end, John would be given the very highest status in heaven---far above that given to most other souls. That is what John believed, what his fellow church members believe and what he wants you to believe. But, that is not what happened at all.

What actually happened, according to Reggie who was present in the room, is revealed in the following pages as John was forced to view the world, not from his own perspective or that of his fellow church members, but from God's perspective.

Chapter 10(b)

Final Judgment

"We must never remain silent in the face of bigotry. We must condemn those who seek to divide us. In all quarters and at all times, we must teach tolerance and denounce racism, anti-Semitism and all ethnic or religious bigotry wherever they exist as unacceptable evils. We have no place for haters in America -- none, whatsoever."

----Ronald Reagan

As John ended his prayer, he was startled. He thought he heard someone call his name. Then he heard it again. "John!" And he instantly knew—he did not know how he knew, but he knew. It was Jesus. So, he answered, "I'm down here on the floor, Lord, where I belong."

Jesus responded, "John, you may rise up off the floor. I've come to escort you to your final judgment. We were a little behind the past few days, so my Father said to let you wait. He hoped that you would learn a few things while waiting. But it's now your time. Let's go!"

With only that brief notice, John found himself facing God. He was overwhelmed. It was simultaneously the most wonderful and most worrisome feeling that he had ever had. He knew that he did not deserve to be in God's presence but was very appreciative that he was.

God got right to the point, "John, we only have a few minutes for your interview. We are really backed up. The problem is that, at the current earthly death rate, we have to process over a hundred souls per minute, twenty-four hours a day, 365 days a year through their final placement. Last month, we averaged processing 106 per minute. Fortunately, we put some fast tracks in many years ago and that has helped a lot."

"Fast tracks?" John asked.

"Yes. These tracks are kind of like big tubes, or pipelines, leading to either heaven or hell and are for souls whose eternal fate has been completely determined by their life on earth. There is absolutely no question where they belong. So, they don't have to go through these formalities. They just go immediately to their final destination. Those, like you, John, whom we're not sure about, get an interview."

John now knew that he faced the most important interview of his life, or rather, of his eternal existence. He absolutely had to get to heaven but knew that he did not belong there. But he just had to see his family, especially Danny again so that he could apologize to them and beg for their forgiveness. Knowing that his interview time was short, he immediately began his plea. "God, while I was waiting for Jesus to come for me, I looked at my life and realized that I had failed my family and Danny my son and, most importantly, I had failed you in almost every possible way. If I could be given just one more chance, I know that I could do better. Please forgive me and grant me just one chance to be with my family again so that I can apologize and ask for their forgiveness. Please, my Lord, just one more chance—just a few moments with them."

God seemed unmoved by his plea and responded, "I understand, John, but you created your own record and that record has now been closed."

In his desperation, John interrupted, "Just one last chance, God. Please. That is all that I am asking----just one fleeting moment to apologize to Danny."

With a voice of sympathy, God responded, "John, my child. I understand how you feel, believe me, but once your record is closed, you can't go back and change anything or even communicate with those left behind. That's just not how things work. Your only chance of ever being able to speak to Danny again is if you meet in heaven someday."

John now realized that he had to quickly learn as much as he could about God's process for judging souls and routing them to heaven and hell. Maybe, just maybe, he could find a way to convince God that he was worthy of heaven, but only so he could apologize to his son. He was willing to accept his fate after that. So, he decided to ask about the fast track system to see if he could, maybe, just-on-the off-chance maybe, be placed on the track to heaven. If not, he definitely needed to find a way to avoid the fast track to hell, his more likely placement.

God responded, "We're actually pretty happy with our fast track system, but I hate the outcomes every day. It's efficient, however, and we think perfect in where it places people when they end their life on earth."

"How many fast tracks are there?" John asked.

"A total of six, but some of the tracks are a lot larger than the others," God answered. "It has been disheartening, but it turned out we needed only two fast tracks to heaven. The first is the sheep fast track. Actually, it's not a fast track at all—even though we call it that. It's more of a meandering path through beautiful gardens alongside gently flowing streams of clear, blue water. Birds are singing, bees are buzzing, and the wind blows softly through the trees as the path leads to a place of wonderful, caring souls who love and care for each other. No one ever condemns another person. Nobody thinks that they're more important than anyone else, and no one is trying to convert anyone else to their set of beliefs. There are no hate emails, text messages or Facebook postings flying back and forth. Instead, all are totally dedicated to loving and serving one another. We're so proud of this track. It's the track for those people who followed Jesus's commandment recorded in Mathew. You remember, don't you John? The sheep are those who serve the least of these. Jesus and I promised the sheep that they would 'inherit the kingdom prepared for them from the foundation of the world.' Some of the most wonderful souls in my creation have traveled this path, people like Mother Teresa, Mahatma Gandhi, David Livingston, Martin Luther King, Jr., and Charlene Grissett."

Then with a look of disappointment, God commented, "We thought that this track would get a lot more use than it does. It breaks my heart everyday as the earthly sheep reports come in and I see so many of my people turn their backs on serving the least of these."

Then, with a smile, God said, "There are days, however, when I get my hopes up. Because even sometimes the Almighty gets a little down, particularly about this. The other day when I was reviewing the list of preprinted tickets for this path I saw lots of members of Christ Episcopal Church on the list, people such as Pat and Buddy Parker, Rev. Borders, Mrs. Rosser, Rev. Love, and Martha Grissett. Oh, and I also saw preprinted tickets for Sally and Aaron, and for JoAnn, Danny, Kenny, Bo, Billy and their families. And on another list, I saw preprinted tickets for your brothers and their wives and for Rev. Young and his wife, Manci."

"Oh, and your friend Chris, we have a dozen preprinted tickets for him. He may be a little gruff on the outside and he doesn't mince words about bigots, but he has a heart of gold. Did you know that he not only volunteers every Monday at the Veterans home making needed repairs and renovations, he also spends several evenings each week when he is not traveling just visiting with those who are sick or need a kind ear? He doesn't boast about it or even mention it to others--bet he never even told you--but he is always out there helping those in need. You guys would have heaven on earth if it were filled with Chrises."

John was totally surprised about Chris's tickets but not surprised, at all, that God did not mention seeing his own preprinted ticket because he knew that he had destroyed that ticket a long time ago. So, he tried again to beg for mercy, but God apparently did not hear him and continued, "The other fast track to heaven is the innocent victims track. It's for people who have suffered due to no fault of their own—like those who are innocent victims of murder, those born with disabling handicaps, and children who die young, including children whose parents abort them. Even though this track is small, we feel that it's extremely important because these people never had a chance."

Moving on to the other tracks, God's mood changed almost immediately from one of happiness back to one of sadness as he explained, "Because of the overall volume, we have to have twice the number of fast tracks to hell. The first one is not large, thank goodness, but it's the fastest one and leads to hottest center of hell. This track is for those who murder people in my name."

"Murder people in your name?' John immediately asked. "Who would do such a horrible thing?"

"Well, it happens. It happens a lot more than I like to admit. That too makes me really depressed. People like John Calvin, who supported the burning at the stake of people who disagreed with his religious beliefs, and Elijah who had the Baal priests murdered after tricking them into coming to a meeting. In total, I think that Lucifer told me that the data show that nineteen percent of the "godly" people mentioned in the Old Testament traveled this track. To their utter surprise, these people who thought they were little gods, claiming that they were authorized by me to murder others, were all fast tracked to hell."

"And it's still going on today. Sadly, we're getting a lot more use out of this track in the last few years for Al-Qaeda and ISIS bombers and mass murderers. The 9/11 suicide bombers, other extremist bombers, and mass murders are really getting surprised. They think they are coming here after being promised a special place in heaven by their bigoted leaders. Instead, they find themselves not only on the very fastest swoosh line to hell, but also to the hottest center of hell where they fry like cracklings forever. Just before they're swooshed, some of them are begging for permission to go back and take out their bigoted leaders. I have to admit, I'm tempted sometimes to let them. But, their bigoted leaders will get their eternity in the furnace soon enough"

Suddenly, John heard a loud "swoosh" sound and God said, "There went another mass murderer to the center of hell. You can almost hear his soul sizzling from here."

Since he had never killed anyone, John was very pleased that he had escaped the first fast track to hell but was still concerned about the other tracks. So, he asked, "What's the next fast track to hell?"—hoping he did not qualify.

God responded, "The next one is for people who murder innocent victims but don't do it in my name, like the guy who murdered those people last month down in Charleston while they were studying my Bible. When you murder someone just for the fun or hate of it, your fast track express ticket to hell has been purchased and is good until you get here."

So far, John felt safe. While he did not fully qualify for the sheep or innocent victims' fast tracks to heaven, he did not fit the requirements for the first two fast tracks to hell. If he could escape the next two, he had a chance of someday being reunited with Danny and his whole family.

So, he asked about the third fast track to hell.

"The next one is our second biggest fast track," God responded. "It's the goat track that's mentioned in Mathew. I'm sure that you remember that verse, don't you, John? It says, 'Then shall he say unto them on the left hand, depart from me, ye cursed, into everlasting fire.'"

John nodded that he did, indeed, remember that verse, responding that he used to use it a lot in his Sunday school lessons back at Christ Episcopal Church. He did not add, however, that he had not used it in the last four years since the split.

God continued, "This track has always bothered me a little because a lot of the people on it are otherwise decent people. They're just people who want to get as much as they can for themselves with no concern about the welfare of others. Some of these people are strong believers. They pray, go to church, and may even teach bible study classes, but never do anything to help the least of these. Unfortunately, we have a lot people using this track—decent people otherwise, like I said, but who do nothing to help others and even condemn them as lazy welfare bums."

"Because we have compassion for these 'do-nothing' people, we have slowed this track down a little. It used to take just thirty seconds to reach hell on this track. We have now slowed it to a full minute! What do you think?"

John was now developing a concern about this track. The only thing that he had done in the past four years to help the least of these was to give that dollar to the homeless man. But he and JoAnn--mostly JoAnn, but him a little--used to do a lot back when they went to Christ Episcopal. He hoped that that was included in his record. *It must be*, he thought, *since God has not yet given me a ticket stamped "Goat Express."*

Just in case, John decided that he needed to try to move God's attention on to the next fast track---no reason to dwell on this track. So, he asked, "What is the last fast track?" He was hoping hope against hope that he did not qualify for this one either. If he didn't, he might have a chance of seeing Danny again someday.

His hope began to vanish, however, as soon as God responded, "Sadly, this is our very biggest fast track. In fact, just last year we had to double the size of the pipe. We're now pushing about 55 souls per minute through this track! Hear that constant swooshing noise in the background? That's the traffic on this track. I think that we're going to have to build another one. This one is getting overheated---not that that makes much difference given where these souls are going."

John was sure he heard a tiny little chortle from the Almighty.

John now deteriorated into a state of sheer panic. Why had he not thought of this before? Given the clarity of God's law in Deuteronomy 23:2 that no bastard can enter the house of the lord for ten generations and the large number of bastards in the world, this track had to be for them. Or, it could be for those who worked on Sundays, which he and millions more had definitely done. Either way, he needed to make a quick move if he was ever going to have a chance to be with Danny again. So, he blurted out, "God, I know your Bible is very clear that bastards are not supposed to enter your house for ten generations. I confess that I'm a fourth-generation bastard, and that I was frequently in your house. Besides that, the pastor of my church was also a bastard, and we not only let him in every Sunday, we let him preach. I know that neither of us should have even entered your house. Please forgive both of us. And I did not know how seriously you viewed working on Sundays. I thought that as long as I went to church on Sundays, that was all that was required to 'keep the Sabbath holy.' Please forgive me for that also."

Apparently, John's comments amused God because with a dry grin, He responded, "John, don't worry about that at all. This track is not for bastards. Nor is it for those who worked on Sundays. So, you're fine on these points; it's these other things on your record that are cause for concern, I'd say."

God then turned to his portable electronic tablet and began to read what John assumed was his life record. After a few moments, God turned to him with another grin and said, "I see here that none of your friends sent flowers to your funeral. That does not speak well of you. I see that you lied to your wife about the size of the mosquitoes that bit you and Joe when you got lost in the woods, claiming that they were helicopters. You exercised very poor judgment in the jokes that you told. In fact, your jokes told me a lot about who you really are. Your hundreds of emails, well, those are even worse. Both are definitely negatives. Did it never occur to you that your jokes, emails, Facebook postings, and texts were being recorded and reveal your true inner self?"

John immediately started a mental review of the hundreds of degrading emails about gays …. and immigrants….and blacks….and Muslims… and Mexicans…and their socialist supporters that he had forwarded to his friends (as well as a few enemies). He suddenly realized that what was funny to him may have been—in fact, almost certainly was—hurtful to the targeted victims. He now wished that he could recall a lot of them but realized that his email and Facebook posting records were also closed and could never be changed.

He was about to ask God for forgiveness for his jokes and emails when God grinned and commented, "Then there was that brouhaha at your burial, which was hilarious. I never laughed so hard in my life. So, that's a plus for you."

But as quickly as it came, God's grin faded back into a look of concern as He said, "John, my problem is not with the minor issues like bastards, or working on Sundays, or the little lies that people tell. It's all the bigotry. I never dreamed that I would have this problem, but humankind has been filled with bigots ever since I created you guys. The Old Testament is filled with bigoted 'laws' that were part of the culture way back then. What ticks me off is that they claimed that I gave them those laws. That's blatantly not true, but they wrote them in the Bible anyhow. Why would I care whether a person has parents from different races? Why would I care if a person eats shrimp? Why would I care if a person loves someone of the same sex? Why would I care if someone wears clothes that have been torn? Why would I ever tell anyone to kill someone else? It makes no sense whatsoever."

With some growing anger in his spiritual voice, God continued, "I've decided that bigotry may be the worst sin of all because it leads to all types of horrible acts, such as kicking people out of churches, discriminating against people, humiliating people, demonizing people—all the way down the line to the torture and murder of millions. Religious bigotry led the Jews to murder thousands of innocent victims in my name in the Old Testament days. It led to the murder of thousands during the medieval Crusades and the Inquisition. It was one of the major contributors to World War II, which sent Jews to torture and death in prisons and the murder of millions. Today, bigotry is the cause of battles between the Sunnis and the Shiites, and the Israeli-Islamic conflict that has killed and will continue to kill thousands. Both sides killing in my name. It's infuriating."

"Bigotry has caused Christians to kill innocent men and women in my name, claiming that they were witches. It has caused Catholics and Protestants to kill each other. It caused extremists to murder little children during the American Civil Rights movement. It has caused people like the son of Don Gravendale, who helped found Zealot Baptist Church, to commit suicide. It has caused parents to disown their children for being born gay. It has even caused good Christian leaders to expel gay members from their churches. Just last week after the U.S. Supreme Court issued its decision striking down laws that prohibit same-sex marriages, good, solid preachers stood in my pulpits and showed their bigotry by condemning same-sex marriages, many just to please the bigots in their congregations."

Funny, John thought, *how bigotry seemed to be such a holy virtue when I joined Pastor Flake and the others to walk out of Christ Episcopal Church to found Zealot Baptist. We were all so smug in our belief that we were doing exactly what God wanted us to do when we condemned our gay brothers and sisters with condescending hatred. We were all so proud of our hundreds of anti-gay, racist, and Muslim jokes and emails. How could we have been so stupid as to believe that we had been appointed by God to condemn any one? Although I hurt terribly inside my soul when I disowned Danny, I was, at the same time, proud of my holy bigotry.*

God's never going to give me an opportunity to apologize to Danny, he thought. *I will receive exactly what I earned, a fast track ticket to hell.*

As John sank into total despair, God continued with growing anger, "What makes it so bad is that bigotry usually starts out with religious and political leaders making bigoted statements in my name. They know that if they just say it in their name only, it will have little impact, so they falsely invoke my name and Jesus's name to give their bigotry a little authority. I get so angry I want to wring their scrawny little necks. It then escalates as other people act on those bigoted statements to condemn and demonize innocent victims, and they do all of this in my name. For my sake! What really ticks me off is that the religious and political leaders who spew the original hate words then act as innocent as newborn babies when something bad happens, piously announcing that they're praying for the victims and their families. Well, they're not innocent. In fact, their fast track to hell tickets have already been printed and posted, just waiting for their imminent arrival."

Having worked himself into an angry froth, God stated emphatically, "John, bigotry is the worst sin of all, especially when it's committed in my name."

Given God's state of mind and his own bigoted record, John decided to say nothing and even thought of hiding except he remembered that one cannot hide from God.

Then, after a few moments of silence, almost as if He was praying, God calmed down a little and directed the conversation to the sixth and last fast track, which John now knew for sure was for bigots and he was right!

"Speaking of bigots, John" God said, "I'm sure that you have guessed it by now. This last fast track to hell is just that. It's for all religious bigots—people who set themselves up as my representatives on Earth and then use the position to condemn, harass, control, belittle, bully, demonize, torture, and even murder other people."

Just then, John heard an extra loud *swoosh*.

"What was that?" he asked.

"We just had a wad of Southern Baptist, Catholic, and Muslim men who have degraded women and forced them into subservient roles go through the bigoted fast track," God responded. "We get that every few days. That's one of the reasons that we have so many more men than women in hell."

Uh oh, John thought, *the Pope and those Baptist guys are not going to like this when they get here.*

Almost as soon as the first swoosh sound faded, John heard another loud swoosh followed by an even louder "They're lying! They're lying! I never even met those women"

"What was that all about?" John asked?

"Ah" God responded again, "Just the soul of another strong Bible believing hypocrite man who spent most of his life sexually assaulting women while promenading around as a strong, holier than thou Christian. We get one of those on the bigot fast track every few days. Funny how they think that just because their fellow

Christians believe their lying denials, we will also. It is bad enough to be a religious bigot, but to be a lying religious bigot hypocrite is just the pits. But they do get a reward for all their effort. They get to move to the head of the bigot fast track line upon their arrival here. Just like on earth, some of these hypocrites never give up. Once they get to hell, they walk around day and night shouting 'They're lying! They're lying'---like they have some mental illness or something. Lucifer says that they really get on his nerves."

Given his own bigoted record, John was now pretty sure that his chances of ever being with Danny again were gone. However, the fact that God was still talking to him gave him a slight hope. So, he decided to try another approach and steered the conversation to the belief path to heaven where he thought that he might have a chance, even though he already knew that there was no belief fast track to heaven. But, still, he thought that he might have a chance for heaven because he was a believer. So, he said to God, "What about John 3:16 which says that all a person has to do is believe in Jesus and they're automatically guaranteed a spot in heaven no matter what? All the bigots that I know certainly seem to believe."

God paused again, just for a second, and, with a concerned frown on his spiritual face, said, "John 3:16 has been a problem for me ever since the books of the Bible were assembled into one volume, and you don't want to get me started on that process, which lasted for centuries as religious leaders argued over which epistles to include and which to exclude. Too many people have totally misinterpreted what John 3:16 says. They believe that as soon as they commit to believing that Christ is my son, they're commissioned to do anything they want under my name."

John, still not quite used to being a spirit, even in the presence of the Almighty, made as if to nod. Yes, he knew a lot of those people.

"Instead of becoming humble, loving, and forgiving servants to those of their fellow men in need of their help, way too many become arrogant bullies condemning as sinners other people who don't believe exactly as they believe. I told John at the time he wrote it that he needed to follow the sixteenth verse with more explanation and requirements. He agreed but never got around to doing so. To his defense, he never thought that his epistle would end up being a part of a Bible. And neither did I."

Obviously, John had hit another nerve, and he thought, *Sure hope that God is not mad at me for asking that question.*

Apparently, the question did not make God mad because he continued, "Fortunately, Mathew covered it very well in chapter 25. It's really simple. Unless you're an innocent victim, you have to be a sheep serving the least of these to get into heaven. Believing is not enough and John should have said so. All types of people believe and then do hideous things in my name."

"Besides, John," God continued, "we tried early on letting all believers into heaven and it turned into hell overnight. We had to go in and clean the whole mess up, sending all the bigots to hell. I don't want to ever have to go through that mess again."

"You see, heaven is home to lots of people with a wide variety of backgrounds. There are, of course, Christians, but there are also lots of Muslims, Jews, Hindus, Buddhists and people who practiced Taoism, Confucianism, and other religions. There are people from all races and there are a lot of gays as well as transgender people. To the surprise of Southern Baptists, Catholics, and Muslims, we even have women. In fact, there are many more women than men. All of these people took my message to serve the least of these seriously and, in doing so, earned the right to spend their eternity in heaven."

John was startled. Non-Christians getting into heaven! How could that be? That's not what he had been told all his life. "I thought that heaven was only for Christians! How are all these other people getting in?" he quickly asked. God responded just as quickly, "John! John! You need to go back and read Mathew 25. It does not say that only *Christian* sheep get into heaven. It says, as clear as a bright day in Montana, in verse 34, 'The King shall say to *them* on his right hand, come, ye blessed of my father, inherit the kingdom prepared for you from the foundation of the world.' The verse does not say '*Christian* thems.' It just says 'them,' which means exactly what it says and that's *all* 'thems' who serve the least of these."

God continued, "With so many gay people, people of all colors, men and women and people from all religions in heaven, we cannot have any bigots, or it would not be heaven. Unfortunately, people do not change their attitudes and behavior when they die. They continue to be the same people that they grew to be before they died."

"Really?" John was startled. Somehow, he had always assumed that when people died they either went to hell where they burned forever, or they went to heaven where they miraculously became warm, caring and loving souls---totally different than they were on earth.

"Absolutely," God responded, "You don't think that Pastor Flake, or Claude Stoner, or Brother Averett, or your national saints, or even Rev. Love or Rev. Borders or Martha Grissett will be any different after they die, do you? They will say the same things, do the same things and treat other people the exact same way they did before they died."

"So, think for a moment, John, what would happen if we had religious bigots in heaven? The airways would be full of condescending tweets, emails, texts and Facebook postings condemning those who did not share their religious and political beliefs. Racial bigots would be standing in the doorways of our heavenly churches with their guns to keep people of other races out. Some would be putting on their hoods and lynching people different from themselves. Some would be kicking gays out of our heavenly churches. Others would be mounting heavenly prayer crusades to castigate both gays and people with other religious beliefs. Some would be demanding that the latest arriving immigrants be arrested and sent back to the earthly hellhole they came from. Still others would be monitoring all bedrooms and then describing the details on their TV shows." God let out a gasp of disgust as he went on with the list, "Some would be walking around making sure women were kept in the lower, subservient caste. Some would even be assaulting women and then claiming that the women were lying when they reported the abuse. And some would even be torturing and murdering those who did not share their specific religious beliefs. In short, it would turn heaven into hell overnight. Like I said, it happened once already, and it was a complete horror to fix."

Then the constant background *swooshing* sound was interrupted with another loud *swoooosh*.

God responded, "We always have this problem during US federal elections when all of the politicians start their hatemongering campaigns. They get their bases all riled up and we have wads of people shouting and posting their own cheers of hate just before they die, clogging the fast track. We had a whole bunch from Texas just last week and are expecting more next week now that this new bigot down there came on the scene with his tour."

When God mentioned a new bigot coming on the scene, John wondered how God knew. So, he asked, "How do you know who the bigots are?"

"It's easy and the sad thing is we don't have to do anything special," God responded. "People do it for us. In fact, they go out of their way first to become bigots, then to publicize their bigotry, and then to recruit others to join them. Not sure why, but bigots love company. So, they take all the tempting work off Lucifer. He does not ever need to tempt people. They do that to themselves and to each other. They're constantly using their emails, Facebook, Twitter, smartphones, speeches, and any other methods they can think of to get other people to join them in their bigotry. In fact, if it were not for his record-keeping responsibilities, Lucifer and his staff would have the easiest job in the universe. The last time that he had to tempt someone was over two thousand years ago when he tempted Jesus, and he even failed at that."

John glanced over at Jesus, who had a spiritual smile on his face.

"Anyhow, it's really sad and I wish that it would never happen. But, given an opportunity, bigoted leaders will quickly step forward and start tempting others to join them. Lucifer calls them bigot baiters.

They love their power roles and--what I don't understand, but it happens--hordes of little bigots quickly line up to follow them."

"Who are these bigot baiters?" John asked. "Do I know them?" "Unfortunately, you know a lot of them, John," God responded. "From the fifties through the seventies, we had the racial equality bigot baiters, people like George Wallace, Ross Barnett, Lester Maddox, Bob Jones, Orval Faubus and lots of Southern Baptist Brother Averett types. When they spewed their words of hate toward the equal treatment of blacks, millions of white bigots cheered them on and shouted their own hate words. Jesus and I were devastated when hundreds took the extra steps to beat, burn, and even murder blacks along with whites who supported equal rights. Those were really busy days for Lucifer and his staff. They took millions of notes, made millions of videos, and placed millions of names on the bigot fast track waiting list. I hoped that many would see their sins and repent before they died, but very few did. Unfortunately, it's almost impossible for bigots to repent because they always think that they have found the truth that only they and their bigoted friends know. Once in a while, some, like George Wallace several years ago, and Klink Cummings down at Holly Hill Lutheran Church just yesterday, do repent. And I'm always so happy for them."

"I had really hoped that after civil rights for blacks were granted, we would see a decline in bigotry," God continued, "but that, sadly, turned out to be a false hope. Instead, a whole new crop of bigot baiters arose around the equal treatment of my gay and transgender sons and daughters. To our total dismay, these new bigot baiters went further this time and organized themselves into a global association named the Association of Sin Searching Saints, which now sponsors an annual ASSS contest to see who can spew the most hate words and deeds. I guess bigotry knows no limits."

John could not help but smirk that the Creator had used the phrase "ASSS contest."

"In spite of all that we, in heaven, could do, lots of national political and religious leaders yielded almost immediately to the lucrative temptation to join ASSS and compete in its annual contests," God continued. "Like most sins, entry requirements set by the ASSS are really low and the contest rewards huge. All one has to do to become a member and participate in the contest is to frequently spew hate words and then feel proud of the pain and hurt placed on the victims. The rewards for political leaders are lots of publicity, huge political donations, and a strong base of rabid supporters. Religious leaders receive huge audiences and big donations. Church memberships and money grow like weeds. As a kicker, the louder and meaner the hate words and the more hurt that they cause, the larger the rewards."

With a large sigh, God lamented, "It has been terrible. For the past decade, bigots have been becoming ASSS members faster than flies gather on honey. Initially, we thought that only a few would yield to the temptation—at most, maybe a few hundred thousand—but millions have joined. And, instead of just the big ASSS leaders, millions of little ASSS members have quickly jumped in with their moral and financial support."

John still could not help smirking, but he knew this was serious, beyond deadly serious.

"What has been so disturbing," God continued, "is that in addition to the hordes of individuals, whole church departments, whole churches, and even whole denominations joined almost as soon as they learned of the ASSS and its contest rewards. Members and their money are just too attractive to most pastors to let this opportunity pass. Instead of showing love and respect for My LGBT sons and daughters, they are jumping at the opportunity to trade that love and respect for more members and their money. There is now a long list of ASSS churches, including your Zealot Baptist Church, John. Even the Cooperative Baptists, for whom I had great hope, jumped on board to protect their sources of money. Money and members—that is the new god that My churches now worship."

It was becoming a lot clearer to John now. He knew about the global association because Pastor Flake had served as its national chair last year, but he had never heard of the annual ASSS contest. He was not surprised, however, that it existed. Based on what God had just said, John now saw that there were millions of religious bigots who were constantly trying to "out-bigot" each other, so it made sense that they were competing in a contest. Some fought for publicity by shouting hate words louder and more persistently. Some gained contest points by displaying their swords and guns to demonstrate their fight against gays. Some constantly used their emails, Facebook, Twitter, and other electronic methods to broadcast their hate. Some organized regional and national antigay prayer crusades. Churches competed by expelling gay members. Some gained points by proudly defying court orders to issue marriage licenses to gay couples; others by refusing to bake a wedding cake."

"While all of this was happening, others raced around the country to get their pictures taken with their bigoted brothers and sisters. Apparently, group pictures of bigots are worth more points than individual pictures. Church associations competed by kicking gay friendly churches out of their association. Christian seminaries competed by teaching that being gay is a sin and by prohibiting the enrollment of gay students thereby ensuring that they produce another generation of religious bigots."

And, to think that I was a part of all of that, applauding every time a contestant racked up more ASSS points, John thought. *But I never saw any of this as sin. Instead, I saw it as a virtue—as doing what was right—what my church and my peers, and even God—well, maybe God--expected of me.*

While John realized again that he had really been sinning when he thought he had been being righteous, God's anger transformed, and in one of the saddest tones John had ever heard, God exclaimed, "John, it has been absolutely horrible. No matter how hard Jesus and I try, the ASSS just continues to grow every week and to thrust more and more hurt on my gay sons and daughters. When I made man in my image and granted him the power and freedom to think on his own, I never thought that he would immediately use that power and freedom to establish himself as a little god over other people, and, even worse, to do so in my name. In all these years, I've kept hoping things would get better, but they always seem to get worse."

"In fact, Lucifer and his staff are now busier than ever taking notes, making videos, and printing tickets for the bigoted fast track. I stay awake many nights worrying. Why in the world would so many people spend so much of their time inflicting hurt on others and think that creating that hurt will get them into heaven when they die? I just don't understand it. It makes me feel like a failure---like I had no idea what I was doing when I created mankind."

For the first time ever, John began to understand the hurt placed on God when man chooses to be a bigot, most especially a religious bigot. He accepted that his own bigotry had hurt not only Danny and really, all gay people, but also made God feel like an idiot. He had joined his fellow Christians in betraying the trust that God had put in him. There was no question that he did not belong in heaven.

John now realized that if he was ever going to see Danny again, he had to find some reason that would cause God to have mercy on his soul. At the moment, however, he could think of no reason. So, instead, to give himself more time to think, he asked, "About how many souls use the different tracks each day?"

"Let me see. Lucifer gave me those statistics for last month just yesterday. Oh, here it is," he said, turning his computer screen around so John could see it. "We report the data by minute, not daily, because of the high volume."

John read the table.

Average Track Volumes Per Minute
July 2015

Track /Destination	Souls Per Minute
Sheep/Heaven	5.4
Innocent Victim/Heaven	0.5
Murder in God's Name/Hell	0.8
Murder not in God's Name/Hell	2.2
Goats/Hell	40.7
Bigots/Hell	<u>55.0</u>
Total	106.3

Looking at the data, God said, "So you can see where the big volumes are. We now know that we made some big planning mistakes early on. Based on our volumes over the past million years, we made heaven far too large and hell far too small. We had just not counted on so many bigots."

Just then, Tina, the most trusted angel in heaven, interrupted with, "Father, Jesus asked me to let you know that Klink Cummings from Holly Hills Lutheran church has been waiting for over an hour and you now have about 75 others waiting in line."

"Okay, thanks Tina, we're wrapping this up," God said hurriedly. He then turned to John and said, "John, I'm sure that you already know that your ticket on the sheep fast track to heaven was canceled about four years ago when you joined that anti-gay group splitting from the Christ Episcopal Church. It was then replaced with an express ticket on the bigot fast track when you disowned your son Danny about three and a half years ago."

John's hope for heaven and ever being able to apologize to Danny vanished for good with those words, and he began to mentally prepare for his big *swoooosh* into hell where he would not only burn but also have to live for eternity with other bigots. He couldn't decide which was worse.

But then, to his absolute surprise, God paused and said, "John, in all of heaven's history, we have never let a bigot who disowned his own son, just for being gay, escape the fast track to hell."

God paused again, and John's spiritual heart skipped six beats. He felt a ray of hope.

Looking directly into John's radio signal spirit, God said, "For the first time ever, we're going to make an exception. We're giving you an interim assignment to see if you can become a loving person worthy of heaven. If you complete this assignment successfully, we will put you on the sheep fast track to heaven."

"To learn, for all eternity, the hurt and humiliation caused by words of hate against other people, for the next two years, you have to listen to every Pat Robertson show, every Mike Huckabee and Ted Cruz political speech, every Pastor Flake sermon, and go to every single one of Franklin Graham's Decision America tour meetings. Whenever another father or mother disowns a gay son or daughter, you must be present to witness the horror and pain as the heart broken child is rejected by those who they thought loved them."

"In fact, where ever religious bigotry raises its ugly head for the next two years, you are to be there watching the pain thrust upon the victims."

"Finally, each evening, you must watch a rerun video of your conversation with Danny the morning that you disowned him. When not involved in one of these events, you're to be present in your son, Danny's home, watching the hurt on his, Kenny's, and their children's faces as they hear and read all the news about religious people condemning gay people. To give you a little flexibility, you do get thirty minutes of free time each day to use as you like. Do use it wisely."

Although John knew that the lessons would be painful, he was deeply appreciative and responded immediately, "Thank you, God. I'm very grateful. I won't disappoint you. I know that I can become a more caring, loving soul worthy of heaven. Thank you."

He knew that he really deserved to be swooshed to hell. He had been granted a reprieve but did not understand why. So, he asked "What did I do to avoid the big *swoosh* to hell?"

Noticing Jesus coming in with Klink Cummings's spirit in tow, God quickly responded, "John, you did nothing. Based on your bigoted life, you should be in hell. It was your son, Danny, who got you a reprieve. He has prayed for you every day—every single day since you disowned him, telling us how much he loves you and asking that we have mercy on your soul. His prayers have been so sincere; Jesus, Lucifer, and I decided to honor them. But we felt that you still had a lot to learn before you could be welcomed into heaven."

God then said, "Good luck, John." and turned to greet Klink, who seemed very appreciative that he had avoided the bigoted fast track and was getting an interview."

Jesus then gave John the schedule for the next couple of weeks that started the next morning with a Pat Robertson TV show followed by Mike Huckabee and Ted Cruz speeches. On Wednesday morning, he is to be present for a Franklin Graham press conference.

On Wednesday afternoon, he is to be in Pastor Flake's home when his daughter, Mary Ann, who is flying in from Denver, will announce to him and Lucretia that she is engaged to her longtime girlfriend. It is a conversation that she has both suppressed and dreaded since her middle school years. Now that the wedding is only a month away, she knows that she needs to tell them. She has prayed long and hard that they will understand and give her the love and support that she so desperately needs from her parents. But she knows, deep down, that it will be the most horrible day of her life and that it will, most likely, be the last time that she ever sees them as they declare that she is no longer a member of their family until she repents of her sin.

Wednesday evening, he is to be at the Charleston, South Carolina jail where the white supremacist, who murdered nine black Christians as they prayed at their church, brags about his accomplishments.

On Thursday morning, John is to be in Gainesville, Florida, where a pastor will burn a copy of the Quran. Thursday afternoon, in Hattiesburg, Mississippi where the Pine Belt Baptist Association will be discussing and voting on dismissing a member church which welcomes homosexual members. Thursday night, he is to be in Hendersonville, Tennessee where the Tennessee Baptist Convention will be showing its love for God by expelling a member church because it has a woman pastor.

On Friday, he is to be in Brookland, Arkansas where a church board will show the world their Christian love for their fellow-man by voting to expel a gay member. On Friday night, in Morristown, New

Jersey, where five predominately black churches will be vandalized by those who have reserved the love of God only for themselves.

Saturday afternoon, he is to be in Montana to watch a skinhead anti-Semitic parade and listen to their Jewish hate speeches. Saturday night, he is to attend a Stone Mountain, Georgia white supremacist rally for God and the confederate flag.

On Sunday morning, he must be back at Zealot Baptist church to hear Pastor Flake's double down sermon condemning the low belly scum LGBT community that recruits innocent young lives into their hell-bound sinful ways.

Sunday night, John must be in Pennsylvania to watch the tragic abuse of a little child by a Catholic priest in a back closet of the church. Monday morning, he is to be present when the bishops try to figure out how to add the new abuse to the hundreds that they are already covering up. At noon, he is to watch the news when the Pope will show the Church's high respect for women by decreeing that they will always be relegated to subservient roles within the church.

Wednesday morning, he is to be in New York to attend the funerals of two children killed by an Islamic extremist.

Wednesday night, he is to be at a Baptist prayer meeting in Tallahassee, Florida where a deacon will be telling a lesbian mother that she, her partner and their two children are no longer welcome at their church.

Thursday morning, he is to watch a video of an Arizona Baptist pastor admonishing those who do not support killing all LGBTs, as commanded by God in His Holy Word. At noon on Thursday, he is to listen to a radio talk show where an Alabama Baptist pastor will ridicule and forcefully damn seven women who "falsely" claim that a good Christian man sexually assaulted them.

Thursday night, he is to be at a major TV network headquarters where one of the network's Christian broadcasters will be sexually harassing one of the female staff. Something he loves to do when he is not smearing the names of the accusers.

Friday, he is to be in Texas to watch a white man kill a black man by dragging him behind his truck.

Friday afternoon, he is to spend all afternoon carefully studying the heart rendering exhibits in the Washington, D.C. holocaust museum. Saturday morning, he is to visit a Seattle synagogue that has just been spray painted by vandals with the words "Holocau$t I$ Fake Hi$tory".

Saturday afternoon, he is to watch an Ohio Muslim father murder his daughter for dating a non-Muslim man. Saturday evening, he is to be in Arkansas for a white Baptist Sunday school class social where a new class member will be explaining that he just moved his membership from a local Presbyterian church because "There is no way that I am going to church with a bunch of queers." Across the room, a long-time class member will be commenting that it would be okay with him if all black people were still in Africa.

On Sunday, he is to be back in Pennsylvania where a Methodist church will be showing its Christian love by voting to leave the United Methodist church because other Methodist churches have accepted LGBT members. Sunday evening, he is to be in an Alabama Baptist church when an alleged molester of teen aged girls will be given a standing ovation in recognition of his strong Christian values.

As John completed reading his list of assignments for the next two weeks, he realized, for the first time ever, the magnitude of the horrors perpetrated on others by religious bigotry. He was devastated. How could religious people be so cruel and inhuman to each other and do so in God's name? No wonder God had to keep all religious bigots out of heaven. They would turn it into hell overnight.

His heart grew heavy as he thought of all the innocent victims who did nothing except be there when the religious bigots damned their lives. He then thought again about his family and what he had done to them---all because he wanted his Christian friends to think that he was one of them. His bigoted image had been more important to him than his family. With tears in his spiritual eyes, he turned to

Jesus and meekly said "Thank you. I don't deserve God's grace, but I will do everything I can over the next two years to learn how to treat every person with respect, dignity, compassion, love and equality."

Jesus replied, "If you succeed, and I hope that you do, we will welcome you into heaven with open arms."

Just like that, John's interview and final judgment were over---well, almost over. He still had a few things to learn. But, he had avoided the bigot fast track to hell and now had a chance of seeing Danny and the rest of his family, at some future point, in heaven. This was all due to the prayers of a son who loved him and had prayed for him every day for over three and a half years—the same son who John had disowned and kicked out of his family had saved him from spending eternity in hell.

Chapter 11

Quick Visit with Martha

"Darkness cannot drive out darkness: only light can do that. Hate cannot drive out hate: only love can do that."

--- Martin Luther King Jr.

John was deeply grateful for his reprieve and decided to use his first thirty minutes of free time to visit Martha's home. He knew that he could not speak to her or give her any messages, but he felt that he needed to at least check on her to show his symbolic appreciation for writing God's message when she was just nine years old.

He zoomed to his aerial chair in Martha's family room near the ceiling. Everything was still in place—the furniture, the hangings on the wall, the pictures—even the purple and white lilies in the vase. Sally and Aaron were still there—although they may have gone home and just dropped by for another visit. Nonetheless, they were there, and the house was filled with smiles and laughter—the way a home should be.

The doorbell rang. Martha said, with surprise because she was not expecting company, "Who could that be?"

As Martha got up to open the door, John noticed the exchange of smiles and a wink of the eyes between Sally and Aaron.

John could not immediately see who was at the door when Martha opened it, but he could hear the conversation. Someone who sounded like his brother Clint said, "We understand that our sister lives here and we want to meet her." Then Clint and Jeremy introduced themselves and their wives.

After the introductions, Clint and Jeremy simultaneously reached out to hug Martha, a big hug filled with years of being siblings but not knowing each other. Finally, they broke the hugs, and everyone laughed and cried together. Martha, regaining her composure, said with the most happiness she had had in years, "I'm sorry. please, please come in."

Martha then introduced Aunt Sally and Uncle Aaron and another round of hugs took place before Martha said, "Please have a seat. I'll get some coffee."

John found himself crying again. *That could have been me if I had not told all those racist welfare jokes over the years that made Martha fear telling me that she was my sister,* he thought.

Martha came back into the room with coffee and said, "How did you know?"

Jeremy responded, "Sally called us last night."

John looked at Sally who was giving Martha that big smile that she used to smile before all the tragedies happened to her and Aaron.

From that point, everyone talked a mile a minute trying to catch up on all that had happened over the years.

While he was disappointed that he could not participate, John was especially happy that Martha was now a part of their family. He knew that Martha was happy, and he could tell from the conversation that Clint and Jeremy and their wives were equally happy. The conversation had already gotten around to planning Martha's first visit to Cleveland.

Then, out of the blue, Clint said, "Martha, I should have known you were my sister when I looked over at you pulling hair out of Pastor Flake's wife's head at the end of John's graveside service. You got a good swatch, too."

"I know," said Martha, "and I still have it." She reached over to grab a wad of long blonde hair off the table next to the couch. Everyone laughed as Martha added, "I was so angry at the way they used John's burial service to promote their hate agenda that I lost control when JoAnn called Flake a 'yellow-bellied bastard.' Before I knew it, I ran directly towards Flake, but before I could get to him, Bo was beating him over the head with the microphone, so I turned and grabbed his wife."

Everyone laughed.

Martha added, "And I should have known that you two were my brothers when you grabbed those two Confederate flag deacons and wrapped the flag around their heads."

Sally then spoke up, "I can't believe we missed all of the fun."

"You also missed a ride in the paddy wagon," Jeremy said.

Clint chimed in, "There was some more fun at the police station. When we got there, Chief Dwayne Doutfield came in and we apologized profusely, telling him how sorry we were that we had caused such a disturbance. After a brief lecture, the chief released us on good behavior."

Martha then added, "Flake, his wife, and the deacons were not so lucky. Pastor Flake immediately confronted Chief Doutfield and accused him of being part of the left-wing liberal conspiracy in this nation, arresting people for trying to exercise their religious freedom. He called Chief Doutfield a minion of the devil himself. Now, anyone who knows Chief Doutfield knows that he is not anything even close to a left-wing liberal and does not particularly like being called one. After listening to Pastor Flake for about five minutes, the chief turned to his sergeant and said, 'Book 'em for disturbing *my* peace,' and walked out."

Clint added, "You should have seen them getting their fingerprints and mug shots taken. It was worth the whole thing just to see that. I'm thinking about having copies of their mug shots framed and sent to them as a present from John."

There was more laughter.

It had been fun to be there with them, but John looked at Clint's watch and realized that his thirty minutes of free time for the day were about up. He needed to shift to Danny's house, where he was supposed to spend the night before starting his schedule tomorrow.

As John was zooming away from Martha's home, he noticed Chris walking up the walkway towards Martha's front door with a huge smile on his face and a bouquet of flowers. *Now what is that all about?* He wondered. But he did not have time to wait and find out.

Chapter 12

Trip after Judgment

"Would 'sorry' have made any difference? Does it ever? It's just a word. One word against a thousand actions."

---Sarah Ockler, Bittersweet

John zoomed to Danny's home, arriving in no time flat at his aerial chair in the family room. He was surprised to see his entire family there—JoAnn and Bo and his family, and Billy and his family and, of course, Danny and Kenny. All the older kids were having a blast playing Snow Rabbit with Joann and Johnny.

With him gone, John realized, they were free to be a family again. He had deprived his family of this happiness for the past three-and-a half years. It was hell to know what he had done not only to Danny but to his entire family by being such a religious bigot.

Because of Danny's prayers, however, he hoped that someday they would all be in heaven together and he could hold his family in his arms once again and say, "I'm sorry. I love you."

Appendix A

Selected Reviews

As you might expect, the reviews of this book have been mixed, as illustrated by the following:

Which Path to Heaven? does a great job of describing life in our beautiful city during its golden age in the 1950s and 1960s. You will really enjoy reading about how we designed and enforced a wonderful lifestyle where our Confederate flags flew proudly, and everyone knew their place and stayed in it. We have been fortunate that, through our social customs and church-sponsored private schools, we have been able to preserve most of that wonderful life style—even until this very day.

Tom Huckleberry, Book Review Editor, *Old Niceville Times*, Niceville, S.C.

Which Path to Heaven? is part of a carefully designed plot by the left-wing liberals to steal our country from us and keep us from preaching God's truth in our churches. I've been told that I am mentioned in the book and that it calls on our nation to endorse the sin of treating all people with respect, dignity, and equality, something that God's people will never do—especially Jews, Muslims, Mexicans, Blacks, Puerto Ricans, women and homosexuals. I, personally, will not stoop so low as to read even one single page of this despicable book and have already sent a damning review to Amazon.

Alex R. Flake, Pastor, Zealot Baptist Church, Columbia, S.C.

Reggie Scot, in his book *Which Path to Heaven?*, does a great job of documenting my experiences during the first four days after my death on July 2, 2015. Although I did not know, at the time, that he was discretely following and documenting my experiences, I am pleased that he did and hope that those experiences will help prepare you for the first few days after your own death. I highly recommend you read it. But, please don't tell Pastor Flake that I recommended it. He seems a little sensitive over his role in the book.

John Willis, Former Accountant, Columbia, S. C.

We Muslim men are delighted to join our Baptist and Catholic brothers in totally rejecting the call by the author of *Which Path to Heaven?* to treat women with respect and equality. We may differ on some beliefs, but not on how we treat our women. Our Muslim-Southern Baptist-Catholic brotherhood will remain united, for all eternity, in treating women as the inferior, subordinate gender they are. No male worth his salt will let his women read this book or any book, for that matter.

Abdul Komal, Imam, Armmpit, Iraq

It's books like *Which Path to Heaven?* that are destroying our nation. We either stand up now to defeat these left-wing liberals or we will have no nation to defend.

"Katfish" Koles, KKK Grand Dragon, Garbage Pit, Missouri

We had no idea that the author would tell the truth when we opened our records for his review. DO NOT READ THIS BOOK!

The Association of Sin Searching Saints (ASSS), Las Vegas, Nev.

Which Path to Heaven? gave me a life that I never knew that I would have and made me a better person. It can do the same for you.

Klink Cummings, Former Member, Holly Hills Lutheran Church, Columbia, S.C.

The deacons of Grace Baptist Church, in keeping with our practice of kicking all openly gay members out of our church, hereby notify all who read the book *Which Path to Heaven?* that you're not welcome in our church. We know the path to heaven and *Which Path to Heaven?* is not the path to heaven. Amen.

Christian Love, Deacon, Grace Baptist Church, Graceville, Arkansas

At first, we were hesitant to let Reggie Scot include our story in *Which Path to Heaven?* but are now glad that we did because the book shows that even in the midst of a climate of hate, it is not only possible, but really easy, to treat all people with respect, dignity and equality---if one really wants to do so.

Pat and Buddy Parker, Owners, Columbia Car Dealership, Columbia, S.C.

Almost everyone in heaven is talking about the wonderful book, *Which Path to Heaven?*, because it lays out so clearly the decision process and criteria on judgment day. The rumor on the street here is that everyone in hell is trying to get word to their friends and family still living on earth to heed the warnings in this great book so that they may avoid spending their eternity in hell. If you have not yet heard from your friends and family in hell, you may want to go ahead and buy a copy of the book.

Elizabeth Scot, Author's Mother, Beautiful Green Meadows, Heaven

Appendix B

Scribe's Experience

By: Ken Boutwell

"Hundreds of wise men cannot make the world a heaven, but one idiot is enough to turn it into a hell."

---Raheel Farooq

A lot of people have asked.... well, not a lot, but some.... well, actually, not any yet, but some might ask "What is it like serving as the scribe for someone who resides in heaven?"

I must admit that the experience was unique---something that I had never encountered before. First and foremost, heaven must be in a different time zone because Reggie chose to send almost all his messages in the middle of the night when I was trying my best to get some sleep. I would wake up around 1:30 or 2:00 AM to go to the bathroom and when I returned to bed there they would be---all these messages from Reggie penetrating my brain. It happened so often that I started keeping a note pad on my nightstand to jot down the thoughts he wanted included. After about two months of this constant after-midnight messaging, I complained that I could not keep functioning with such little sleep, but he kept right on transferring his thoughts.

Finally, I had had enough and submitted my resignation. Reggie very calmly responded, as he had done before, "Fine. Tomorrow I will send the message to your church friends that you are a left-wing liberal." As in all previous cases, I caved in, reached over to my night stand, picked up my pen and pad and started writing. It went this way for months. Fortunately, Reggie received a special assignment from God for about two months to go help Lucifer add some fuel to a bigoted religious fire down in the underworld. As Reggie explained, to keep hell as hell, Lucifer has to sometimes stoke the fires by telling one group of bigots what the other group of bigots said about them.

Upon Reggie's return, however, the late-night messages continued for almost a year and then came the time for revisions. Now Reggie never slept, constantly sending his revisions while I was driving, while I was trying to work, while I was taking a shower---he never let up. Frequently, my wife would ask during dinner, "And just where are you now?" I couldn't say that I was receiving a message from Reggie. She would think that I had lost it. So, I would say "Just thinking about a revision to the book."

So, my advice is that if you are asked to serve as a scribe to a heavenly spirit, think long and hard before agreeing. The spirit will work you to death and then you will be one of them---which, come to think about it, is not all that bad.

Beyond the long hours and frequent thought interruptions, the biggest problem was Reggie's and my frequent disagreements. Having been raised in a Southern Baptist church and being an active member all my adult life, I have a very strong set of beliefs. Perhaps, more importantly, many of my friends are strong Christians with, sometimes, even stronger fundamentalist beliefs. There was no way that I could write things that disagreed with their beliefs. At least, that is what I thought until Reggie threatened me again with his blackmail.

Frequently, however, I would tell Reggie that what he wanted me to write was against my beliefs and, particularly, the beliefs of my church friends. This was especially true about my friends' beliefs on whether LGBTs and non-Christians go to heaven. Finally, one day, Reggie had had all that he could take and pitched a heavenly fit. "Ken," he shouted about 2:00 AM one morning, "You earthlings are not in charge of who goes to heaven. God is. So, get over it. Beliefs are not facts. Religious people have more stupid bigoted beliefs than Carter has little liver pills. I have lived in heaven for over 400 years and I know what the facts are. My next-door neighbor is a Muslim, the family in the mansion across the street are Jewish and I play golf with a close transgender friend every Thursday. There are Buddhists, Hindu, Catholics and Baptists in my civic club. All these people are the most wonderful, caring, loving, and serving souls you will ever meet. So, don't tell me who is in heaven. I know. I see them every day."

I talked with my pastor and went right back at Reggie the very next day. "Reggie," I said, "I talked to my pastor yesterday and he said that he didn't care how wonderful, caring, loving, and serving your heavenly friends are, as soon as he gets to heaven he's telling God and all you guys, except the straight Baptists, are outta there." Reggie responded not so kindly, "Ken, I am tired of arguing with you, just write what I tell you to write or you know what will happen."

From that point on, I did what I had to do to keep Reggie from telling my church friends that I was a left-wing liberal, but I still do not believe all that junk he was telling me. Every true white Christian knows who goes to heaven and it is not all these other people who don't believe as we do. It is only those of us who keep women in subordinate roles, demonize other beliefs, condemn the entire LGBT community, admire men who sexually assault women, smear the names of the women who report the abuses, refuse to help refuges, relegate Blacks, Mexicans and other minorities to the "lower class" and fight governmental welfare programs for lazy welfare bums.

Despite all the conflict, however, I must admit that the overall experience of serving as Reggie's earthly scribe for this book changed my life forever. I am sure that some of the messages in the book may conflict with your beliefs as they do with mine. However, I have done my job. I wrote what Reggie told me to write. Now, it is all in your hands, you must wrestle with the question: **what if Martha is right that there are no bigots in heaven?** (If she is, wonder if being a bigot about bigots will be a problem?)

APPENDIX C

As You Will, My Son

Reggie reminded me, a few moments ago, of a story that I heard many years ago.

A young boy approached his grandfather with his hands behind his back. In his hands, the boy held a small baby bird.

The boy said to his grandfather, "I have a baby bird in my hands. Is it dead or alive?"

The grandfather quickly realized that if he said "alive," the young boy would squeeze the bird to death and hold out a dead bird. If the grandfather said "dead," the boy would hold out the live bird.

So, after a few moments of thought and with a smile, the wise old grandfather answered, "As you will my son, as you will."

---***************---

To my fellow Christians, you hold the future of Christianity in your hands. It will be, "As you will, my son, as you will."

Ken

www.ingramcontent.com/pod-product-compliance
Lightning Source LLC
Chambersburg PA
CBHW071904290426
44110CB00013B/1274